## Chris Ayres

Chris Ayres, 29, is the West Coast correspondent for *The Times*. He was born in Newcastle upon Tyne, grew up in Northumberland and was educated at the University of Hull and City University, London, before joining *The Times* in 1997. Ayres held the positions of media business correspondent and Wall Street correspondent, based in New York, before taking up his current position in LA. He was an embedded reporter with the United States Marines during the 2003 Iraq War, his coverage earning him a nomination for the British Press Awards 'Foreign Correspondent of the Year'.

D1124782

# War Reporting for Cowards

*Between Iraq and a Hard Place*

## CHRIS AYRES

JOHN MURRAY

© Chris Ayres 2005

First published in Great Britain in 2005 by John Murray (Publishers)
A division of Hodder Headline

The right of Chris Ayres to be identifed as the Author of the Work has been asserted by him in
accordance with the Copyright, Designs and Patents Act 1988.

1

Extract from 'Borderline' composed by Reginald Lucas, published BMG Music Publishing Ltd.
Used by permission. All rights reserved.

A CIP catalogue record for this title is available from the British Library

ISBN 0 7195 6001 2

Typeset in Bembo

Printed and bound by Clays Ltd, St Ives plc

Hodder Headline policy is to use papers that are natural, renewable and recyclable products and
made from wood grown in sustainable forests. The logging and manufacturing processes are
expected to conform to the environmental regulations of the country of origin.

John Murray (Publishers)
338 Euston Road
London NW1 3BH

For Lucie

# Contents

The events described in this book really happened.

I wish they hadn't.

Some conversations have been written from memory.
(It's hard to take notes when you're running away.)

Some names and biographical details have been changed.

'The war correspondent has his stake – his life – in his own hands, and he can put it on this horse or that horse, or he can put it back in his pocket at the very last minute . . . being allowed to be a coward, and not be executed for it, is his torture.'

Robert Capa, *Time–Life* war photographer,
killed by a landmine in French Indo-China, 1954

# *Preface*

What follows is a confession. It is also a memoir, of sorts – although I like to think it could be about anyone. Anyone, that is, who prefers the warm loo seat to the shovelled hole in the desert, or who would rather experience the great outdoors on a comfy chair, behind tinted, re-inforced glass. Feel free to flip through the excuses about character and motive, and on towards the action – the falling buildings in New York City; the biological attack; the near-misses in the Iraqi marshlands; and, of course, my final, shameful act, 90 miles south of Baghdad.

I should also mention that this is not an anti-war book. I enjoy the guilty thrill of a televised war as much as the next civilian. Bring on the gun-cam, the bomb stats, the 3D battle map, and the reporters in flakwear standing, as they always do, on hotel balconies in distant, crumbling cities.

No, this is not an anti-war book – this is an anti-sending-me-to-war book; an I-didn't-want-to-go book. I left Iraq dumbstruck at the sacrifice made by Rick 'Buck' Rogers and his fellow United States Marines. I also left Iraq with a desire never to be trapped in a Humvee with them again.

But nor is this a pro-war book. Whether the war of March 2003 was right, or wise, is not for me to decide here. Instead, I see this as a 'how-to': a practical guide for those intrigued by the extreme tourism of conflict journalism. Most war reporters are brave, selfless types – more interested in the news story at hand than their own physical dis-comfort and fear. Not me. Which is why this book is dedicated to those who find themselves running in the opposite direction to the action. Yes, *you* know who you are: my fellow cowards out there.

C.A.

London, 2005

xi

al–Diwaniyah, Iraq

2003

# I

# How to Deal with a
# Dead Media Representative

The day, like most of my days in Iraq, had got off to a bad start. I awoke that morning, as usual, shivering violently and aching from another night in the Humvee. Waking up, of course, shouldn't be a difficult or traumatic process. For the first twenty-seven years of my life I had done it every day without even thinking. Open eyes. Yawn. Scratch balls. Look up at ceiling. Climb out of bed. Waking up in a Humvee on the front lines of an invasion, however, is different. The first thing you notice is the contortion necessary to sleep inside the vehicle: the head dangles inches from the bare metal floor; the right leg is somewhere behind the left ear. The spine feels as though it has been splintered like a cocktail stick. If the war doesn't kill you, sleeping in the Humvee might. Look what happened to David Bloom, the newsman from NBC: dead at thirty-nine from 'deep vein thrombosis' – a.k.a. Economy Class Syndrome – after spending one night too many in his 'Bloom-mobile'. In a Humvee, it's more like Cargo Class Syndrome.

Then comes the mental replay footage from the night before – the hollers of 'Lightning! Lightning!'; the absurd 3 a.m. fumble for the gas mask, welly boots and rubber gloves; the casualty reports over the radio. And then you remember the almost hallucinatory dreams: corny, sepia-tinted images of parents, aunts, uncles, grandparents. With that comes a gutful of guilt – at what you're doing to the little boy they spent years nurturing. And, of course, what you're doing to *them*, as they try to hold down undigested food every time they switch on the television. Oh yes, the battlefield dreams are best forgotten. Quickly.

From the outside, the gap-toothed Humvee looked as though it belonged on Sunset Strip: an oversized pleasure wagon with a camouflage-paint gimmick and room in the back for a hot tub and

PlayStation. Inside, however, the 2.3-ton vehicle was jammed with radio equipment, ration packs, and a large circular footplate for the machine-gunner, an earnest and ageing first sergeant called Frank Hustler, who could have been a PE instructor in a different life. His desert boots danced to the rhythm of his anxiety somewhere next to my right hip. The gun on the roof was a 50 calibre – the kind they used to shoot down Spitfires during World War II. A single shot to the abdomen would rip you in half like a Christmas cracker.

In front of me sat the young Irish-American driver, 'Fightin' Dan' Murphy, and the half-Trinidadian captain of our unit, Rick Rogers, known to everyone but his mother as 'Buck'. Directly behind my head were two filthy olive-drab Iraqi Republican Guard uniforms and a sloppily maintained Kalashnikov, all confiscated during a violent, terrifying house raid outside al-Nasiriyah. The Humvee's narrow seats, stuffed with cheap foam and covered with ripped, muddy canvas, were an afterthought. After two weeks, my buttocks felt badly bruised.

At one point I could have sworn they had started to bleed.

'Holy *shit*, look at the size of that scorpion!'

This was Murphy, a few nights earlier. He had just discovered the downside to sleeping on the desert floor: it glistened and squirmed with an encyclopedia's worth of creepy-crawlies. The Marine, who was barely old enough to buy alcohol and spoke with a profane Irish drawl, starred with incredulity at the creature that had just disturbed what passed for sleep in an Iraqi bomb zone.

He jabbed at the grumpy arachnid with his rifle.

'Cap'n, did you see that? That mother*fucker* could have crawled into my sleeping bag. It coulda crawled up my ass!'

Buck was lying on the Humvee's bonnet, staring at the gleaming constellation above. The distant thuds of bombs being dropped on Republican Guard positions echoed through the infinity of mud and sand.

'Sleep on *top* of the vehicle, Murphy,' he said, impatiently. 'There ain't nothin' gonna crawl up your ass up there.'

'Where's the media dude?' asked Murphy.

'In the back. First serg is in the front. *Sleep on the roof.*'

From the back of the Humvee I could hear tobacco being spat, a sleeping bag being unzipped, and a short, tightly-wound Marine scaling the side of the vehicle. With a clatter, Murphy pulled himself on to the Humvee's roof. Somewhere, another bomb went off and more Iraqis died, horribly.

'Some fuckin' stars,' said Murphy.

'Like being on vacation,' muttered Buck.

In front of me I heard Hustler's chemical suit rustle. 'Personally, I'm thinkin' of buying myself an Iraqi retirement home,' he declared. 'Either that, or I'm gonna open the first goddam Starbucks in Baghdad.'

There was, of course, another downside to sleeping on the ground: it was the risk of making an unlucky roll on to a landmine – probably intended for the Iranians, back when the Americans were on the Iraqis' side. Getting my legs blown off, I thought, would really interfere with my morning schedule. And it would ruin the goose-down sleeping bag I had bought in Beverly Hills – back when I was supposed to be writing about celebrity parties and film premieres.

Not that my morning schedule was anything to look forward to. This particular morning, as on most other mornings in Iraq, my first task was to dig a coffin-sized 'foxhole' in the baked mud of the marshlands, the endless no man's land where the Euphrates and Tigris rivers meet.

In theory, if you jump into a foxhole during incoming fire, your chances of survival increase by 80 per cent. It was this statistic, rather than any desire for hard labour, that made me dig foxholes whenever we moved position. But, for anyone who has studied the theory carefully, the foxhole, rather like the illuminated emergency exit in a Boeing 747, is hard to take seriously. For a start, unless you're in it when the mortar or missile hits, it's probably too late. And then I remembered what the instructor from the SAS – a squat northerner with cruel eyes and a mechanical handshake – had told me back in the journalists' training camp: 'Even if yer in yer foxhole,' he said with a smirk and a hint of silver-capped enamel, 'it'll protect you only if the shrapnel from the mortar explodes *up*wards.' He raised his eyes to the ceiling. 'But some mortars are designed to explode *down*wards.' He frowned. 'That's when yer foxhole becomes pointless.' It also becomes pointless, of course, if the mortar that explodes in your camp contains a vial of smallpox, or a canister of poison gas.

If Fodor's ever gets around to publishing a guide to Iraq, the entry on the marshlands will be brief. They are, after all, an apocalyptically bleak part of a country that's lacking in charm to begin with. After the first Gulf War, Saddam drained the marshes and sent his henchmen on a murderous purge of the Ma'dan, or marsh Arabs, who had lived there for 5,000 years. The moustachioed madman considered the peaceful Ma'dan a threat to his Ba'ath Party.

Within less than a decade, the Ma'dan were virtually wiped out, and their former home became a windy wasteland of dried mudbanks, deserted tank trenches, and the occasional lonely, malnourished goat.

The few surviving Ma'dan look like apparitions, bones jutting out of their sackcloth robes. We had thrown a few bright-yellow 'humanitarian-relief' packages to them as we first rolled into the area. The irony, of course, is that the ground the Ma'dan owned had enough oil trapped underneath it to buy Microsoft, leaving enough change for General Electric. Thanks to the post-Gulf War I sanctions, however, the Iraqi leader couldn't turn a profit from his genocide.

On this grim morning, as I started to dig my foxhole, all I cared about was that the top layer of mud had the consistency of cake batter, while deeper down it became as hard as frozen toffee. With mud and sunblock running down my forehead and into my eyes, I hacked away at the earth for what seemed like a Sisyphean eternity. It was an excruciating exercise regime: the marshlands had been freezing cold that night, hardening the tightly packed ground. Iraq has a reputation for being hot, but, as the future Fodor's guide may eventually inform more peaceful visitors, the cold is just as extreme: in fact one member of the SAS died from *hypothermia* during the infamously botched Bravo Two Zero mission into Iraq in 1991.

As the sun rose, and the mud still felt like masonry, the temperature climbed stoically towards 100 degrees, forcing me to strip off the layers of trendy North Face climbing gear I had stuffed inside my ripped chemical suit. I didn't dare take off the gas mask strapped to my waist, however, or the sealed canteen of drinking water on my hip. My heavy blue flak jacket, with the word 'PRESS' inscribed on it in large reflective white lettering, also stayed on.

Buck, Murphy and Hustler would find it amusing to walk up to me, poke me in the chest, and say, 'I'm pressing!' They also enjoyed pointing out that my jacket was possibly the only blue thing anywhere in the southern Iraqi desert – if not the entire country – and was therefore guaranteed to draw fire from even the most junior and inexperienced Iraqi marksman. I could even make the blue target area bigger by unclipping and lowering a special plate of upholstered Kevlar to protect my balls. Now that *really* made the Marines' day.

At least, they joked, I would be able to find out first-hand whether the jacket lived up to its promise of being able to stop a round from an AK-47. None of the Marines, I noticed, stood next to me for very long.

Time passed. I kept hacking at the ground.

I noticed there was an unusually fierce wind, which blew up the dried mud from the marshbanks, giving the world a strange orange-brown tint. Just what I needed, I thought: the world to get more surreal.

As I dug my foxhole, I recalled the gross act of cowardice that had landed me in Iraq in the first place. I was fast asleep in Los Angeles – where I had been posted by *The Times* to write lighthearted and quirky stories about the West Coast – when the floor underneath my bed began buzzing and shaking. It was the phone. On the other end of the line was Martin Fletcher, *The Times*'s foreign-news editor and my boss. My bedside alarm clock read 6.30 a.m. In London, however, it was 2.30 p.m. Fletcher had already been up for at least eight hours and, worse, had just had lunch. Fletcher often had ideas over lunch. And they usual meant work for me.

'Ayres, do you want to go to war?' Fletcher asked cheerfully, as Alana, my girlfriend, lay fast asleep beside me, oblivious that the conversation I was having was about to change everything, for ever.

I tried to summon blood to the brain cells that dealt with Fletcher's often baffling questions. However, the hangover from the previous night, and the lack of espresso, were working against me. 'Yes!' I blurted. 'Love to!' My brain, unable to process the incoming data, had automatically called up a standard response, like an internet browser calling up a home page from its memory when it's not online.

Respond in the positive, my brain remembered. *Be enthusiastic.*
Foreign correspondents are supposed to love wars, after all. What kind
of journalist would prefer to lie by the pool in West Hollywood,
drinking cappuccinos from Urth Café and writing about post-Oscars
parties with Donald Trump and Elton John? And didn't Homer write
in the *Iliad* that every man should experience war, because war, like
love, is one of the central mysteries of life? Or was that Hemingway?
Hang on, didn't Hemingway say that in war 'you'll die like a dog for
no good reason'?

Now I was awake. Fletcher continued. 'The Americans seem to
have some kind of scheme . . . Make sure you get on it, Ayres. Good.'
I reflexively made another positive noise, and Fletcher hung up. *Shit*,
I thought to myself, and went back to sleep. I dreamed of Sunset
Boulevard, the Hollywood sign, Mulholland Drive. When I awoke
again, I realized what I had done. Was Fletcher serious? Probably not,
I reasoned. Why would he send a twenty-seven-year-old Hollywood
correspondent with no combat experience to war? The very idea was
absurd. No doubt I would end up writing a 'colour piece' from Qatar
about an Army chef preparing scrambled eggs for the troops. That
would be my contribution to the paper's war effort. Just in case
Fletcher *was* serious, however, I came up with an ingenious escape
plan – it would make me look enthusiastic, *heroic* even, and yet would
also keep me far away from any live bullets. I would get assigned to an
aircraft carrier. I didn't care what Homer or Hemingway had said. No
one ever died like a dog for no good reason on an American aircraft
carrier.

It was hard to concentrate on the digging, out there in the Iraqi
marshlands. Even though I had been at war for nearly a fortnight, I
still hadn't become acclimatized to the man-made thunder sending
pressure waves through the mudbanks every few minutes. The tremors
were so violent they would surely have registered on the Richter scale.
I was, however, beginning to learn the difference between them: the
distant rumbles were bombs dropped by F-15 fighter jets; the face-
slapping pops were rounds from our own unit's 155-mm howitzer
cannons; the *pfut-pfut-pfuts*, meanwhile, were incoming Iraqi mortars.
Of all the noises, that one was the worst.

Naturally, I tried to react with a mixture of machismo and non-chalance. It didn't work. Nearly every blast made me drop my shovel and involuntarily scream, 'WHAT THE FUCK WAS THAT?' The Marines would turn to look at me, squint into the weak, dusty sun, and explain, '*Someone's gettin' some.*' Then they would shake their heads – possibly out of frustration with the 'media dude', or more likely out of awe for the sheer force of the firepower around them.

'Boy, would I not like to be gettin' some of that,' they would add, thoughtfully, with another head shake.

'That shit would *suck.*'

It was hard not to agree. 'Yes,' I would offer, 'that would certainly be unpleasant.' I mentally pictured the bloodbath a few miles away, as rounds the size of petrol cans from our howitzers whooshed overhead and separated into scores of mini-bomblets, raining down pure misery on those below. 'Good work, Marines,' I had heard a major say the day before. 'The tanks upfront had nothing to fight but body parts.' It was no surprise that the Marines to whom I had been assigned proudly called themselves the Long Distance Death Dealers. They were as efficient as factory workers – a disassembly line, churning out Iraqi body parts.

There's no doubt about it: I should have just said no to Fletcher. But my competitive instincts got the better of me. In other words, I didn't have the guts. Fletcher is an old-school *Times* man. Tall and marathon-runner lean, with tousled dark hair, a billion-gigabyte brain and an inscrutable smile, he is an English foreign correspondent from central casting. Although he is technically an executive, he turns up to the office on a bicycle and never wears a tie. He is, needless to say, irritatingly dashing for a man entering his fifth decade, with a wife and three teenage children. ('Fletcher's yummy,' a female colleague once confided in me.) His career has been relentlessly brilliant: educated in Edinburgh and Pennsylvania, he spent the best part of a decade as *The Times*'s Washington bureau chief and American editor – the journalistic equivalent of being the lead singer of the Rolling Stones – before reporting from Belfast and publishing a bestseller about his US travels called *Almost Heaven*. It's no secret in London that Fletcher hates being wedged behind a desk. As he towers over his computer terminal, he makes it look like some trivial toy. Fletcher belongs out in the field. Preferably an exotic and dangerous field.

Fletcher could barely suppress the envy in his voice when he sent me on assignments in far-flung corners of the US. 'Go! Enjoy!' he would cry. 'It'll be great fun! And think of us poor souls back here on the desk . . . OK? *Good.*' Fletcher ended almost all his conversations with 'good', delivered so quickly and sharply that the double 'o' became almost redundant. It was as though he was so busy he had to abbreviate his speech, like a hastily written email: 'Gd.' I desperately wanted Fletcher to respect me. And if I turned him down, I thought, he would no longer consider me a 'proper' foreign correspondent and would send someone else – making a mental note to recall me from Los Angeles as soon as possible.

So I had only myself to blame for the fact I was digging harder than a convict in an Arizona chain gang, while toting a suffocating camouflaged chemical suit, a gas mask, a water canteen, and a heavy blue flak jacket that was probably visible from space. Every few minutes I would reflexively check to see if my gas mask was still in place and, more importantly, if the holster still contained the self-injectable 10-mg canister of diazepam that had been given to me in Kuwait. The diazepam was to give me a happy death in the event of an Iraqi chemical attack.

'The time to use it's if you start dancin' the funky chicken,' I had been told with a giggle by the butch female Army instructor back in Kuwait City. She did a jerky dance routine to illustrate her point. The 'funky chicken', I assumed, would be my final, violent convulsions, as I clawed at my eyeballs while the blister agent inside my lungs choked me with blood and vomit. On several occasions since entering Iraq I had been tempted to self-administer the diazepam pre-emptively.

Eventually, with the sun near the top of its upward arc, I had created a hole the size of a small bathtub. Then I smoked a Marlboro Light – one of my last before the carton of 200 that I had impulsively bought in Kuwait City ran out. Every time I inhaled I sucked up airborne mud, which at this point was running out of my nose and making my eyes water. The gusts of wind were getting more powerful by the minute, and the orange-brown tint caused by the mud was deepening, making it hard to see. I wondered, not for the first time, if the foxhole would become my grave, or if we would move position again, forcing me to burn another 3,000 calories digging a new one. Our unit, which called itself Katana, after the samurai sword – because it had been stationed on Okinawa island in Japan before moving to Iraq – had never stayed in any one position for more than a few hours since crossing the border into Iraq. As I leaned on my shovel and smoked, I saw Buck approaching me through the mudstorm. My day might have started badly, but it was about to get a lot worse.

Rick 'Buck' Rogers was thirty-one, black and athletic, with family in Trinidad and Britain. I liked him a lot – he wore a hunting knife strapped to his flak jacket, and talked about English football and cricket in a sing-song staccato that reminded me of Will Smith – but I could tell he wasn't happy about having a foreign journalist riding with him on his first combat mission. Especially not a terrified Brit whose luggage took up vital water and rations space in the Humvee.

To be honest, I didn't blame Buck for getting frustrated. During my time in the Humvee I got to know Buck – and Hustler and Murphy – pretty well. Well enough, at least, to know that what they wanted more than anything else in the world was exactly what I was trying to avoid: a fight. Later, much later, when I was convinced that Buck had lied to me in a muddy camp by Highway 8, about 90 miles south of Baghdad, I understood: I really did. It was what he had to do. And perhaps, in some strange way, Buck was looking out for the media dude.

Since leaving northern Kuwait, Buck had been promising to show me the guidelines he had been given on dealing with journalists – to prove, he said, that he wasn't withholding any information from me.

'I found it,' he declared, pulling a creased and muddy booklet from his camouflaged flak jacket. He handed it to me. It was pretty thin. 'Everything is "on the record",' it said, somewhere near the beginning. I soon lost interest in that, however, when I found the far lengthier section entitled 'How to Deal with a Dead Media Representative'. 'Treat a dead or wounded media representative as you would one of your own United States Marines,' it advised.

'Thanks,' I said, spitting out more orange filth, but Buck was already sprinting away, back towards the Humvee.

I heard shouting, enfeebled by the increasingly powerful gale. Then more shouting. I could see a blur of activity around the howitzers.

It could mean only one thing: we were on the move again. I looked sadly at my foxhole. When I climbed into the back of the Humvee, Buck was clearly agitated. The weather made finding a new position almost impossible – but the commanders had ordered it. Our unit's GPS devices – which used satellites to track our position – were unreliable even in good weather. And the night-vision goggles, essential for driving off-road at night, didn't work in a sandstorm, so they probably wouldn't work in a blizzard of dried mud either. But orders were orders. I tried to take notes, but my laptop's battery icon was flashing red and my spiral-bound reporter's notebooks were ripped and filthy.

The routine of finding a new position went something like this: the captain's Humvee – our Humvee – would be the advance party, finding a piece of ground where the Long Distance Death Dealers could set up shop, churn out a few hundred more Iraqi body parts, then move on quickly. Being the advance party – not *in it*, actually *it* – had redefined the concept of terror for me. And it was the reason my bruised buttocks had remained clenched since leaving Kuwait.

Every time we swerved off fresh tracks I expected us to hit a landmine, or some Iraqi 'irregulars' to jump out of the bushes with grenade launchers. Capture was what I feared most. In Pakistan, the *Wall Street Journal* reporter Daniel Pearl had been beheaded, on videotape. Perhaps the Iraqi Republican Guard would do the same to me. Also, I carried with me a copy of *Bravo Two Zero*, Andy McNab's account of his SAS unit's failed Gulf War I mission – not the wisest choice of reading material, given its long description of McNab's torture by the Iraqis. When we eventually found a firing position, we could be alone for hours before the howitzers, towed by all-terrain trucks, eventually turned up. Often we would just drive around in circles, the first sergeant scanning the horizon through the sights of the Humvee's machine gun, his heavy boots tap-dancing on the circular footplate next to me. He would chew gum so loudly I could hear it above the diesel groans of the Humvee's engine.

After receiving our orders to move, the Long Distance Death Dealers started to pack up their howitzers, and we roared off into the eerie orange glow in search of a new position. Darkness was only a few hours away, but the mudstorm had already reduced visibility to just a few feet. I sat grimly in the back of the growling, rattling Humvee, staring at the gun rack in front of me.

I might not have been given a weapon, but I had been unofficially taught how to fire a standard-issue M-16 rifle by Murphy. Not that I had wanted to take the lesson, of course. 'I think there might be an ethical problem with this,' I laughed nervously, aware that my English accent probably sounded pompous and absurd to the musclebound Vermont Marine. Of all the men in Katana, or 'Kilo', Battery, Murphy was perhaps the one I spent most time with, largely because he kept stealing my Marlboro Lights. He told me his nickname was 'Fightin' Dan', because of the number of nightclub brawls he had been involved in. 'Do they do a lot of fightin' in London?' was his opening conversational gambit on the first morning we met.

Murphy, who possessed one of the filthiest vocabularies I had ever heard, was no amateur philosopher, and he certainly didn't understand my ethical dilemma. He just looked me in the eye and drawled, 'So if there's a shitstorm, and you can shoot an Iraqi and save my life, or NOT shoot an Iraqi and let me die, *what you gonna do*?' It was more of an instruction than a question. And I had to spend the rest of the war sharing a Humvee with Murphy. I internally sneered at the notion that 'embedded' journalists – reporters such as myself, assigned to US military units – were in any way impartial. I wanted Buck and his men to beat the Iraqis as much as they did. After all, my own life was at stake. 'I'd shoot the bastard,' I said quickly.

Then I took the weapon from his hands.

As we crawled up a partly built motorway, our faces now orange from the mud, I wondered if I would finally get to use the M-16. I noticed that Saddam had built ugly concrete picnic stops, complete with concrete umbrellas, at regular intervals along the road. I made a mental note never to complain about Little Chefs again. Meanwhile, the blizzard of mud intensified. By this time we were coughing up orange phlegm and reaching for the painters' masks we'd brought for oil-well fires. They weren't much use. Eventually the storm brought us to a halt.

The howitzers were somewhere a long way behind us – perhaps still in the old firing position. Only a couple of other Humvees from our unit had caught up. We waited. We appeared to be alone, and stuck. Over the radio, we heard reports of trucks overturning in the wind, and of Humvees shunting into the back of each other. It would have been insanity to continue driving.

It was now getting dark. Buck picked up the radio and ordered the Marines to stay put and not leave their vehicles – they could have been lost in seconds, and the search parties would have been lost equally quickly. And who knew what lurked over the berm to our right, or in the marshbanks to our left?

I remembered how the Marine commanders in Kuwait had boasted that the Marines were an 'all-weather fighting force', unstoppable by anything that Iraq's annual spring storm season could hurl at them. But the wind and the mud made me feel like a character in one of the Wilfred Owen poems I had studied in the sixth form. (Owen, unluckily, was killed by German gunfire a week before the Great War ended; his mother received the telegram on Armistice Day.) At the time, those poems had seemed so old, so irrelevant. Modern war, after all, was clean, quick and efficient. The Americans could move across entire countries in the time it took the Germans to advance 3 feet during the Battle of the Somme. To me, the five-day Gulf War I had seemed like a thrilling video game, fought with laser guidance and aircraft that looked as though they had been designed and built on Mars.

This, however, was no video game. I imagined what my face must have looked like, caked, like everything else, with orange-brown slime. Just to make matters worse – quite a feat in the circumstances, I thought – a thunderstorm arrived from the north, making us flinch with every rumble.

The lightning created a problem: the radio code name for a chemical Scud-missile attack was also 'lightning'. As a result, every time Buck mentioned the storm, everyone reached for his gas mask. By this point it was so dark I couldn't even see my gloved hand in front of my face. I felt short of breath. 'If I was an Iraqi, this would be my *ideal* time to attack,' muttered Buck.

Then came a blast of radio static and some catastrophic news. This was, indeed, a very bad day. 'We have contact,' crackled a distant bass monotone. 'Contact', in the language of the Marines, where all emotion is surgically removed to avoid collateral damage to troop morale, means being attacked by the enemy. When fire is returned, it becomes 'engagement'. A nuclear exchange, presumably, is a white wedding. I attempted to reassure myself that since the first night of the invasion we had been 'contacted' only by amateurish Iraqi fighters – they drove Toyotas and Nissans with machine guns fitted to the roofs. They wouldn't be a problem.

*Wrong.* We were being contacted, the radio informed us, by a dozen Soviet-built Iraqi tanks: probably Republican Guard. I immediately thought of home and family. This was serious – more serious than anything that had happened to us since we left Kuwait. We couldn't see more than a yard or so. We were blind and lame and alone in the dark. It might have been my imagination, but I was sure I could hear the grinding of the tanks' engines being carried on the wind. The tanks had been spotted only because one of the artillery batteries behind us had illuminated the battlefield by firing a round of white phosphorus into the gloom.

Each round of 'lume' effectively turns 250 acres of night into day and can last for up to two minutes. Its brightness is measured in 'candlepower', a bizarre anachronism, with each of our white phosphorus rounds the equivalent of one million naked flames.

Ahead of us, the infantry clenched their muscles for a fight. Behind us, another artillery unit began preparing to cover them. After an agonizing five-minute delay, the howitzers began their bombardment. For the first time, I hoped they would be as deadly as possible. To hell with my delicate, anti-war sensibilities: I wanted the Iraqis destroyed, turned into body parts. The explosions sent violent tremors through the marshlands. I felt sorry for any random camel-herding Ma'dan or Bedouin who might have set up camp in the wrong place. I also felt as though a pressure hose of adrenalin had been hooked up to my central nervous system. I wondered what it would feel like to die – and how it would happen. Would I even have time to know that we'd been hit? What kind of damage would a round from a Soviet-built tank do? Would I be burned alive or just blown into a 'pink mist', as the Marines like to say. What would that feel like? I curled up in the Humvee's seat, wrapped my sleeping bag round me, and closed my eyes. With my right hand, I created small hole in the Velcro opening of my gas-mask holster and checked that the vial of diazepam, the happy-death juice, was intact. I apologized to the God I didn't believe in for having ignored him all my life, but I was already in a sort of hell. I prayed for sleep, precious sleep. None came.

Another round of lume showed that the howitzers had missed their targets – hardly surprising, given the wind, which had probably blown the rounds off course by miles. The Iraqi tanks were still chewing up the mud and heading straight for us. Their commanders probably thought they would get a chestful of medals from Saddam for this: taking out half a convoy of US artillery, stranded in the dark. I imagined Saddam, his Big Brother features crumpled into a dictatorly smile, tenderly pinning honours to the Iraqis' olive-drab uniforms. Tears would well up in their puppy-dog eyes. 'You destroyed the American infidels!' Saddam would say.

Then, over the radio, came the message we had all wanted to hear – but thought was impossible because of the weather. 'We're sending in some F-15s,' said the bass monotone – meaning fighter jets, probably from one of the American aircraft carriers I had so desperately tried to get on.

Buck, who had been silently staring at the crucifix hanging from the Humvee's dashboard, slapped his camouflaged thigh. 'Ladies and gentlemen,' he said, 'The F-15s are in da house!'

Then came the catch. 'They'll be thirty mikes,' said the monotone – meaning thirty minutes. There was a fizz of static. Then silence.

# 2

# A Proud Line of Cowards

My name is Chris Ayres, and I never wanted to be a war correspondent. To me, war reporters were a different species: fearless and suntanned outdoors types who became Boy Scout leaders at school, studied Latin and Urdu at Oxford, and probably knew the correct way to eat a sheep's penis at the table of an African warlord. I felt a mixture of envy and bafflement at their careers. Before I was sent to Iraq, I could have imagined doing John Simpson or Walter Cronkite's job no more than I could have imagined becoming an Olympic javelin-thrower.

Growing up, the enduring image I had of a war correspondent was Martin Bell, the BBC man in his trademark white linen suit, who took a direct hit from mortar shrapnel while reporting live from Sarajevo in 1992. 'I'm all right, I'll survive,' were Bell's stoic words as he collapsed into a pool of his own blood. There was a thrilling, implicit machismo to Bell's work, betrayed by the title of his memoirs: *In Harm's Way.* Bell, always the self-deprecating hero, could barely bring himself to mention the incident in the book. I hated to think of the piercing, girlish squeal, followed by the involuntary bowel movement, that would have been broadcast into the homes of BBC viewers if it had been me in Sarajevo instead of Bell. The profanity I would have unleashed upon being hit, however, would probably have ensured that the satellite feed was cut long before it reached London.

When I first joined *The Times*, the paper's best-known war correspondent was a lunatic called Anthony Loyd – a heroin addict who had left his job as a platoon commander in the British Army for a career in journalism because, he later confessed, he saw it as a 'passport to war'. To me, Loyd's life seemed like an endless, heart-pounding sequence from *Apocalypse Now* – but with no 'stop' button to end the action. Loyd's motivation for joining *The Times* was very different from my own. If I saw journalism as a passport to anything, it was *fun*. I wanted to meet celebrities, dine at Michelin-starred restaurants, and feel important at parties. I fantasized about pontificating on world events, penning witty op-ed columns, and profiling politicians and rock stars – all from the comfort and safety of an air-conditioned London office.

Most of all, perhaps, I wanted my writing to impress exotic, intellectual girls with exciting curves. It's fair to say that taking mortar fire didn't feature, at all, in my decision to seek a job in the news business.

To me, war reporting was a guarantee of a premature single-column obituary, printed alongside an unflattering headshot, in my own newspaper. I remembered reading about Ernie Pyle, the all-American farm boy from Indiana, who forced himself, out of duty, to live on the front lines during World War II. Pyle described his chance to cover the D-Day landings in 1944 as 'like an invitation from the White House: something you don't refuse'. He was less lucky than Bell. After making the front cover of *Time* magazine and winning a Pulitzer Prize for his dispatches from the European battlefront, Pyle's career at the powerful Scripps-Howard newspaper chain ended abruptly with a bullet from a Japanese machine gun.

When I returned to Los Angeles from the Gulf, I searched for books by Pyle, and other war correspondents, to convince myself that my conduct in Iraq hadn't been a total disgrace. The book jackets, however, provided little reassurance. There was Pyle, his woolly hat and goggles pulled down over his military crew-cut, the cigarette wedged between his cracked lips. He was an 'aw-shucks' Everyman – one of the boys. And the boys, of course, loved him. Then there was the cover shot of the *Washington Post*'s Neil Sheeham, the veteran Vietnam correspondent. He was wearing black aviator shades and sitting, shirt unbuttoned and notebook poised, in front of a rifle rack. Sheeham's expression, like Pyle's, betrayed his role: the pen pausing for thought; the lip curled in disbelief and disillusionment.

And then I thought of the picture of me, somewhere in those miserable, windy marshlands, stuffed into an oversized chemical suit with a stupid blue helmet on my head, squinting myopically into the dust and the sun. I had even taken my glasses off, because I thought it might make me look cooler. But the message of the photo is clear: *I want to go home*. When I look at it now, I think of my brief and largely inept stint in Mesopotamia.

And I wonder how on earth I became a member of Pyle and Sheeham's elite, noble and fucked-up profession.

My father hates fairground rides, aeroplanes and fast cars. In fact he enjoys joking that I come from a long and proud line of cowards. This is odd, given our family name. The first Ayres was, in fact, a Truelove, and a follower of William the Conqueror, the Frenchman who successfully invaded England in 1066 at the Battle of Hastings. In the sweat of battle, William was flung off his horse and saved only by the fearless Truelove, who pulled him up from the mud and wrenched off his battered helmet, which was suffocating him. According to an entry in the royal land deeds of Battle Abbey, East Sussex, William told him, 'Thou shalt hereafter from Truelove be called Eyre, because thou hast given me the air I breathe.' Eyre, however, didn't have a good war, and was found in a ditch with a leg and thigh cut off. The King ordered him to be looked after, and, in reward for his loyalty, gave him land in Derby and a family crest featuring an amputated leg and thigh, clad in armour. The name Eyre eventually became Eyres, before mutating into the modern form, Ayres.

Fearlessness wasn't an Ayres family trait that survived into the twentieth century. When I was a child, in the eighties, my family would spend three brutal days driving to southern France for our annual summer holiday, largely because Dad was afraid of flying. On the motorways and autoroutes, we did a steady 65 m.p.h. in our little Renault 9. And when the funfair visited our home town my father would always refuse to take me on the Ferris wheel. 'I'm not going on that bloody thing,' he would say, after taking one look at the pot-smoking carney operating the machinery. Later, when I was learning to drive, my dad was the worst passenger imaginable, stomping his foot on a phantom brake pedal when even the gentlest of bends approached. Once, when I accidentally reversed my chocolate-brown Austin Metro into a wall, I thought he was going to have a cardiac arrest. He hated physical danger.

Being scared, however, is not the same as being a coward, and my father is wrong to portray himself as one, although he probably sees it as a good-humoured way of shrugging off his lack of machismo. Perhaps it's also an excuse for his own father, a manual labourer for twenty-five years, who avoided World War II because of a vague problem with his hands which meant he couldn't grip a rifle. It's odd, however, that Dad doesn't try to plume his male feathers once in a while. He is, after all, a natural sportsman, who once boxed and played semi-professional football. In fact his first job was as a PE teacher, before he took an Open University degree and was promoted to head of a first school in Wooler, a farming village in Northumberland, near the Scottish border.

Before he retired, in 2005, my dad was the kind of firm-but-fair teacher that everyone liked. He would amuse the children by walking down the hallways on his hands, or by giving them all silly nicknames. But if anyone so much as uttered a swear word, or touched another pupil, he unleashed a wrath so terrifying that the incident was never repeated. Even in the old days he wasn't much of a fan of 'Big Bertha', the disciplinary slipper he kept in the bottom drawer of his desk. Instead, he used verbal assaults to put the fear of God into wayward pupils. 'Son, if you do that again, you'll be in so much trouble *you won't be able to handle it,*' was his favourite threat. Generally, and in spite of his featherweight's build, the pupils believed him.

When it came to physical violence, avoidance was nearly always better than engagement as far as my father was concerned. Once, at the family dinner table, he told me a story of how he was attacked by a gang of older boys when he was growing up in the back streets of Warrington. After the gang circled him and his brother, one of the older boys pulled a knife. I asked my dad how he escaped, expecting a heroic tale. 'I cried,' he said, without pausing. 'The fact that I cried made them realize that I wasn't worth bothering with, so they left us alone.' The thought of my father crying was enough to silence me for the rest of the meal.

Given that I had no talent for fighting, it was probably wise that I adopted my father's avoidance strategy. I blamed my lack of school-yard combat technique on the fact that I had an older sister, rather than an older brother, and so didn't have anyone to practise on. Later, my body awash with the furious chemicals of adolescence, I began to question my dad's pacifism. My maternal grandmother, a redoubtable woman who admired Margaret Thatcher, had always told me that if Britain hadn't waged war with Germany we'd all be living under Hitler's National Socialist Party, and the Jews would be an extinct race. And so, as a teenager, when another boy in my class took a dislike to me, I decided to confront him – physically.

At first it worked. On the bus journey back home from school, I wrestled him to the floor and put him in a headlock until it was time for him to get off. The next morning, however, as I was sitting on the bus reading – feeling both macho *and* intellectual – the boy appeared out of nowhere and pummelled my nose into a bloody pulp before I had a chance to raise my fists in defence. I could, I suppose, have retaliated a few days later. But it seemed pointless to continue the circle of violence. My father's strategy, I realized, was not to avoid standing up for yourself, but to fight only when it was worth it. My bloodied nose was the reason why: fighting has consequences. Not for the first time, I realized my dad was right.

Islington, London

1997

# 3

## The Lunch Tutorial

The lounge of the Red Lion was warm and dank, and the thick, blue-tinted air carried a strong odour of salt-and-vinegar crisps and tobacco. It had just gone noon and, as usual, we were drinking heavily. An ageing waitress with a poor memory of both the menu and our orders occasionally clonked an unwanted pork pie or cold lasagne between the sodden beer mats. The date was early June 1997 – nearly six years before *The Times* would send me to the Middle East.

'This can't possibly live up to expectations,' I declared, to no one in particular.

'Right,' said Jamie.

'Why not wait and see?' offered Georgina.

Me again: 'Where *is* he anyway?'

There was a contemplative silence. Glasses clinked. Then Chris said, 'He's on deadline, probably. A busy man.'

'He's more than busy,' snorted Jamie. 'He's a celebrity.'

All of us around the table were enrolled at City University's postgraduate journalism school, a kind of Fame Academy for aspiring reporters. In fact City regarded its only serious rival as Columbia in New York. Whether or not this was bullshit was beside the point: City was a brutal place to study, partly because of Linda Christmas, the matriarch who presided over the course (her second name was a gift to young writers with a flair for cruel puns), and partly because of the ferocious rivalry between the students – something we tried to hide with forced camaraderie. Between classes we would fix our fake smiles and discuss how much we *loved* our classmates. The competitiveness was unavoidable: all thirty of us wanted one of the handful of junior positions that came up every year on national newspapers.

The crowd at the Red Lion, which was the nearest drinking establishment to City's red-brick entrance on St John's Street in north London, also had something else in common: we had all opted to take City's 'financial-reporting' specialism, which in theory meant we wanted to write about stock prices and corporate takeovers. That, of course, was a joke. No one still in their twenties, and broke, goes into journalism to write about money – a subject in which they have zero practical experience. Journalism students don't get excited about GDP fluctuations or the price-to-earnings ratios of widget-makers. No, they want to bring down the Prime Minister, meet Robert De Niro, or expose human-rights violations in Guantanamo Bay. Under the Christmas regime, however, everyone had to specialize. Which was why we were in the Red Lion, waiting for Robert Cole, our finance tutor.

As far as I was aware, no one, apart from me, had taken the financial module as first choice. On the geek-o-meter, it was the equivalent of taking a night class in Klingon. Most of our group had been forced on to the financial specialism by early indecisiveness and then a shortage of places on other, cooler, courses – such as crime, fashion or, most glamorous of all, foreign reporting. Unlike the other students, I had no interest in the last of these whatsoever. I couldn't speak a foreign language, and I hated any kind of physical discomfort. I had flown only once before, on a high-school skiing trip to Switzerland, and wasn't keen to repeat the experience. The idea of covering a famine in the Sudan, or a civil war in a failed Balkan state, was enough to bring me out in a hot, prickly sweat. I had never even been camping – unless I counted a trip to a caravan park in France, or a couple of Cub Scout outings to youth hostels. There were many reasons for my lack of adventurousness, most of them physical: I had a sensitive stomach, for a start, and my forehead turned crimson if exposed to sun. It had been hard enough enduring my family's annual holiday to France.

I was easily the least cool student at City. Part of the reason was my age – at twenty-one, I was one of the youngest – and another part was the fact that I had never lived in London before. I also looked a mess. My ginger hair, which had been long and greasy at university, had been cut into a failed attempt at a floppy Hugh Grant style, and

I sported a scruffy ginger beard, an incongruous throwback to the days when I wanted to look like Kurt Cobain. My eyesight, meanwhile, had recently deteriorated to the point at which I had to wear my glasses all the time. My specs were a nasty eighties design, with gold, circular rims. I couldn't yet afford to buy a new designer pair or, even better, switch to contact lenses. My clothes, like my haircut and beard, also confirmed that I was lost in a fashion wilderness somewhere between university and adulthood. I wore steel-capped boots with blue Levis, and a patterned, designer-label work shirt, tucked in instead of out – an aspirational gesture towards grown-up respectability. My unfortunate concession to the dance-music-inspired fashion of the time was a purple jacket made from rubbery waterproof material. The ensemble looked ridiculous. Needless to say, I was single, and doomed to remain so for a long time.

But even for me the finance specialism was a compromise. I took it largely because I had a good contact on *The Times*'s business desk – a result of having won a student essay-writing competition, sponsored by *The Times* and the NatWest Bank, on the oxymoronic subject of business ethics. I had won the contest almost by default, because only a handful of other students had bothered entering. I picked up the £3,000 prize from Lindsay Cook, *The Times*'s petite and fashionable business editor, at a surreal ceremony in London. My plan was to use the cash to pay for the City course, then beg Cook for a job on *The Times*'s business desk. If she gave me one, I thought, I could later decamp to a more interesting section of the paper.

It was, of course, a catastrophically successful scheme.

The finance geeks, being the lepers of the City course, stuck together. There was Jamie, a tall, curly-haired five-a-side footballer who looked like a cross between a Greek god and Jesus Christ; Chris, a scholarly and urbane wit with an intimidating arsenal of degrees from Oxford University; and Georgina, an English rose whom everyone fancied. An honorary member of the group was Glen, an acerbic public schoolboy from Suffolk, who had already managed to get himself on *The Times*'s graduate trainee scheme, allowing him to sit out the competitive shuffle of the other students. I admired Glen because he had a better Hugh Grant hairdo than mine, and also because of his devotion to a grungy Islington nightclub called The Garage, which he patronized every Friday and Saturday without fail. Glen and I became good friends, sharing many a Garage night together, and later a squalid flat in Clapham.

There were upsides to being a finance geek. One of them was avoiding the dreaded 'off-diary' classes given by Linda Christmas. The purpose of these was to teach students what hard-working reporters did when there were no scheduled press conferences taking place. In reality, of course, reporters get drunk and smoke cigarettes when there's nothing to do. But Christmas would give each student a grid reference on the *A-Z* map of London, then instruct us to go to our location and find two 'exclusive' stories. 'Get out there and talk to people,' was her only advice on how to complete the task. 'This is *real* journalism, folks. This is what you should be doing, instead of rewriting press releases.' The grid reference always just happened to be in one of the most violent, piss-reeking slums of the East End. We had to get the stories, write them, and file them – all by 4 p.m. the same day. Some students gave up before even getting on the Tube, despite knowing they would have to endure a 'private talk' with Christmas – who always power-dressed in monochrome trouser suits – and also probably a public humiliation in class the next morning. There were, however, more serious consequences to displeasing Christmas: she regularly had lunch with senior newspaper editors, who would quietly inquire about the performance of individual City students.

To me, the jargon and statistics of the finance specialism were infinitely preferable Christmas's 'real' journalism. It might not have been a particularly glamorous form of reporting, but it seemed civilized and dignified – like a *proper* job. There was no way, I concluded, that a business reporter would end up being dispatched to anything more traumatic than a bankruptcy hearing.

'He's here! The man himself!'

Jamie stood up and raised his pint glass as Robert Cole made his entrance. A low cheer went up from the table. Cole was in his usual outfit: wool suit, trench coat and hat, the latter resembling a cross between a farmer's flat cap and a French beret. He carried a leather briefcase. All this made him look like a 1930s Fleet Street caricature, and about a decade older than his real age, which was somewhere in the mid-thirties. Cole completed his image by smoking Silk Cuts, twirling an umbrella, and affecting an ironic Old Etonian accent, calling people 'old boy' and 'dear chap'. In fact Cole had grown up in Surrey, and, like me, had gone to Hull University, a red-brick institution favoured by *Socialist Worker* types.

'Righto, chaps,' he said, removing his coat and sitting down. 'Time to get this over with. Sorry I'm late: deadlines.'

I sucked on my pint of warm Stella Artois and felt my forehead become flushed with alcohol. I was a terrible boozer – a one-pint wonder. But it was important I fought off the drunkenness. Today's lunch, after all, was business, not pleasure. It was the culmination of nine months of tutorials, assignments and disappointing grades, scrawled in red ballpoint across inkjet printouts.

Cole, a portly and sometimes moody fellow with a bald pate and round, bookish glasses, was a senior financial editor of London's *Evening Standard*. He was one of City's 'visiting' tutors, which meant he was a professional journalist who took one day off a week to give a specialism class. Cole was also our hero. We read his columns in the *Standard* with awe. His technique was to tackle tedious money matters using the matey first-person persona of a pub raconteur. He used man-of-the-people metaphors and a slap of irreverence to enliven complex, technical arguments. Cole's populist writing style had even produced a book, albeit one with the rather off-putting title of *Getting Started in Unit and Investment Trusts*. To us he was a genius. He was also a celebrity. And we all desperately wanted his attention.

Like many journalists, Cole was an odd mixture of self-confidence and insecurity. Both traits, I later learned, are necessary in a good writer. Without the former, you would never believe your thoughts worthy of publication; without the latter, your thoughts would never be worthy of publication. Cole was also a Catholic, who saw it as his duty to stand up for the private investor – the 'little man'. I even suspected he was a bit of a class warrior, what with his ironic 'old chaps' and the fact that he once referred to investment bankers as 'those marble-halled bastards'.

On the first day of term, Cole had blustered into our Victorian-era lecture hall and scratched the names of some of his former students on to the blackboard. All of them were now writers on national news-papers. Having expected the finance specialism to be a career junk-yard, our mood improved. He then told us that if we turned up for his weekly lectures, and handed in our assignments on time, our names could also one day appear on the blackboard. And then came the best part: Cole said he always gave his favourite students a special end-of-term tutorial – which, to mark the occasion of our imminent graduation, would be held in the Red Lion.

No one skipped Cole's lectures. Meanwhile, the end-of-term tutorial became our own private folklore. Word came back from other graduates of Cole's class that it involved an all-day boozing session. Others said it held the secret to getting a job at a major paper. The subject, however, remained a mystery. We would spend entire short-hand classes speculating about its content.

The end-of-term tutorial, Cole promised us, would be a practical, hands-on 'workshop', unlike any of the other lectures he had given. It would be a guide on how to extract stories from secretive billion-aires, arrogant bankers and nerdish stock-market analysts. The very thought of it made me shudder with excitement. If I became a jour-nalist, would these business behemoths really want to meet me? And would they really give me 'exclusive' stories? I had yet to learn that, if used correctly, a career in journalism can be a licence to meet anyone, or do anything that takes your interest. In journalism, no expertise is required. In fact I don't think I truly understood that concept until I ended up in the Iraqi desert.

Eventually, the week before we were due to graduate, Cole came clean and told us what our final lesson would be. Clearly, it would be a momentous occasion – the curtain call of the Robert Cole Show to which we had become so addicted during our time at City. 'So, you 'orrible lot,' he announced one Friday lunchtime, with his best faux-Dickensian sneer, 'my effort to educate you is, thankfully, about to come to an end.' We listened in blank silence, notebooks and pens quivering with anticipation. 'That means you're ready for the *final tutorial*.'

Cole crushed a piece of chalk into the blackboard, then drag-ged it. After his loopy handiwork was complete, he used his umbrella to point to the white letters he had formed. He cleared his throat.

'In this, your last lesson, the date and location of which you already know, you will learn the primary information-gathering technique of the successful business reporter. After this,' he said, 'you will be able to go to your future newspaper employers with confidence – knowing you can cajole and bully a story out of even the most hardened, miserable bastard of a business executive. Chaps, you're finally ready. See you down the pub.'

With that, he picked up his briefcase and left.

We stared at the dusty letters Cole had just drawn on the blackboard. They spelled out the words 'The Lunch Tutorial'.

Cole raised his pint glass and ignited a Silk Cut. This was it – the moment we had been waiting for. 'Let's begin,' he said. We leaned in over the table, desperate to hear his wisdom over the din of a Kylie track.

The business lunch, Cole told us, was the key to financial journalism. The best tables at London's best restaurants were our workstations. The waiters and sommeliers were our technicians, helping us work on our raw material – our billionaire dining companions – until we had extracted the precious stones of information within. We could spend as long as we wanted polishing those stones back in the office, but it was at the lunch table that we had to dig for them. 'Never underestimate how much someone will tell you while stuffing a salmon blini into their face,' said Cole – 'especially after they've drained a bottle of 1990 Gevrey Chambertin.'

I was nervous, however. Since the age of eighteen I had been suffering from panic attacks, the main symptom of which was a powerful tide of nausea. I spent one entire term at university making steam-hammer convulsions into the philosophy department's toilet bowl. What if that happened at lunch?

'Just follow the simple rules, chaps,' Cole told the table. 'You sit down and make small talk. Discuss the weather, the traffic, the bloody route you took in the cab – *whatever*. Order the starter. Make more small talk. Talk about the news, the book you're reading, anything you want. Move on to the serious stuff over the main course.' Cole extinguished his Silk Cut in an empty wineglass. Then a thought struck him: 'Oh, and if you're having lunch with anyone in public relations, always order the most expensive thing on the menu, because *PRs always pay*. For your guidance, anything lobster-related is generally at the top of the price list. Oh, and don't *ever* order skate. Too many bones. Impossible to eat. I nearly choked to death on one of those fuckers once. And no one wants to give a choking man a story.'

And that was it: the lesson over. Thus educated, I made an appointment with Cook at *The Times*. She didn't give me a job, of course. But she did the next best thing: she invited me in on 'work experience'.

# 4

## 'You Haven't Got a Bloody Hope in Here . . .'

Before we move any further towards the blood and the horror (it won't be long now), I should probably tell you what happened on my first day of work experience. My plan was to stride through the door to the business section as confidently as possible and proceed immediately to Lindsay Cook's office, in the hope that her familiar face would help calm me down. After tripping over the step, however, and launching myself into an undignified recovery dance in front of a row of grimacing sub-editors, I noticed that the door to her office was shut. *Bollocks.*

When I looked again, I realized why the subs were so downcast. Behind the blinds of Cook's office I could see the flickering outline of the business editor, a tissue pressed to her face. With her other hand she was shakily transferring the contents of her desk to a brown cardboard box.

To this day, I have no idea what happened. But Cook, my best Fleet Street contact, and perhaps my only chance of a job on a national newspaper, was gone. As I trudged downstairs to the office vending machine, wondering whether or not to go home, I almost collided with Robert Miller, *The Times*'s banking correspondent. I didn't know it at the time, but Miller, a dapper City gent with a boxer's frame and a rhinoceros-hide complexion, was one of Cook's closest office allies. 'Still want to be a journalist, son?' he sneered, brushing past me.

In fact I did. Having blown my prize money on tuition fees and paid for more than a year's worth of living expenses with the kind of high-interest debt that would make a South American central bank nervous, I had no Plan B. The only free accommodation available to me was 400 miles north in Wooler, but I didn't much fancy a return to Sheepsville. I had wanted to be a journalist because it seemed the closest thing to being a rock star without having to be either good-looking or talented. As a petulant, hormone-saturated teenager living in Wooler, the one thing that kept me sane was my family's daily delivery of *The Guardian*. It was the only proof I had that there were other people in Britain who read the same books, watched the same films, and bought the same records as I did. I might not have managed to get a work-experience gig at *The Guardian*'s arts desk (a task I considered impossible), but I had come close with *The Times* – albeit via the Most Boring Section. It seemed too depressing to give up now, having come so close to career nirvana.

So I spent the rest of the day just hanging around. I didn't have a desk, so I shuffled my feet by the newspaper rack; drank frothy, muddy tea from the vending machine; and sat quietly beside the shelves of index cards that served as a kind of pre-internet database. I didn't ask anyone's permission to stay, or to go, assuming that if they wanted rid of me they would tell me. Every hour or so I would go downstairs to see Glen, who was at that point working on the foreign desk and designing an elaborate graphic of an exploding volcano on the island of Montserrat. With his Hugh Grant flop, brilliant white shirt, Greek-island tan and posh drawl, Glen was a *Times* natural. I, on the other hand, had suffered a catastrophic breakout of stress acne, and my pale skin seemed to have become paler from shock. Anyone in the newsroom could have identified me as 'the work-experience kid' from 400 feet. If Glen hadn't been downstairs, I'm not sure I would have had the guts to stay all day.

Eventually, at 6 p.m., I left *The Times*'s office – which was then in a windowless former rum warehouse inside the News International printing compound in Wapping – and began the lonely, miserable trek to Tower Hill tube station. From there, I made three connections until I ended up back at my tiny, disgusting flat-share on Caledonian Road. The next day I turned up for another unwanted, unpaid shift. The day after that I did the same again.

Finally, on Thursday, I was busted.

'Jesus *Christ*, are you still here?'

*Oh no.* I dropped the newspaper in my hand and turned to face Martin Barrow, *The Times*'s deputy business editor. During my week as a ghost in Rupert Murdoch's machine I had already learned all about Barrow. He was infamous on the business desk for his relentless sarcasm, delivered in a nasal sneer that could puncture the most inflated journalistic ego. He was, I would later learn, the opposite of the 'other' Martin: Martin Fletcher, the foreign-news editor. While Fletcher was a well-bred scholar, fond of debating government policy and fine-tuning his correspondents' work to emphasize intellectual points, Barrow was a workaholic with no formal university education who enjoyed ridiculing the pretensions of his colleagues. One of the many ways he did this was by using tradesmen's terms for what many considered the sensitive art of writing stories. 'Could you bash me out five pars while I shovel some more copy through the system?' was a typical Barrow request.

Later, much later, I would ask Barrow whether he had many friends who were journalists. 'Nah,' he said. 'They're all plumbers and cab drivers.' If anyone else had said it, it might have sounded like inverted snobbery. But with Barrow, whose bullshit detector was one of the most powerful on Fleet Street, it seemed natural. If Barrow thought an article was shoddily written, he would say so, often directly to the author's face. 'Mucky – *very mucky*,' he would tut, with a slight downward curl of his upper lip. 'Do you want to have another go at it, *or shall I clean it up?*' In Barrow's universe, there was nothing worse than mucky copy.

It was obvious that Barrow relished his job as The Cleaner: the journalistic equivalent of The Wolf, the character played by Harvey Keitel in *Pulp Fiction*. His ability to 'tidy up' copy was all the more impressive given that he was brought up in Peru and spoke Spanish as his first language. His appearance matched his role: with his Marine buzzcut and rectangular, steel-framed glasses, he had the slightly sinister look of an MI5 bureaucrat. During my week of invisibility, I noticed that he spent his lunch hours taking five-mile runs around east London rather than eating lobster on the expense accounts of obsequious PRs. Barrow, clearly, had never been given The Lunch Tutorial. When he returned from his noontime exercise break, saddlebags of sweat visible through his grey T-shirt, he seemed to fizz with static from his high-voltage energy. He was always in good humour in the afternoon – the kind of good humour, at least, that a drill instructor might have after ordering you to do 300 sit-ups. Perhaps Barrow was happy because he was pumped-up with endorphins while everyone else was trying to sober up after their three-hour sessions in Coq D'Argent and Pont de la Tour. At 3 p.m. the foreheads of the business-desk reporters, almost hidden behind their egg-shaped computer monitors, glistened with booze-sweat.

Barrow, meanwhile, looked taut and tanned. Every so often his villain's cackle would echo through the newsroom. When Barrow laughed, I thought, it didn't seem like something to be very happy about.

As Barrow stood in front of me and laughed until the veins on his forehead started to tap-dance, I definitely knew it wasn't anything to be happy about. 'What's your name again, son?' he asked, eventually.

'Ugh, Ayres,' I told him, with a worrying stammer.

'OK – *Urquerz* . . .? Follow me.'

Barrow sprint-marched me back towards his desk, his long, stiff arms swinging like a sergeant major's. He sat down and began thumping and slapping his way through a pile of faxes. Finally he held up a press release with an unfamiliar logo at the top. It said, 'Pressac'. The fax didn't seem to have any words on it at all – only numbers, pound signs and what looked like computer code.

'Here you go . . . erm, mate,' said Barrow. 'Write this up as a nib. Hundred words? Shout when you're done.'

With no further explanation, Barrow went back to his copy-cleaning, his long, thin fingers attacking the computer keyboard with urgency, as though he were programming the flight trajectory of an intercontinental ballistic missile. Before I could ask a question, a pretty, motherly secretary seized me by the arm and led me towards an unmanned computer terminal, which looked as though it pre-dated the microwave oven. She sat me down, switched on the green LED screen, and patted me on the shoulder. 'Here you go, love,' she said in a northern accent as thick as gravy. 'You've got to get used to Martin – he's very busy, y'know.'

I felt relief wash over me like warm Mediterranean sea water. The secretary was the first person I had met at *The Times* without a terrifyingly posh accent. I almost wanted to call my mother and tell her that everything was OK. I gripped my press release tightly and began to fantasize about the Pulitzer Prize I would win for the thrilling, witty and brilliantly researched piece of broadsheet journalism I was about to produce. It would surely be the best nib ever published by *The Times*! Then a thought struck me. I turned and called out to the retreating seam of the secretary's blazer. 'Excuse me, erm, miss, but what's a "nib"?'

She stopped dead, and I thought I could hear her heels grind into the carpet as she turned. Her face looked very different now.

'If you don't know that, you haven't got a bloody hope in here, have ya?' she said. 'Nib means NEWS IN BRIEF. *Duh!*' She rolled her eyes, turned 180 degrees, and stalked back towards the news desk.

'YOU'LL NEVER GUESS WHAT?' I heard her screech as she sat down. 'THE BLOODY WORK-EXPERIENCE KID JUST ASKED ME WHAT A NIB WAS!' Again, Barrow's cackle echoed.

This is the nib I filed to Barrow:

> PRESSAC, the electronics group, is set to make another major move forward in the automotive industry with the purchase of Italamec, the Italian mechanical and electronic components manufacturer, for £20.7 million. The acquisition will be funded through a one-for-three rights issue of up to 12.5m new ordinary shares, priced at 180p each. Existing shares rose ½ p to 215p yesterday.

The nib had taken me the best part of three hours to write, and I didn't have a clue what it meant. I had, however, managed to translate some of the computer code into English by means of a red manual called *How to Read the Financial Pages*. Robert Cole had ordered all his students to buy the book during his first class at City. I remembered the class well, because it was then that Cole had also ordered me to shave off my beard before setting foot in any Fleet Street newsroom. 'Is anyone else going to tell him, or shall I?' he asked, as Jamie, Chris and Georgina snickered. 'Ayres, get that bum-fluff off your face, old chap,' said Cole. 'No one trusts a man with a beard. Just look at Richard Branson. And he's got a billion pounds. You don't have diddly-squat, dear boy.' Cole mimed a shaving action. 'Time to get rid of it,' he said.

★

Cole's advice – on both the book and the facial hair – appeared to have worked. But wasn't a job on the business desk supposed to be more glamorous than this? Why hadn't I had lunch with a billionaire yet?

'Cheers for that,' said Barrow, as I headed towards the door at 6 p.m. 'That was a pretty clean nib. Not bad at all. See you tomorrow?' There was no mention of pay, or any kind of job offer, but at least I had survived the week. In fact I was already well on my way to becoming a war correspondent.

Greenwich Village, New York City

2001

# 5

## Fight or Flight

'I don't think there's anything wrong with you,' said the female voice, from an unusual position behind me. I felt an index finger slide out of a place it definitely didn't belong and heard a latex snap. '*Done*,' the voice said. 'You can pull your jeans up now.' I bent down and wrestled with my Levis.

As I fastened my belt buckle, I turned to face Jeane Ruth, my local Greenwich Village doctor. She was a short, crumpled-looking woman in her forties, who always dressed for extreme comfort. Today she was wearing a red tracksuit bottom, hiking shoes, and a hand-knitted cardigan in Christmas-tree colours. I wiped a film of dirt and sweat from my flushed brow. Outside, the amplified squawk of an NYPD squad car competed with a fire engine to drown out the throb of the heater, which was wedged below the only window in Dr Ruth's tiny clinic.

'Bet you love doing this first thing on a Monday morning,' I said, in an effort to unwind the awkward tension. I couldn't, however, look her in the eye. She had, after all, just pushed her finger up my anus.

'I don't know what to tell you, Christopher,' sighed Dr Ruth. Her use of my full name, as it appeared on my health-insurance card, reminded me of visits to my childhood doctor in Wooler. It was strangely comforting. 'There's nothing unusual up there as far as I can tell. Y'know, stress can cause a lot of phantom symptoms. There's certainly nothing to suggest colonic cancer. It would be unusual for a twenty-six-year-old with your health to have colonic cancer. *Very* unusual.'

I suddenly felt winded with guilt. Since arriving in New York I had visited Dr Ruth's clinic almost every other week. Each time, I was convinced I would leave in an ambulance, doomed to spend the rest of my tragically short life in the death-watch ward of St Vincent's Hospital. My symptoms were varied, exotic and, from Dr Ruth's point of view, maddeningly non-specific: *my right leg keeps shaking*; *I need to urinate all the time*; *I feel dizzy*; *my back is sweaty; my skull bone aches*. With the help of the internet, I would always self-diagnose in advance of my appointments. Once I had diabetes; another time Parkinson's. Then, of course, there was my near-miss with Creutzfeldt-Jakob disease, caused by eating a hamburger made from mad cow. I later decided it was the premature onset of Alzheimer's.

In three months, Dr Ruth had literally got to know me inside out. On every visit, she would give me a weak smile before setting to work on me with her tools. Once her tests were complete, she would take notes in a pretty longhand, then declare me to be in unusually excellent health. At first I didn't believe her. I demanded blood tests, urine samples, MRIs and CAT scans – the full hypochondriac's boot camp. I consulted arm specialists, leg technicians, ear-nose-and-throat experts. I received diagnostic bills from laboratories as far afield as Alaska. Before long, however, her verdicts started to act as their own medicine. I would stride out of her clinic on 14th Street feeling suddenly symptom-free. Sometimes I would smoke an ultra-light cigarette in celebration. But within days it would start again, the symptoms returning, in a different combination. A long, sweaty session on the internet would confirm the very worst. Then it would be time for another visit. By the time I got to her clinic, I would have already planned the music for my funeral.

'So I'm OK?' I asked, looking at the heavy white plaster cast on Dr Ruth's leg, which she had broken on a skiing trip to Vermont. Of the two of us, I internally conceded, she probably had the more serious medical problem. In fact I wondered whether she resented the whole colon thing.

'Yes,' she said, wearily. 'You're OK. Absolutely fine.'

'What about you? That leg looks painful.'

'Fine. It's an inconvenience, that's all.'

She threw the used latex glove into the bin with only slightly more force than necessary, then hobbled across the room using the window sill for balance. Her metal crutch, I noticed, was propped up by the door. Dr Ruth really didn't look very well at all. She coughed into her hand, picked up a tissue, and emptied her nasal passage. I noticed that her nose was raw with blowing.

'Stress can do a lot of things to your body, Christopher,' she croaked. 'And I think your body is susceptible to it right now. Moving from London to New York is a big change. I know you're used to dealing with stress with your job, but you can't underestimate the effects of culture shock. You probably have an intestine that reacts badly to anxiety, which is causing you to experience the symptoms you describe. Try not to panic so much. It's just anxiety.'

*One* intestine? Surely, *one* broken entrail couldn't cause me so much discomfort. Then another thought struck me.

'But how can I be stressed? I have nothing to be stressed about! I have a nice apartment. I have a girlfriend. My job's going well. It's not like I'm being sent to war, for God's sake. *I'm a spoilt yuppie.* And I don't even feel all that stressed. It's just that I feel so . . . so bloody *wretched* all the time.'

Dr Ruth sat down heavily. 'Christopher, listen to me. Anxiety doesn't work like that. It can just build up in your system without you realizing it. That's what's happening to you right now. Your mind is channelling all your stress into phantom symptoms. Think about it: you need to pee all the time. *Anyone* can convince themselves they need to pee all the time – just like *anyone* can convince themselves they want to throw up. I can give you something for it if you want. It depends on how bad you think it is. I have no problem prescribing you some Zoloft.'

The thought of taking antidepressants depressed me. 'No, absolutely not,' I muttered. 'I'll be fine. I'll deal with it.'

'Zoloft isn't only for depres—'

'No, no. Really, no,' I said.

Dr Ruth gave me a long look, then shrugged. 'Oookay,' she announced, before hauling herself out of her chair and limping towards the door. 'Here, take this with you,' she said, picking up a leaflet entitled *Facts about Irritable Bowel Syndrome.* 'You should also try this.' She handed me a square paper bag of brown gunk, labelled 'fibre supplement'. 'Just add water and drink it in the morning,' she said. 'It's unpleasant, but it might help.' She gave me another low-wattage smile as she leaned on the doorknob. 'Good luck, Christopher. And come

back if you need anything. Not that I need to tell you that, of course.'
I walked out with a worried grunt, signed insurance documents at the
reception desk, then jammed myself into the creaking lift with some
of my fellow patients, all of them toothless and geriatric.

They all looked so damn healthy to me.

So how did I end up in New York? The nib I completed for Barrow
on that traumatic Thursday was followed by more nibs, then, in a
profound development of my *Times* career, by some 'lead' nibs.
Eventually I was trusted with a few proper news stories, which carried
my name at the top of them. My copy of *How to Read the Financial
Pages* meanwhile became ripped and bent with heavy consultation. By
August, Barrow had agreed to pay me £30 for a weekly Friday shift.
I soon became fluent in finance, able to riff confidently on price/
earnings ratios, dividend yields, 'Pac Man' defence strategies, stock-
option trigger prices and 'discounted-cash-flow' balance-sheet analysis as though I knew what it all meant. I watched and rewatched Oliver
Stone's *Wall Street*, with Michael Douglas as Gordon Gecko, in the
hope of eventually understanding the plot. Then the lunches started.
My first was with the chief executive of Treatt, a fragrance manufac-
turer. It was held not in a restaurant, but in the catered offices of a PR
firm. I followed Robert Cole's advice to the word. As homework,
I read the novel *Perfume*, by Patrick Süskind, so that I would have
something to talk about over the appetizer – after, of course, I had discussed the weather, the traffic and the route my cab had taken. It
worked flawlessly, as Cole had said it would. By the time the fish
course arrived ('Hope you like skate,' whispered the PR woman), my
nerves and nausea had gone. I had, however, drained half a bottle of
Cabernet by then.

As the weeks passed, I became a veteran of the business lunch.
Cole's tutorial had liberated me from the nervous dyspepsia that had
ruined countless social occasions since I left home at the age of eighteen. Now I had some catching up to do. I consumed fields of lamb
shanks, oceans of lobster tails, and pints of gazpacho. I snacked on
blinis and shards of parmigiano reggiano. I scoffed steak tartare, with
fried, garlic-soaked bread, for breakfast. In short, I became fat. My
head, with its permanent sunburn and sheen of booze-sweat, inflated.

My waistline bullied my trouser seam. By the time a new business editor was appointed I had become a restaurant snob, never to be tempted again by the colour photographs in a Pizza Hut menu.

Cook's replacement was a redoubtable woman called Patience Wheatcroft, a middle-aged mother with a teenager's figure who had previously worked at the tabloid *Mail on Sunday*. Her wardrobe was sensational. She would click into the office on Manolo Blahnik stilettos, wearing a short leather skirt and a chequered red-and-black Chanel jacket, accessorised with oversized gold buttons. Her stilettos, the office soon learned, came in a variety of violent shades: blood red, furious purple and death black. Once she turned up to the office in a cowboy jacket with tassels. She reminded me of one of Donald Trump's ex-wives: a flamboyant eighties anachronism in the sleek, monochrome nineties. From the day she was appointed (she introduced herself to her subordinates by asking them, in turn, '*What exactly do you do here?*'), Patience was known only by her first name: she was too terrifying to be dismissed as 'Wheatcroft'. She did, however, earn an unofficial nickname – 'Margot' – which was whispered only after particularly heroic lunchtime boozing sessions. It came from the 1970s BBC sitcom *The Good Life*, in which Margot Leadbetter (played by Penelope Keith) is the prim Little England conservative who lives next door to two hippy, downwardly mobile neighbours, earnestly trying to opt out of the rat race by raising their own livestock and growing vegetables. Some on the business desk also liked to joke that when Patience went home at night she swapped her aristocratic warble for broad Brummie – switching back into character at ten o'clock the next morning.

I liked Patience a lot, even though she made my palms sweat. She, in turn, saw me as cheap and motivated labour (i.e. poor and indebted), so she gave me a temporary six-month contract worth £9,000. I was immensely grateful. Unable to get excited by banking, insurance or heavy industry, I suggested stories on media and new-technology companies. Barrow, who had made his name in business journalism by covering the oil industry during Gulf War I, was not very impressed. 'But, Chris, they don't *make* anything,' he said, with a pinched face.

Regardless, the media beat was a good way to get invited to parties in Soho with B-list celebrities and 'it' girls. In the technology industry, meanwhile, something very curious was happening. I began writing features on the wildly out-of-proportion stock-market success of firms such as Yahoo!, whose young founders had each made millions after going public. It seemed as though the Americans were getting excited over nothing. At the time, I used the business section's computer to go online; it had a dial-up modem the size of a breezeblock, which downloaded web pages at a rate of one frame per day, making it a useless research tool. How could this be the future? As the dot-com boom started to echo across the Atlantic, however, I became converted, and my contract was upgraded to a staff position. Patience eventually gave me a technology column, and, as the speculative bubble inflated, some of my stories started to appear on the front page. On a few occasions, PR firms flew me first-class to Silicon Valley to interview the billionaire chiefs of Oracle, Intel and Cisco Systems. I even met Bill Gates. (So did Patience. 'Not even $45 billion can guarantee freedom from dandruff,' she clucked on her return.) By 1999 my responsibilities had been expanded to cover telecommunications, and by 2000 I was also editing a weekly section on 'e-business'. My career, like the careers of so many other young and hopelessly inexperienced dot-commers, had been built entirely on the funny money of the hyper-inflated internet economy. I was, in short, a fraud. But when the position of Wall Street correspondent became free in late 2000 I was in the ideal position to seize it.

'You're probably too young for this job,' Patience told me. 'But it's yours. Just don't muck it up. *I'll be watching you.*'

I had lobbied Patience for the New York job without really thinking about what would happen if I got it. And so the enormity of my move to Manhattan really sank in only as I stood outside my new office at 1211 Sixth Avenue, or, to use its official name, Avenue of the Americas. The building is one of several imposing skyscrapers that make up the Rockefeller Center in midtown Manhattan. The seventies-style behemoth, which looks like a scaled-down version of the former World Trade Center, is also the headquarters of Rupert Murdoch's News Corporation in America. The Fox News studio is on the ground floor, the *New York Post* headquarters on the ninth and tenth, and Murdoch's executive suite somewhere between the two.

On any given day, even during the most violently cold weeks of December, there is a crowd of woolly-hatted tourists and hot-dog sellers outside 1211 – partly because of the celebrities being escorted in and out of the Fox studio, and partly because of the 'news ticker', an LED display that wraps around the front of the building and displays scrolling news headlines twenty-four hours a day.

I felt like a celebrity myself as I pushed my way past the gawping and munching throng and through the revolving doors to the security desk. As the lift pulled me up to the ninth floor with a metallic whine, I concluded that it made sense for *The Times*, one of News Corp's most prestigious properties, to open its New York bureau at 1211. I pictured myself, white napkin tucked into my shirt collar, at weekly power lunches with 'Rupert' and his inner power circle. Just in case The Boss was in the office, I had worn my least stained tie and business suit.

Although I had never been inside 1211 before, I had formed an impression of it from the weekly column of Joanna Coles, *The Times*'s sassy and witty New York correspondent. It appeared under terrifying headlines such as 'Englishmen v. American men: Good Fun but Better Sex' and 'It's Official: Men are the New Single Women.' Joanna's weekly missive was accompanied by a picture of what looked like the star of several Hollywood romantic comedies: she had a knowing, sceptical pout (she was from Yorkshire), and an immaculate blonde hairdo which undoubtedly cost several hundred dollars a month to maintain. I secretly fantasized that she might be single and interested in a younger, slightly overweight reporter with receding hair. (She was in fact engaged to a world-renowned author.)

Joanna was infamous in Wapping for having negotiated a contract with the editor, Peter Stothard, that excused her from the menial task of writing news stories. The deal, envied by almost every journalist in Fleet Street, meant she could concentrate exclusively on her column and on splashy features for the tabloid section. It was like an air steward refusing to serve drinks to anyone other than first-class passengers. I could only imagine how bored she would be by the prospect of working with someone who wrote about Wall Street mergers and acquisitions.

In the lift, I imagined the glamour that awaited me: the huge *Times* logo above the reception area, the pristine glass walls, the splatterings of modern art, the chic office assistants, and the Conran furniture.

With a mechanical clank, the lift's chrome curtains opened. There were two smudged glass doors to either side of me, one leading to an open-plan work area and the other to a reception desk with a *New York Post* sign above it. The *Post's* logo – leaning forward, as if in a hurry – made me feel like Clark Kent reporting for work at the *Daily Planet*. Behind the reception desk sat a stern-looking African-American woman, wearing white surgical gloves. I approached, scanning the walls for the distinctive royal insignia of *The Times*. There was none.

'Hi,' I said, rather breathlessly. 'I'm the new man at *The Times*.'

'The what?' The woman didn't look up. She appeared to be using a machete to open post. There was ink on her white gloves.

'*The Times*,' I repeated. Then, unnecessarily, 'The *London* Times. *The Times of London. The Times – erm, newspaper.*'

The knife continued its work. The woman's frown deepened. I noticed there was a television set hanging from the ceiling, blaring out the military-sounding theme of the Fox News channel. I felt suddenly self-conscious and dizzy, like a schoolboy visiting the head teacher's office. Did she not understand my English accent? Was it that strong? My God, I thought, maybe no one in New York – or the United States – would understand me. *Perhaps I'm doomed to failure.*

'FAIR AND BALANCED!' declared the television.

'*The Times's* bureau is on this floor, isn't it?' I asked, as politely as I could.

Still no reaction. A muscular Fox News anchor began talking over the clatter of drums. Had I offended her somehow?

'Excu—'

'I DON'T KNOW, SIR.' She dropped the knife, threw open a drawer, and thumped a telephone directory down on her desk – all in one flawless angry motion. '*TIMES?*' she said, accusingly.

'Erm, yes.'

'Not listed.'

'That can't be right.'

'Who is it, *sir*, you wish to see?'

Finally, a chink of light in the dark. 'Adam Jones,' I blurted. Adam was the *Times* reporter whose job I was taking.

'Oh – *you mean Adam!*' The trenches in her forehead disappeared, and her barbed sneer became a gleaming wall of enamel. I felt an inappropriate amount of relief. 'Let me call him for you. Please, take a seat.' One white glove picked up a telephone handset, and the other dialled an extension number. The woman gestured towards a cheap-looking black-leather sofa. Next to it was a plastic potted plant. I was too nervous to sit. Perhaps, I thought, I had made a terrible mistake.

Eventually, Adam appeared from behind the reception desk. He was a bookish man with angular spectacles and an overnight growth of stubble. 'Welcome,' he said, and shook me firmly by the hand. I thought I could detect a hint of irony. He produced an electronic swipe card, and used it to take me through the second glass door and into the office area. 'This is it,' he said flatly.

The office looked like the set from an old episode of *NYPD Blue*. Its negative aura would have been enough to put a feng-shui consultant in hospital. Underfoot there was a sticky, matted carpet, on which had been placed brown metal-and-plastic office furniture. There was a strong whiff of burned percolator coffee and pretzels. A handful of plants wilted under fluorescent striplights. There was no sign of a *Times* logo anywhere – or, indeed, of any staff, apart from a couple of young, bored-looking African-American messengers and an ancient post-room worker, who was coughing violently while grumpily sorting through envelopes. His coughs were punctuated by the occasional 'GodDAMNit!', followed by self-pitying groans. Bundles of post – everything from handwritten letters to bulky brown UPS packages, most of them addressed to 'THE EDITOR' – were stacked everywhere.

Adam winced.

I had known Adam in London. During my hellish first week of work experience, he had reminded me of an intimidating third-year student at university who occasionally hands out insider advice to freshers. Because he seemed slightly distant and phlegmatic most of the time, I was immensely grateful whenever he warmed up and gave me one of his fireside chats. After a two-year stint in Manhattan,

Adam seemed ready to leave, and I got the impression he was puzzled that I would want his job. I was surprised, however, that he'd agreed to go back to London to take my old position on the business desk. In fact, he'd been secretly offered a job at the *Financial Times*, and had no intention of returning to the Wapping printing plant.

Adam escorted me to my 'office', which turned out to be a cubicle, cordoned off from the empty cubicles next to it by a brownish plastic-and-cork wall, which also doubled as a noticeboard. This is what Douglas Coupland had meant when he talked about 'veal-fattening pens' in *Generation X*, I thought. Behind the cubicle was a long table-top covered in yellowing copies of English and Australian newspapers. 'The loo's that way,' said Adam, pointing towards an LED display hanging from the ceiling. It read, '31 calls waiting'. I peered over the plastic and cork cordon and came face-to-face with woman sporting a New Jersey perm and a leather miniskirt. She was painting her nails. She looked up and smiled. This surely couldn't be . . . Joanna? I felt as though I had stumbled into an episode of *The Twilight Zone*. 'No, Julie,' came the nasal reply, followed by a squawk of laughter.

'Oh, right,' I said, offering a pale, trembling hand. 'Chris. The *Times* man.'

She gave me a blank look.

'Ad sales,' explained Adam. The New York bureau of *The Times*, it seemed, was a single cubicle wedged between the post room and the advertising-sales departments of the *New York Post*. In fact the *The Times*'s bureau was actually *in* the post room. And no one seemed to know it existed.

Adam hadn't yet cleared his desk (which was meticulously tidy, in maximum contrast to the surrounding chaos), so he showed me to spare cubicle next to it. I lifted a pile of undelivered post from the broken swivel chair and sat down. 'This is your computer,' he said, pointing to a device which looked as though it pre-dated the vacuum cleaner. I had to kneel down on the sticky carpet – avoiding someone's dusty, half-eaten croissant – to locate the 'on' button. 'Don't look at the keys,' came Adam's voice from above. He made an 'ew' face.

I looked.

The keys had turned almost black with newspaper ink from hundreds of deskless IT support staff, freelancers and secretarial temps, and the gaps between them served as gutters for spilled drinks and crumbs. The desk was slick with rings of congealed coffee and grease from countless lonely take-out lunches. I would later learn that my dead-line was 3 p.m. – which made lunch breaks almost impossible, unless they were taken at 4 p.m., while the waiters cleared the tables around you. I noticed that in Adam's cubicle there was a heavy, 38-inch Sony television set – a late 1980s model, tuned permanently to CNBC, the American business-news channel. I wondered how Adam had time to watch television during the day.

'You'll find that the Aussies sometimes use this desk,' he said, pluck-ing an empty can of Foster's from behind my computer monitor and dropping it in the bin. 'They share the bureau with us.'

The Aussies, I later learned, were two New York reporters for News Corp's Australian papers. The brutal thirteen-hour time difference between Manhattan and Sydney meant they kept very odd hours. Sometimes, clearly, cans of Australian lager were required to keep them motivated.

Before my spirits had time to sink any further, Adam offered to introduce me to Joanna. I stood up and turned around, catching a glimpse of blonde hair through a glass office door. *Thank God*, I thought: *the bureau is larger than my cubicle*. I wondered if Adam had also fantasized about an office romance with Joanna. Then I remembered he was married. Adam swung open the door to her office, which had little more charm than my cork enclosure. 'Joanna, this is Chris,' he said, then jogged back to his desk, where his phone was ringing.

'Hiiiiiiiii,' said Joanna, with impressively feigned interest. I noticed she was also watching television – CNN – and had a copy of the *New York Times* open in front of her. She was wearing stretchy trousers, a heavy sweater and no make-up, but she still looked glam. 'So, you're the new Wall Street guy,' she said, in an enthusiastic but motherly tone that reminded me of my old high-school English teacher and imme-diately destroyed any serious notion of a Mrs Robinson affair.

'So I expect you'll soon be getting used to lift and view,' she said.

'I'm sorry?'

Why was she talking about the lift? And there was no view – we were a long way from the window and, besides, we were on a low floor. Once again I felt like a schoolboy.

'Lift and view, Chris, is what we do here.' Her sentences, I noticed, were emerging fully formed from her mouth, as though they were part of a pre-written column. Had she researched this speech? Or was she as intimidatingly bright as I feared she might be? 'We lift from the *New York Times*.' She held up the copy on her desk. 'And we watch the news.' She pointed to CNN. 'We *lift* . . . and *view*. If you get the hang of that, you too can be a foreign correspondent.'

Her blue eyes bored into me.

Was this a test? Was she serious?

I laughed and said something about exclusives and working 'off diary'.

'Good luck,' she said.

The next few months proved Joanna's point. Foreign reporting from New York, it seemed, involved an awful lot of following up stories from the *New York Times* and watching CNBC. I had imagined something more glamorous. Given the number of stories I had to write, and the wide range of subjects, it was almost impossible to make insider 'contacts' – the PRs, bankers and analysts who supply journalists with the occasional scoop. Joanna, of course, had been deliberately provoking me with her 'lift and view' comments (she had, after all, managed to get the first interview with O. J. Simpson following his acquittal), but I wondered how Adam had found the time to leave the office and interview everyone from Donald Trump to Jeff Bezos, the nerdish founder of Amazon.com. Patience and Barrow, however, seemed impressed with the hasty rewrites I produced for them every day, like a robo-reporter.

I tried to distract myself from work by creating a social life. My initial attempts at meeting women didn't go well, however: my first date was with an Upper West Sider called Sady Smith, who spent the evening quizzing me about Prince William and telling me about her plan to produce a stage adaptation of a porn film. (It later became an off-Broadway hit.) Meanwhile the dizziness I had felt on my first day in the office kept returning. And that was when my sessions with Dr Ruth began.

By spring I had found a girlfriend. A tall, graceful Midwesterner with a concave stomach and hair cut into a Cabernet bob, her name was Alana. She voted Democrat and wore pointy-collared shirts with pinstripe trouser suits. For a girl who'd grown up in rural Ohio, she'd adapted well to city life. For a start, her apartment was so small it barely had four walls. And then there was her New Yorker attitude: on one of our early dates, at a West Village pavement café, she had attempted to ward off an abusively drunk hobo by picking up a heavy ashtray and threatening him with it. The hobo fled. I found Alana's confidence reassuring. She was, in fact, the alpha male in our relationship. Not that I would have ever admitted that.

But I still wasn't happy. I couldn't work out what was wrong with me. Why, for example, was I was so frazzled by nerves? After all, my generation – the fat, spoilt offspring of the seventies – have nothing, or at least very little, to be nervous *about*. Take disease: we're so doped-up at birth with flu jabs and pox shots that the only life-threatening illness we're likely to get is a self-inflicted one. As for hunting and gathering, the nearest we get is the remote control and the takeaway menu. Then there's our day-to-day safety: last century, a car crash at anything over 30 m.p.h. would have been a guarantee of death – or at least of a coma and an off switch. Today you can lose control of a cheap Korean saloon travelling at 110 m.p.h., down a hill, *in a monsoon*, and suffer only minor air-bag bruising. We're virtually indestructible.

Then, of course, there's war. The children of Thatcher and Reagan – my generational brothers and sisters, on both sides of the Atlantic – are war virgins: never drafted into military service; never invaded by a foreign army; never expected to defend their countries with their lives. The few conflicts we've lived through – the Falklands, Gulf War I, Bosnia – lasted only a few days, or weeks, and were fought by volunteers, not schoolyard conscripts. The Allied forces, it seemed, could win any war with a few Stealth bombers and an A-10 Warthog. Air offensives could be conducted online, like banking: one click of a mouse in the Pentagon, and a Kosovan village disappeared. Casualties, on our side at least, were extraordinarily low. On the first day of the Battle of the Somme in 1916 the British lost 19,240 men; during the entire Gulf War the British death count was 47. As teenagers watching television at home, it was tempting to regard these latter-day conflicts as entertainment: real-life video games. Perhaps it was because we had grown up being told that a *proper* war would involve 50-megaton nukes. The Soviet arsenal alone, we learned in the eighties, could kill 22 billion – and yet there were only 4 billion people in the world to kill. Back in the winter of 1991 it was almost a relief for us to discover that war was still possible without Armageddon.

So why, as a generation, are we so drenched in adrenalin? What could explain the $3.4 billion that Pfizer made in 2004 by selling its anti-anxiety drug Zoloft (known as Lustral in the UK)? For us war virgins, the adrenal cortex should be an obsolete piece of biotechnology. Our lives are safe, pampered and free from almost every kind of stress that troubled our ancestors. Perhaps, I often wondered during my treks to Dr Ruth's clinic, the human body will produce adrenalin regardless of the circumstances. And perhaps, without mortal danger, our adrenal glands get bored and start firing at random. It's not so much a disorder as a malfunction – a trip to the shops becomes as fraught as a tiptoe through a minefield, a new job as terrifying as trench warfare.

There is, however, a more troubling explanation: that the adrenalin is coming from our subconscious. After all, we war virgins know that our lifestyles can't last: that our comfort and safety are unsustainable. At school, our teachers were the first to break the news – about the dwindling oil reserves, the leaking ozone layer, the Third World. Even rock stars, those icons of the short term, started lecturing us about starving Ethiopians and disappearing rainforests. Our parents, it seemed, had not thought things through. In fact they'd really fucked up. Cheers, Mum. Thanks, Dad. And so, as much as we enjoy our modern invincibility, we wait for it to end. We wait for the inevitable. Even war, we know, will come eventually – probably from those at the wrong end of the First World's consumption binge. Technology will one day turn against us. The Moore's Law that gave us cheap PCs, video games and iPods will also make possible the homemade atomic bomb, detonated in Trafalgar Square.

The nineties, of course, were an attempt at denial. With our graffitied chunks of Berlin Wall on the mantelpiece, we stopped worrying about global politics. The Cold War was over and, as one of the most influential books of the decade said, it was The End of History.

Our Greenpeace subscriptions lapsed; we bought luxury German SUVs. As for our unsustainable lifestyles, we convinced ourselves that the New Economy would solve everything. Oil? It was so *Old* Economy. We took jobs in advertising and marketing, and tortured ourselves with images of the nearly but not quite obtainable. We blamed our anxiety on money, or sex. We stopped thinking; we bought shares in dot-com companies; we skimmed through the stories about missing suitcase-sized nukes and tifillated ourselves instead with Bill Clinton, the intern and the cigar. We were distracted; borderline delusional. But it wouldn't last.

'It's fight or flight,' Dr Ruth told me during one of my hypochondriac's work outs. 'It's also called the acute stress response. You're a journalist, you should look it up: Walter Cannon, born in Wisconsin in 1871, went to Harvard Medical School. He said animals react to threats with a general discharge of the sympathetic nervous system: in other words, the release of epinephrine and norepinephrine from the medulla of the adrenal glands. So your muscles tighten; the heart rate increases; your blood vessels constrict. Young men used to need that on the battlefield, Christopher. And, as much as your problems might seem, well, completely *trivial*, they are still causing the same animal fight-or-flight response. We call it an anxiety disorder. Which is why you come here so often. And why I tell you to take Zoloft.' The word 'trivial', I remember noting at the time, was emphasized rather too heavily.

My malfunctioning body, concluded Dr Ruth, was permanently stuck in 'flight' mode. It was telling me to empty my bowels, turn on my heels, and run as fast as possible: away from the West Village.

I was a clinical coward.

While we're on the subject of war and virginity, I should probably tell you about my other granddad, on my mother's side. Ross Selkirk Taylor was a smart and particular young man with black-rimmed spectacles and rather too much Brylcreem in his hair. His idea of a good time was a packet of full-strength Player's, a date with my future grandmother, Florence (or Flo, as he sometimes called her), and Tommy Dorsey on the gramophone. Unlike my father's father, granddad Taylor had no problem gripping a rifle. And so, at the age of twenty-one, he was drafted into the Royal Army Service Corps and handed a gun, six rounds of ammunition and the keys to a 3-ton Bedford lorry. The first order given to 121357 Dvr Ross Taylor was to drive to Boulogne, northern France, where he would help the British Army fight off a German invasion – if one ever came. The date was February 1940.

My grandfather had never been abroad before. That might explain the entry he made on Saturday 2 March in the brown-leather Automobile Association diary that my grandmother had given him as a Christmas gift: 'Not very impressed by France at present. Although it may get better.' He wrote this in pencil, being careful not to make a mistake, or use up more than the square inch of space allocated to each day. France, of course, did not get better: it got a lot worse.

Dvr Taylor went on to disclose that he had tasted his first glass of champagne in France and was 'confined to barracks' for smoking Player's in the Bedford's cab. In fact his incarceration in the barracks was ended only by compassionate leave, when he was ordered home to Newcastle upon Tyne to visit his dying mum. 'Doesn't seem much hope for mother,' he wrote, on the weekend of 23 March. 'Said nothing to nobody though!' Two days later, my great grandmother, Margaret Taylor, had died from a kidney infection.

After returning to France, my grieving grandfather was cheered up by good weather and a football match with the French, which, against all the odds, the British won. He even spent a day at the Berck Plage seaside resort – later to become the subject of one of Sylvia Plath's bleakest poems. Looking back, the day at the beach was a terrible omen. That night there was a terrifying air raid. Then, on 15 May, Dvr Taylor was ordered to drive south-east to pick up the 7th Battalion Royal West Kents, an infantry unit. That was when Hitler invaded. My grandfather and the West Kents were ordered to meet an advancing Nazi panzer division, head-on.

These were Dvr Taylor's diary entries after leaving the Boulogne barracks:

SATURDAY: Set off at 1.30 a.m. to proper hellhole. Found we were in front line. Machine gunned. Discovered we were surrounded all night. Enemy know nothing of us. Luckiest people on Earth to get out.

SUNDAY: What a morning. Expecting enemy to move in on us any minute. Retreat 3.30 a.m., 20 miles back.

MONDAY: Moved up to Albert. Got blasted to hell. Captured in Afternoon. Rode on horseback to village.

Each diary entry, of course, tells only one square inch of the story. The West Kents had met the German Army near the town of Albert, came under heavy fire, then retreated. It was then that my grandfather realized he'd never been shown how to fire his rifle, and that its barrel was still full of grease. After being told by a commander that the Germans were moving backwards, the West Kents motored forward again, only to run into an ambush in Albert's village square. The square was famous for its church, which had been flattened by the Germans during World War I, leaving only a wobbly statue of the Madonna standing. The West Kents were standing near that statue, smoking cigarettes, when a German Messerschmitt fell out of the sky and started spitting out lead. My grandfather managed to stomp on the Bedford's accelerator pedal before being hit. He swerved down a boulevard, only to meet a German blockade with a machine gun in the middle of it. He threw himself out of the lorry before the gun opened fire. Then he ran, eventually meeting up with three other surviving West Kents. The shell-shocked soldiers tried to hide in a line of French refugees, but seeing their British Army uniforms and bloody faces, the French shooed them away. Later the Luftwaffe opened fire on the unarmed civilians anyway. The West Kents had nowhere to go, and soon enough my grandfather and his friends were captured.

That evening the Germans decided to transport Dvr Taylor on a horse, without a saddle, to the nearest town. Fearing he would fall off, my granddad tied a piece of string around one of the animal's ears, hauled himself on to its bare back, and set off nervously. At that very moment, however, a machine gun went off and the horse bolted, catapulting my granddad into a razor-wire fence. Bloody, terrified and exhausted, he finally made it, on foot, to the camp. The next morning he was ordered on a death march to Germany, covering 18 miles a day and sleeping in cattle fields. What little food he ate was given to him by locals who pitied the starving prisoners. In the town of Trier he was shoved into a railway truck, and he eventually arrived in Poznań, a port on the Warta River in Poland. There, as British Prisoner of War No. 4552, he joined a working party that tore down Poznań Zoo so that it could be turned into a military airfield. He also operated a crane in a quarry. (At one point, the PoWs tried to kill the Nazi guard by dropping a boulder on him.) He spent rest of the war as a labourer near Freiwaldau – now called Jeseník – on the Czech-Polish border.

Within two weeks of returning to Newcastle, Dvr Ross Taylor married Florence and was put on paid leave by the British Army. Then he came down with tuberculosis, caused by five years of malnutrition. Doctors treated him by collapsing one of his lungs and putting him in a sanitorium for nine months.

He survived all this, needless to say, without the need for Zoloft, trauma counselling or French existential literature. After recovering from TB, he put himself through night school and set about making himself a member of the English middle class. Sometimes, on my way to Dr Ruth's clinic, I would think about my grandfather and I would feel guilt – the heavy, suffocating kind.

It wasn't just my health that was bothering me in New York. I was also thoroughly sick of lift and view. I met up with other English foreign correspondents to see if they shared my frustration with rehashing other people's stories. Toby Moore of the *Daily Express* told me despondently that foreign reporters were a dying breed: the paper's proprietor, the one-time porn magnate Richard Desmond, had decided to get rid of all overseas bureaux apart from New York. Ironically, the *Express* had once been famous for its global reach, and in 1936 had had the largest circulation of any publication on earth. In place of foreign correspondents, Desmond used young, poorly paid reporters in London to follow up stories from the online editions of overseas newspapers. Clearly it wasn't just Joanna who knew about lift and view. Within weeks Toby had returned to the UK: Desmond had shuttered the New York office to save more money. This made Toby the last staff foreign correspondent ever employed by the newspaper founded in 1900 and bought sixteen years later by Lord Beaverbrook. I feared *my* job could also disappear. The dot-com boom, after all, had turned into a financial catastrophe, and the American economy was coming down with a nasty bout of recession. The New Economy, it seemed, wasn't that new after all: it was just a plain old speculative financial bubble – no more sophisticated than tulipmania in seventeenth-century Holland. Patience started to reject my expenses claims and, in one curt phone call, warned me to cut the overheads of the New York operation. Manhattan, however, was in denial: the hedonism of the nineties, as epitomized by *Sex and the City*, was still the norm.

There was, however, a palpable sense of foreboding. Repossession trucks towed Porsches from outside fashionable loft apartments, such as the one I lived in at 666 Greenwich Street. The West Village's trendy, candlelit restaurants started to feel emptier on week nights. The homeless multiplied. And the cheesy Europop of the nineties had been replaced by the depressive bleeping of Radiohead's *Kid A*. Then, of course, there was George W. Bush – a president no one in New York seemed to like. The war virgins, I concluded, had been spoilt for too long.

Part of me wondered whether it would be stress or Patience's budget cuts that ended my stint as Wall Street correspondent. I decided that a holiday in England – my first return to Britain after moving to New York – might help clear my mind. So I booked myself a ticket through News Corp's travel department and turned up at John F. Kennedy Airport, only to discover that the company had automatically put me in first class, at a cost to Patience of $5,126.32. That was it, I thought, *I was done*. The travel agent had assumed I was a News Corp executive travelling with Rupert Murdoch's entourage. I couldn't face telling Patience about it in person, so I emailed her instead. 'Oh dear,' was her two-word reply, followed by a week of silence. I spent the rest of my holiday convinced she would fire me. In the end, however, she let me off, even though I had offered to pay the difference in fares, which amounted to $4,739. For the first time since Patience had arrived at *The Times*, I wanted to hug her.

By the time I got back on my United Airlines jet at Heathrow I was exhausted, still unwell, and not sure I was happy about going back to New York. But weren't people supposed to love New York – The City That Never Sleeps? I tried hard to feel love, but none came. At least, I thought, I could savour a guilt-free, first-class flight.

I needed all the sleep I could get.

The date was 10 September 2001.

# 6

## The Accidental War Correspondent

*It's 8.45 a.m. the next morning. I'm in my apartment at 666 Greenwich Street, wearing only a pair of white boxer shorts, debating whether or not to go into the office. I'm suffering from a mild stomach upset, probably caused by yesterday's seven-hour flight from London. I fear, however, that it might be more serious: gall-bladder disease, perhaps. I make a note to call Dr Ruth.*

*Above me, to the north-west, an American Airlines Boeing 767, piloted by an Islamic terrorist called Mohammed Atta, is travelling at 470 m.p.h. towards lower Manhattan, at an estimated altitude of 2,000 feet. In the aircraft's coach-class cabin, Amy Sweeney, a flight attendant, is talking on a mobile phone to a colleague at Boston's Logan Airport. 'I see water and buildings,' she is saying, in a low voice. 'Oh my God! Oh my God!' At this point the aircraft is probably now directly over 666 Greenwich Street – a mile and a half south of the World Trade Center and one block east of the Hudson River. In Boston, 216 miles north-east, Amy Sweeney's colleague is unaware that one of Mohammed Atta's suitcases is currently circling, unclaimed, on a baggage carousel only a few yards away from him. He doesn't know who Atta is; nor that the terrorist passed through Boston that morning after a connecting flight from Portland, Oregon. Atta's suitcase contains airline uniforms, flight manuals and a four-page document in Arabic. It instructs him to 'feel complete tranquillity, because the time between you and your marriage in heaven is very short'.*

*President George W. Bush, at this freeze-framed moment, is 1,217 miles south-west of New York in Sarasota, Florida. He's in a motorcade, on his way to a photo opportunity with a group of local schoolchildren. He intends to read them a story entitled 'My Pet Goat'. He has not yet been told by the Federal Aviation Administration, the North American Aerospace Defense Command, the National Military Command Center, the Pentagon, the White House, the Secret Service or Canada's Strategic Command that at least one commercial aircraft has been hijacked. He is, in fact, remarkably ill-informed for the leader of the free world.*

*In my apartment, I am also ill-informed. I return to bed, yawn, scratch, and then stare at the ceiling. As I lie there, another Boeing 767, this one operated by United Airlines, is diverted from Los Angeles to New York. The pilot doesn't know about the diversion because he is currently being murdered by one of Atta's fellow members of al-Qaeda, an Afghanistan-based terror group.*

*I list the arguments against going to the office. Number one: Joanna Coles no longer works for* The Times *– she left yesterday, after being offered a top job at a New York magazine. That means a solitary lunch at 1211 Sixth Avenue. Number two: Joanna's replacement, Nicholas Wapshott, is currently on the deck of the QE2, probably 1,000 miles off the eastern seaboard, having decided to use a 100-year-old mode of transport to get to his new foreign posting. That means no one will know I'm working from home.*

*As I talk myself into doing just that,* The Times*'s only other correspondent in New York, James Bone, is a mile south-east, finishing a cup of coffee at an Egyptian news-stand on lower Broadway. He's running late. He's about to get the front-page story of a lifetime.*

*The nanoseconds and seconds tick towards 8.46 a.m. Another aircraft, a Boeing 757 operated by United Airlines, idles its engines on the runway of New Jersey's Newark Airport, 16.5 miles south-east. The pilot, who has just received clearance for take-off, is unaware that he has only forty-one minutes left to live. He has never heard of al-Qaeda, or a Saudi billionaire called Osama bin Laden. A passenger on the plane, Tom Beamer, has no idea that he is about to inspire a Neil Young song entitled 'Let's Roll', or that his family will publish a book in his honour.*

*I jump out of bed: I will go to the office. As I make this decision, another Boeing 757, operated by American Airlines, nears cruising altitude. It is twenty minutes into its journey from Washington Dulles to Los Angeles. The pilot of the plane has nine minutes to live. The passengers have fifty-two minutes.*

*The plane will not reach Los Angeles.*

*It is now 8.46 a.m. Outside, I hear a distant crashing noise. The world changes. In an instant, my generation loses its war virginity – and I become a war correspondent. But I don't know any of this yet. I'm still worried about my gall bladder. I assume that the noise outside is the metal shutter of the kebab shop opposite my apartment. The shop is owned by an Iranian family. I can hear sirens now; the city whines into an echo chamber. Nothing unusual in*

*that. There's a strange, acrid smell. I curse New York. I can see clear blue sky
outside. It's hot for September.*

*I put on my clothes — dark-blue denims, light-blue work shirt, aviator sun-
glasses. I open the front door of my apartment and pick up the* New York
Times. *The lead story is this: 'Arsenic Standard for Water is Too Lax, Study
Says'. I wonder if my gall-bladder problem is in fact arsenic poisoning.*

*In a few minutes I won't care.*

I stepped into the lift at precisely 8.50 a.m.

'Down?' I asked.

'Did you hear anything about the trade centre?' came the unexpected reply, from a middle-aged woman dressed head to heel in
Prada. Her jaw was locked with worry. She was gripping a Motorola
phone.

Me: 'No.'

'I heard it on the radio,' she said. 'An explosion — or something. My
husband's there. He's not . . . *he's not picking up.*'

She stabbed at the Motorola.

At first the words 'trade centre' didn't mean anything to me. It was
early, after all, and I hadn't had my morning espresso.

'Yeah, *I heard that too*,' said the gay investment banker next to me.
By the end of the sentence his voice had risen an octave. 'I think
there's been an accident with an airplane,' he speculated. '*Ohmagod!*'

I wondered if this was a news story. If so, I was ill-equipped to cover
it: I kept all my pens and spiral-bound notebooks at work. The 'trade
centre' still didn't mean anything to me, even though I had recently
taken my parents to the observation deck on top of the south tower.
In fact I had been invited to a party at the Windows of the World
restaurant in the north tower on Thursday. The invite was currently
sitting on my kitchen table. 'Cocktails at 1,350 ft,' it said.

I needed coffee. My stomach ached.

The lift jerked to a halt. I strode passed Walter and Carlos, the
building's doormen, and out into the sunshine. I cursed as I realized
I'd forgotten my dry cleaning. Then I searched for a cab, catching a
glimpse of something unusual as I turned. I looked right, towards the
familiar view of downtown Manhattan, dominated by two gigantic
silver towers: an inverted Bugs Bunny smile poking out of the gum of

the skyline. '*That's* the trade centre,' I scolded myself. 'The *World Trade Center*.' But something was wrong. There was a black gash about three-quarters of the way up the north tower, and a trail of smoke coming from it. I could see an orange glow from deep within the hole. An accident, I thought – probably an amateur pilot in a small plane. I remembered reading about the Army Air Corps B-25 bomber that had somehow managed to hit the side of the Empire State Building in 1945.

A yellow cab pulled up beside me.

'*Man*, that pilot must have been on fuckin' *crack* to crash into somethin' that big, on a day like this,' said the driver. 'Holy *crap!*'

I waved him away and called my friend Karen, who worked for Deutsche Bank somewhere within the Trade Center complex. Perhaps she would have the real story. No answer – she was probably late for work, as usual. It didn't occur to me to be worried. I knew she was on a low floor: she complained about not having a view. Wearily, I called the business desk. 'Something's hit the World Trade Center,' I said. 'There's a bloody great hole in it.' I felt myself wanting to exaggerate – to sell the story. This could be a way of avoiding the office, after all.

But, as I looked at the flames, I suspected I didn't need to embellish.

'Yeah, we've heard something about that,' came the distant, vague reply. Barrow was clearly knee-deep in mucky copy.

'Shall I take a look?' I asked.

Barrow: 'I'll put you over to foreign.'

I immediately tensed. The foreign-news desk represented the exotic, dangerous world outside financial journalism.

I heard eight bars of Vivaldi, then another voice. It was posh, and clipped.

'Chri-*is*?' My name had a dip in it, signalling the need for information.

'Hi, yes. There's a hole in the World Trade Center.' I coughed. 'Small plane probably.' I hoped this sounded informed.

'H*mm*. We're watching it on Sky. Can you get down there? James Bone's already on his way.' The voice was impatient, harried. There were probably much bigger stories to be worrying about, I thought. What with the arsenic in the water supply, this would probably make only a few hundred words: a photo story, perhaps. Maybe it would be a lead nib. I was good at those.

'Yes, I'm not far fro—'

'Good, *good.*' The voice was distracted.

Me: 'I'll call in later.'

I hung up, eager to cause the least possible inconvenience.

In front of me, of course, was the biggest American news story since 7 December 1941, when the Japanese attacked Pearl Harbor. I was young, ambitious and – after months of lift and view – desperate for what Linda Christmas called *real* journalism. So what did I do next? Run towards the flames? Hitch a ride on a passing fire truck? Jump into a cab and order the terrified driver to step on it?

Alas, no. At 8.53 a.m. on Tuesday, September 11, 2001 I strolled back inside 666 Greenwich Street and took the lift up to my apartment, where I collected some pens and hunted for a notebook. I congratulated myself on getting out of a day's work at the veal-fattening pen on Sixth Avenue. I was ignorant, of course, of one crucial fact: the World Trader Center had been attacked before, in 1993. The alleged bomber, Ramzi Mohammed Yousef, who had entered the US with a fake Iraqi passport, was currently residing in the 'Supermax' correctional facility of Florence, Colorado. Yousef was a close friend of Khalid Sheik Mohammed, who at this moment was watching the burning north tower from a bunker in Afghanistan. No doubt he was whooping, cheering and doing whatever else terrorist chiefs do when they've successfully murdered a few thousand innocent men, women and children.

At home, I looked in the mirror and took some multivitamin tablets. Unable to find anything to write on – not even a napkin – I snatched the red, leather-bound diary that Alana had bought for me as a gift from Italy, along with my dry cleaning, and headed for the door. As an afterthought, I also grabbed my digital camera, which I jammed into my jeans pocket. It didn't occur to me that the fire in the World Trade Center would be the most photographed event in history. I thought *The Times*'s picture desk might appreciate some amateur snaps. By the time I staggered back out on to Greenwich Street – coat-hangers in my teeth, a bag of laundry over my shoulder, and blankets and sweaters under my arms – it was 9.02 a.m. I checked the World Trade Center again: the burning had intensified. I reassured myself that I had plenty of time to get down there before my deadline. The truth, however, was that I was deliberately stalling: I was apprehensive about the prospect of having to interview real people, instead of doing the usual lift and view. Part of me was tempted to go back upstairs and cover the story from CNN. Sweating, I ducked inside the dry cleaner's, which was next door to 666 Greenwich Street, and dropped everything on the counter. The Asian shop owner, unable to pronounce or spell my second name, was struggling to label my clothes when I heard another distant crash. By the time I made it outside, there was another gash in the World Trade Center – this time in the south tower.

I looked again.

*I'm hallucinating*, I told myself.


I got Alana on speed-dial. She was having breakfast with her father, who was visiting from Ohio. No, she hadn't seen the World Trade Center. 'Switch on the television,' I told her, adrenalin now starting to feed through my nervous system, dissolving the grogginess. I had already forgotten about gall-bladder disease and arsenic poisoning. Alana, who had an irritating but understandable habit of never believing anything I told her until she had independently verified it, sounded uninterested. 'I'm heading down there,' I said, trying to sound brave. I wanted her to tell me – or, better, beg me – *not* to go down there. She didn't. 'Give you a call in a bit,' I said. 'Enjoy breakfast.' I hung up. I tried to call the foreign-news desk, but it wouldn't connect. Karen's office number, meanwhile, just rang off the hook.

Now I was worried.

I jogged south, passing tables set up outdoors for voting in the mayoral elections. The winner would replace Mayor Rudy Giuliani, who was standing down after two controversial terms. There were people wearing sandwich boards with the names of candidates and campaign slogans daubed on to them. 'HE HAS COMMERCIALS, I HAVE CREDENTIALS,' read one. Behind the campaigners, plumes of stinking black smoke rolled out over the Hudson River. The sirens of emergency vehicles wailed hysterically. New York is deafening on a good day. On that day it was unbearable. It was as though the city itself was howling.

The campaigners and voting officials didn't seem to know what to do. They sat on their camping chairs and watched two steel volcanoes erupt less than a mile away. Later, much later, some of these same people would criticize President Bush for continuing to read 'My Pet Goat' to the children in Florida even after he had been told about the south tower. Inaction, however, was an almost animal response: like rabbits caught on a six-lane highway under a xenon glare.

By this time I was in Tribeca, an empty warehouse district that had been gentrified with 'white-box' lofts, furniture shops and Robert De Niro's Mediterranean restaurant. There were pedestrians everywhere, all of them speed-walking north. It looked like Fifth Avenue at the weekend. Then it hit me: the pedestrians were evacuees from the World Trade Center. There were hundreds, perhaps thousands of them – the men dressed in Italian pinstripes and Thomas Pink shirts; the women in smart trouser suits and low heels. They were possibly the world's best-dressed refugees. I stopped one of them, who told me his name was John Fratton.

'What happened?' I asked. 'Was there an accident . . . *with a plane?*'

Fratton, a grandfatherly figure with thick grey hair, was agitated. 'This wasn't some two-bit propeller job from Teterboro Airport,' he said, waving his arms at the burning towers. 'There were two jetliners! JETLINERS!' He wasn't looking at me as he spoke. It was as though he was trying to explain to himself what had just happened. 'The cops said the second one came in over the East River – and then, SLAM!' He shook his head, as if something were trapped inside.

His pupils were pinpricks.

For some reason the word 'jetliner' clicked. I thought of the silver tube of a Boeing 767 and the damage it would do to a skyscraper. It didn't occur to me that a Boeing 767 would also have nearly 24,000 gallons of high-octane jet fuel in its wings and body. I was, however, a little sceptical: did Fratton really know what he was talking about? There were plenty of amateur pilots, after all, who flew small private planes from Teterboro Airport in New Jersey. Surely it was possible they could get their navigation so muddled that they hit a 110-storey building. But *two* planes, into *two* buildings, *on the same day? On a clear and sunny September morning?*

'Thank you, sir,' I said, giving him a quizzical stare.

John Fratton didn't look like an exaggerator.

At this point, of course, I hadn't seen what the rest of the world had already watched live on CNN: United Airlines flight 175, from Boston to Los Angeles, making an unscheduled stop between the seventy-eighth and eighty-fourth floors of the south tower. The aircraft had seemed to twist as it cut into the building.

As I continued jogging south, the refugees began to look more ragged. Some of them had specks of white dust on their business suits. The election officials, meanwhile, were starting to hurriedly pack up their tables. There was an overwhelming stench of what I assumed to be jet fuel . . . and something else. I stopped one of the evacuees. She seemed calm and together. She said her name was Diane Rieck, and that she worked for American Express in the World Financial Center, one block north of the twin towers. 'I heard a big bang and then saw a . . . a huge red *fireball*,' she told me, her hand over her face to shield it from the sun. Rieck continued, 'But the worst was seeing the people jump – three or four from this side, two or three from the other.' She pointed matter-of-factly to the inferno of the north tower. I finished my jerky writing – in longhand – then began to process what she had just told me.

'What? *There are people jumping?*'

Rieck didn't answer; her face was suddenly awash with tears and mascara. A colleague held tightly on to her arm.

'Interview over,' he said.

*It's now 9.45 a.m. This is what I don't know: the fire caused by the 24,000 gallons of fuel in the plane that hit the south tower is weakening the steel core of the building. It will collapse in twenty minutes, nearly killing me. A total of 642 others will not survive: 18 of them on the ground, 618 above the impact zone between the seventy-eighth and eighty-fourth floors, and 6 on the floors below. The north tower, even though it was hit earlier than the south tower, will take another forty-three minutes to fall. A total of 1,466 will be killed: 1,356 of them at or above the impact zone between the ninety-fourth and ninety-eighth floors, and 100 below. This is what else I don't know: at 9.30 a.m. President Bush described the events in New York as 'an apparent terrorist attack'; at 9.40 a.m. the Federal Aviation Administration grounded all flights in the US; and at 9.43 a.m., 213 miles south-west of Manhattan, in Washington, DC, an*

*American Airlines Boeing 757 nose-dived into the west side of the Pentagon. I also don't know, of course, that at this very moment, 2.6 miles north-east of the burning Pentagon, the White House is being evacuated.*

*I have jogged from Tribeca to Murray Street, three blocks north of the World Trade Center. I'm facing east, with the sun searing into my forehead. Beside me there's a man sitting on the kerb, his back to the inferno, and his son on his lap. The boy, barely more than a toddler, is shielded by his father's body from the unbearable horror behind him. The man is holding a book of nursery rhymes and reading into his son's ear, not once giving in to the temptation to glance over his shoulder. I wonder where the mother is. Then I look up at the flames.*

*There's a police blockade in front of me. NYPD officers and FBI agents have gathered around their cars, watching helplessly. There are four burly and uniformed men around one vehicle, thumping their fists on its roof and stifling sobs. They're listening to something on the police radio. 'People don't see shit like this in wars,' says one. A yellow school bus grunts eastward. Some of the cars on Murray Street have shunted into each other, a disaster-movie visual cliché, as their drivers stare at the spectacle above. Already the crowd on Murray Street has witnessed scores of people suffer one of the most wretched deaths imaginable. Here they come: black shapes, writhing, turning and grasping as they make the quarter-of-a-mile journey from the top floors of the World Trade Center to the concrete plaza below. They fall silently: the sirens scream for them. I tell myself they have passed out with shock; but why are they moving? Why do they seem to be clawing at the acres of glass?*

*I remind myself that I have been to the observation deck of the south tower three times. Each time, I felt a chill of fear as the lift doors revealed Manhattan and New York Harbor as if viewed from space. I remember the sickly sensation of the building swaying in the wind; I also remember reading that the 1,350-foot towers swing a few feet every ten seconds, their giddy movements counter-balanced by gigantic steel pendulums in the centre of each structure. The last time I was up there I wanted to be back on the ground immediately. The lift operator cracked stupid jokes all the way down. I wonder if he is one of the terrible black shapes.*

*Now they're falling in clusters; two of them appear to be holding hands before gravity takes over. I glimpse a flapping necktie. The cloudless blue sky makes for perfect viewing conditions. Someone in the crowd says he has just escaped from the building. He says he saw bodies in the treetops.*

68

*The clutter of the skyline makes it impossible to see where, or how, the black shapes land. Then a terrible thought strikes me: the human shrapnel must be deadly for those trying to evacuate the building. Again I think of Karen. The plaza itself must be a vision of hell – God, I hope she was late for work. The crowd gasps, weeps and whoops as the human confetti continues. Every so often a bystander falls to the ground, shaking and praying, unable to watch any more. This happens to me after perhaps the sixth faller. I'm a godless soul, but praying seems appropriate. I'm willing to try anything to help the poor bastards falling from the building.*

*At first it seems inexplicable that they would choose to jump. Then comes the slow realization – the furnace of jet fuel, the charred skin, the toxic fumes. And then the conclusion that there is no choice at all. There's a helicopter hovering close to the mast on the south tower. I wait for it to land on the roof, but it backs away and circles. Some trapped office workers are waving brightly coloured rags out of the shattered windows. 'What the fuck are they doin', man?' someone next to me shouts at the retreating helicopter. 'Why don't they land on the roof and save them?' No one is able to supply an answer. And then it starts to happen.*

*There's a crunch, a boom, and the sound of several thousand windows exploding. A section of the north tower comes loose, like a melted ice shelf falling into the ocean. The impact creates a wave of debris that crashes through the streets, channelling itself between buildings and sweeping pedestrians off their feet. Then comes a terrible realization: it's heading for Murray Street. For the first time in my life I experience mass hysteria: everyone starts to run. Head down, my notebook in one hand, camera in the other, I sprint north-west, towards an apartment complex near Chambers Street. I stop noticing other people. I find an enclosed square and a doorway facing north, away from the collapsing building. There are perhaps ten of us in the doorway – we look at each other, but say nothing. The smoke clears; we're OK. I jog east to where Chambers Street meets the West Side Highway. I walk slowly backwards up the highway, staring at the disintegrating skyscraper ahead of me. Then a police officer shouts something. There's a loud pop: did someone fire a gun?*

*Then another crunch, another boom – this time, much, much louder.*

*I think of the man sitting on the kerb with his son.*

*I'm running again.*

I got back to 666 Greenwich Street at some time before noon: deadlines seemed like an abstract concept after what had just happened.

I didn't stop running until I was about halfway up the West Side Highway: only then did I dare turn round to confirm what had caused the seismic boom behind me.

The south tower of the World Trade Center had disappeared. In its place was an acrid mushroom cloud, slowly billowing northward and upward: black ink spilled on a blue canvas. I wondered what had happened to the police officer who screamed at the crowd to move. I could have sworn I heard him fire his pistol into the air. I concluded that the people only a few yards behind me as I ran north must have been killed: at one point, when I looked over my shoulder, I saw them being sucked into the wall of smoke. There were, however, some survivors, their suits ripped and matted with dust. They ran, walked and stumbled north, occasionally pausing to throw up in the gutter or spit out gobs of filth. None of us had even thought about what would happen if one of those 110-storey towers collapsed. After all, the Empire State Building hadn't keeled over after the B-25 hit it back in 1945. *You bloody idiot*, I thought to myself. *What were you thinking?* But I hadn't been thinking. I had been watching.

I turned east on to the cobbled part of Greenwich Street, and then north again, back up towards my apartment building. By the time I got to the massive UPS warehouse on the border of Tribeca and the West Village the throng had stopped and turned to look at the burning north tower. A brown UPS truck, its doors and windows wide open, had parked in the middle of the street, the radio in its cab cranked up to full volume. A hot-dog seller, who had presumably wheeled his rusty cart all the way up from the financial district, was offering snacks. There were curses of disbelief as the K-Rock DJ, who had stopped playing back-to-back Led Zeppelin for probably the first time in his career, announced that the Pentagon had also been hit by an airliner, and that another aircraft had come down in Pennsylvania. 'This is fuckin' World War III,' shouted a teenager on a skateboard. At that moment the north tower fell – all 1,350 feet of it sucked into the bedrock of southern Manhattan.

Each tower, I learned later, created 900,000 tons of rubble when it fell. And each Boeing 767 released one *kiloton* of raw energy – the equivalent of 1,000 tons of TNT, or a twentieth of the power of the atomic bomb dropped on Hiroshima – when it hit the World Trade Center. The scale of the destruction, it seemed, could be described using only the metrics of nuclear Armageddon.

So there I stood on Greenwich Street – watching a 110-storey skyscraper being razed, for the second time in one morning. It was then I realized that this was a deliberate act of cruelty, not a freak double accident. Perhaps, I thought, this is the beginning of the end for us war virgins. Perhaps our adrenal glands weren't malfunctioning: they were trying to tell us something all along. But who would have wanted to vandalize the world's most famous skyline? What could they hope to achieve? I felt my first flash of anger. Only one name seemed obvious: Saddam Hussein. I thought of President George W. Bush, and I thought of his father, President George H. Bush. And I thought of the inevitable revenge ahead. There is a war coming, I told myself – and this time it won't be over in five days. My only comfort, out there in the ash and the smoke, was that, wherever the war was declared, I wouldn't be there to cover it.

Little, of course, did I know.

Even now, I can't remember the final steps into my apartment. Did I say anything to Walter and Carlos on the door? Was there anyone in the lift with me? My memory resumes its narrative with me trying to call the foreign desk, then Alana, with no success. The mobile-phone masts had jammed with 21 million New Yorkers calling their mothers. Instead, I emailed. Luckily my internet service was still working; it was hooked-up via cable, not through the dead phone line.

This is what I sent to Barrow:

Subject: Hell
Must say the whole thing has been traumatic. Not only do I have a friend who works there (can't contact her), but I also sat and watched at least 20 people jump out of the W.T.C. from the top floors because they were being burned alive. I stayed as long as I dared, but when the first tower collapsed and a huge mushroom cloud engulfed the financial centre, I'm afraid to say that I legged it as fast as I could. I'm not going anywhere near the financial district again, too dangerous.

With hindsight, those final two sentences were probably not the best way to begin a career as a war correspondent. Legging it, after all, is not what war correspondents do: they hold fast; stand firm; head back into the action. The email did, however, establish a theme for my later work. I also emailed Alana and Glen. I told Glen to call my mother. She would have assumed the worst.

Finally I emailed Karen:

Subject: OK
Are you okay?

I imagined the message pinging into the inbox of her computer, buried beneath 1,800,000 tons of melted steel and plastic. Perhaps she would be able to access her work email account remotely, I thought. I remembered that she used to carry a Palm Pilot around with her.

After clicking on Send, I noticed I had a new message, highlighted with a cheerful yellow envelope icon. It was an email from the foreign desk:

Subject: [Blank]
Thousand wds please on 'I saw people fall to death,' etc.

I felt a twist of anger at its almost comic insensitivity. '*Fuck you!*' I mouthed at the screen of my laptop. Part of me, however, felt pleased with the request. To the foreign desk, I was a dull, egghead business reporter – and a young and inexperienced one at that – not a trusted 'colour' writer. But the rest of me felt disgusted at the thought of using the Trade Center's destruction as a career opportunity. Nevertheless, I could only imagine the agony of Wapshott, having to watch or listen to reports of the destruction of New York from the *QE2*. I wondered if the cruise liner was even within range of satellite televison.

Poor bastard.

My most pressing concern, however, was that I was in shock and unable to summon a single emotion, never mind a pleasing turn of phrase. The final deadline for the first edition was in about two hours, meaning I would have to file my 1,000 words within an hour to guarantee it a place in the paper. I got up, washed my face, and spat dust and phlegm into the kitchen sink.

Then, somewhat belatedly, I threw up.

Next to my laptop was the red, leather-bound diary I had grabbed before running towards the World Trade Center. I opened it up. On the first page I had unimaginatively scrawled 'Independence Day!' – a reference to the Hollywood film in which aliens destroy the White House. I felt a shudder of incompetence – not the first of the day. My notes ended with a quote from a random bystander: 'Dude, there's *no way* that tower will collapse,' it said.

I sat on my cheap, pretend-leather chair and stared at my laptop's postage-stamp screen. Behind me was the only window in my apartment. I stared harder at the LCD, and felt light-headed with anxiety, as though the morning's terror had dissolved the sugar in my blood. I jiggled my feet in an effort to revive myself. Then I typed, 'At first, we thought it was burning debris falling from the upper floors of the World Trade Center. Then we noticed the debris had arms and legs.'

By 1 p.m. it was done. Twenty years ago the deadline would have been and gone; I would probably have been frantically jogging uptown in search of a working telephone on which I could cough a few lines from my notebook. Perhaps my story would have made it into the following week's paper.

I tried to watch the television, but kept being distracted by an unusual noise. It sounded like distant cheering – not constant, but in irregular bursts, as though David Beckham kept approaching the goal at Old Trafford. Then air horns and applause, like a ticker-tape parade. For the second time in a few hours I thought I was hallucinating. There it was again. I stood on my window sill, cupped my hands against the filthy glass, and tried to see what was going on. Nothing: just an empty street, trees, and that awful smoke. I grabbed my keys and headed for the lift. Outside, as I reached the corner of Christopher and Greenwich Street, the noise came again, louder. Then I saw where it was coming from: on either bank of the West Side Highway was a crowd of perhaps two hundred people, waving American flags and holding placards with 'OUR HEROES' and 'GOD BLESS AMERICA' painted on them. As the ambulances and fire engines hurtled south down the highway, towards the mouth of hell, the crowd cheered, hooted and wiggled the signs. I felt a sudden and unexpected swell of patriotism for a foreign country. There was no traffic going in the opposite direction. The vehicles blasted their horns. Their occupants, I noticed, looked more like soldiers than emergency workers. Some of them raised their fists and shook them in defiance. Some just waved. The rest, soot-faced and sipping sticky energy drinks, stared blankly at the missing Manhattan skyline. Perhaps, like me, they felt angry.

Later, my mobile phone managed to connect for the first time since 9 a.m. I talked to my dad, who told me I was lucky to have witnessed such an historic event: I could tell, however, that he was just trying to find something positive to say. He was also trying to hide the fact that he was hugely relieved. My mother said that she and my sister had cried all day. I spoke briefly to Alana, who was still with her own dad. She said she would come over to the apartment later. Then I got through to James Bone, who had written the day's lead story. I found his cheery tone both hugely reassuring and slightly irritating. 'This reminds me of Afghanistan,' he said casually. Bone, of course, was a *real* war correspondent. *He hadn't legged it.*

After another few restless hours in the apartment I decided to take a walk, but there was a police blockade at 14th Street. No one without ID was being allowed in or out. On my way home I saw a Vietnam veteran draped in an Old Glory flag standing on the corner of 7th and West 13th. He was shouting; crying; pleading – I made out something about God and the 'fucking Arabs', but his words didn't form coherent sentences. It didn't matter: words had been put out of business on this particular day. I headed south, and the terrible fog thickened; my walk broke into a run. A light rain of ash made my contact lenses sting. There were American flags draped over the brownstone buildings on Charles Street: *Christ*, I thought, *I'm in a foreign country in a time of war.* The US had never really felt foreign to me: it did now.

The same thought had clearly struck others: there was a Muslim cab driver, who had probably escaped his own war-torn country to come to New York, buying an 'I LOVE THE USA' bumper sticker from the Asian-owned news stand on Hudson Street and West 10th. He wouldn't look me in the eye.

The Italian restaurant on Christopher and Washington Street had wrapped its outdoor tables in plastic and put its winter snow canopy over the front door – but there were still people inside, eating and drinking, as ash rained against the windows. It seemed odd to order pasta and swig Chianti with a blazing mass grave only a dozen or so blocks away. But then what else were we supposed to do? Sit at home, sober and hungry, waiting for the next jetliner to hit? I ducked into my monolithic red-brick apartment building and felt relieved to be inside.

Back in the apartment, I logged on to *The Times*'s website – I couldn't stand another second of television. It was about 3 a.m. in London, and the first of tomorrow's articles were going online. The 12 September edition was turning out to be an almost unbearable mix of the world as it was and the world as it had become: 'Clingfilm Attack Lover Jailed for Five Years' was next to 'She Sat at Her Desk and Watched an Airliner Flying Straight at Her'. I skimmed through several other articles – all probably written before lunchtime on Tuesday in London – but developed a fixation with a single item, halfway down the nib column. It said:

> Some like it hot: Thousands of volunteers from the Women's Institute and Women's Royal Voluntary Service have knitted the world's longest scarf – 22 miles. The scarf, which would cover two football pitches if laid out, took five years to make and involved 500 million stitches.

How long would it be, I asked myself, before another story like that made it into *The Times*? Weeks, months . . . years?

*It's 11 p.m. I'm lying on my mattress, sweating and tangled in the blue cotton sheets, waiting for Alana to arrive. I would phone, but the phones don't work. Nothing bloody works, apart from cable television. All 897 channels have become one: the terror channel. I don't want to watch it. Not again – not ever. My apartment looks much the same as it did yesterday; nothing else does. Outside, there are pedestrians wearing gas masks. The amber fuzz of the street lamps through the terrible, stinking fog makes Manhattan look like Victorian London. The fog, with all the microscopic particles of horror within it, is being carried up the wind tunnel of Greenwich Street from downtown, which has today been renamed 'Ground Zero' by the news networks. That, apparently, is what scientists used to call the impact zone of a thermonuclear bomb. Perhaps, as the skateboarder said, this is World War III.*

*Today Manhattan became a target in a war no one knew had been declared. And today I became an accidental war correspondent. I can't get the smell out of my clothes. And the NYPD officer's words are still trapped in my head: 'Get the fuck out of here!' His handgun was raised and his face was stretched and twisted into a drenched mask of panic. But his scream was silenced by the tidal wave of smoke and debris crashing towards Chambers Street. 'How do you know it's over?' he mouthed. 'Go home! GO HOME!' There was a gunshot, or perhaps the sound of steel and glass hitting concrete, and then the simultaneous realization of several hundred people that they were about to die. That was when the running started.*

*I keep having to wash my face and spit gobs of grit and dust and God knows what else into the sink. I snapped, and bought a carton of cigarettes an hour or so ago: cancer can try as hard as it wants, but it's not going to scare any New Yorkers today. Let's see if civilization survives tomorrow first – then the cigarette smokers can start worrying about their ruined lungs.*

*Still no word from Karen. I reflexively dial her home and mobile numbers, but my phone can't or won't connect. I call her office again, and listen to a cheerful recorded voice telling me the number's temporarily unavailable. How about permanently unavailable, I think, along with an entire Zip code of southern Manhattan? I imagine Karen's melted desk in the inferno still blazing less than a mile and a half from my bed. From Greenwich Street, the floodlights erected by the rescue workers look like a distant rip in the space–time continuum, a blinding white doorway to another dimension. Even from this distance I can hear the groans of the machinery. Karen would probably have been late for work, I reassure myself. She always was – is.*

*Alana is on her way from Midtown: 40th and Lexington. It's close to Grand Central; I hope she's OK. Maybe that'll be next. It's hard not to speculate. I haven't seen her since I left for England two weeks ago. I can barely believe I landed at John F. Kennedy Airport only last night. Alana must be walking, or taking the subway: the cab drivers have all gone home, and who can blame them? Who'd want to be an Iranian or Afghan – the prayer beads hanging from the rear-view mirror; the Holy Koran on the passenger seat – picking up angry Americans on the streets of Manhattan tonight? There's a gospel song playing on the clock radio next to my bed: 'I keep on falling,' goes the lyric. The bass notes make the radio's casing rattle. I close my eyes and think of black shadows against blue sky and reflective glass.*

# 7

## *Bacillus Anthracis*

'Business new-*ews?*'

This was how Martin Barrow answered the phone. He would often claim he was world's best-paid receptionist.

'Martin?'

'Hello Chris. *Having fun?*'

I marvelled at the power of Barrow's sarcasm, and the fact that it could travel 3,500 miles down a telephone line and emerge into my right ear with 100 per cent of its original force.

'Martin . . . they've found some spores of, erm, *anthrax* in the Rockefeller Center.'

'Really? Wow . . .'

I could hear Barrow's keyboard clacking. He was distracted. It was close to deadline; Barrow was shovelling hard.

There was a fuzz of transatlantic static, then more clacking.

I tried again. 'Martin: the Rockefeller Center in NEW YORK. On Sixth Avenue. WHERE I WORK.'

The clacking stopped.

'N-*ohh* – really?'

There was a pregnant silence as Barrow decided how best to respond.

'Chri-*is*,' he began. 'Wherever you go, bad things seem to happen.'

Now I could hear chuckling in the background.

Barrow was on a roll. 'First it's falling buildings; next it's biological weapons of mass destruction,' he said. 'Next time you come to London, Chris, could you, like, let us know in advance? *We might all take a holiday.*' He let out a delighted nasal yelp, followed by a schoolboyish giggle. I could hear the other staff on the business desk guffawing in the background. It was like listening to the 'morning crew' on a radio talk show, through my telephone's earpiece.

'Martin. This isn't *fucking funny*.'

I knew, of course, that this was Barrow's way of trying to calm me down. But it wasn't working. Nothing, in fact, would work.

Barrow coughed.

'Sorry, Chris. Where has it been found? Anyone infected?'

Me: 'It's in the NBC building, opposite 1211. The victim's name is Erin O'Connor, she's the assistant to Tom Brokaw, the news anchor. CNBC is saying she got the skin version after opening a letter.'

I glanced around at the landfill of post surrounding me. I felt a shudder. Some of the *New York Post*'s messengers were watching the television over my right shoulder: they looked blank, uncomprehending.

'ANTHRAX IN NEW YORK,' was the CNBC screen caption.

'OK, Chris,' said Barrow. 'Hold tight.'

He hung up.

Perhaps Barrow was right. Perhaps bad things did happen to me. For a journalist, of course, this could be considered a good thing. Take the film *Bruce Almighty*, starring Jim Carrey. The hero is Bruce Nolan, a hapless television reporter for Channel 7 News, who is dispatched by his editor to cover a dull story about the biggest cookie ever to be baked in the town of Buffalo. Bruce curses God, and, in a curious form of revenge, God gives Bruce divine powers. So what does Bruce, the failed hack, do with his powers? On his next assignment, during an interview with a contestant in a fancy-dress 'Chili Cook-Off', Bruce summons an asteroid to fall out of the sky and land in blazing fireball yards from where he is standing, turning his report into an eye-witness scoop. Bruce becomes 'Mr Exclusive', and is promoted to anchor.

This, of course, is a perfect demonstration of the inverted logic of the news reporter and, even more so, the war correspondent: safety is bad, danger is good. It was a *good* thing I was nearly killed by the falling south tower of the World Trade Center, and a *bad* thing that Wapshott was trapped on the *QE2*. This much was clear from the gloating of *The Times*'s arch rival, the *Daily Telegraph*. 'The new New York correspondent for *The Times* spent the first week of the crisis chugging around the Atlantic on board the *QE2*, arriving in America just as the story moved to the Middle East,' the paper sneered in its 'Media Diary' column. 'Last week, his byline appeared on only three stories, leading some to worry about his current whereabouts. We can only pray that the cruise wasn't a round trip.'

There was, I suppose, some logic to the anti-logic of wanting to be near 'the story', even when the story involved mass destruction, some of which might destroy you. But it didn't feel like a good thing to be in New York on, or after, September 11. After all, there were nearly 3,000 dead; the world's most powerful economy was crippled; and the 'War on Terror' had begun. As I sat at home, spitting out the carcino-genic dust that had cartwheeled upwind from Ground Zero, being stranded in the choppy waters of the Atlantic seemed like a good idea. Besides, what little journalistic capital I had earned with my 'I saw people fall to death' story I immediately spent with a second one, wrongly identifying the impact zone in the south tower as the offices of the investment bank Morgan Stanley. Then, of course, there was the state of my mental health. Whenever I closed my eyes, I saw the father and his little boy sitting on the kerb. They were reading nursery rhymes together, black shapes falling behind them. And I heard the police officer shout, '*How do you know it's over?*'

Perhaps it *wasn't* over.

At least my friend Karen had survived. She had, as I suspected, been late for work. She ended up getting off the subway before the World Trade Center stop, after being warned of delays. She emerged into the sunlight to see her office, along with her computer and Palm Pilot, destroyed by a terrorist who lived 6,700 miles away. Within a week her company had relocated to New Jersey.

For the first two weeks after September 11 adrenalin kept me going. My adrenal glands, useful for the first time in my adult life, had given me an almost transcendental energy. I felt superhuman, better than at any time since leaving London. My body had finally disengaged from 'flight' mode. I was borderline cheerful. Then, inevitably, it ended. Sleep became a wrestle with soaked bed sheets; I developed a terrible bowel pain. Wearily, I resumed my Dr Ruth habit.

It was 12 October when I called Barrow to tell him about anthrax. There were, I suppose, two ways to look at it: first, as another huge story on my home turf; second, as another way in which I could die horribly. I veered, inevitably, towards the latter view. And, to be honest, I'd had enough of nearly dying horribly. It was, after all, only a month and a day since the twin towers had been demolished – not, as it turned out, by Saddam Hussein, but by a Saudi terrorist called Osama bin Laden. And I wasn't in the mood for any more terror. Or for any more war reporting.

I already knew all about anthrax. In Florida, it had killed Bob Stevens, a sixty-three-year-old photo editor at *The Sun*, a supermarket tabloid. That gave him the unhappy distinction of being the first American anthrax fatality since 1976 *and* the first person on US soil to die in a bioterror attack. (Stevens was actually born in Britain, but had emigrated to the US in 1974.) His terrifyingly swift deterioration from feeling fluey to lying in the Boca Raton morgue was a result of him contracting the inhalation, or pulmonary, form of the disease, as opposed to the less dangerous skin variety. I knew from my extensive internet-based research that skin anthrax, also known as cutaneous anthrax, could be treated effectively after infection with Cipro, a powerful antibiotic. Inhalation anthrax, however, seemed to be in a disease league of its own. Its mortality rate of nearly 100 per cent was right up there with Aids, late-stage bubonic plague and marsh fever. And it operated on an even more hectic schedule: it could have the whole thing wrapped up in ten days. Anthrax was a hard worker. There just wasn't much work for it to do. Until, that is, Bob Stevens was wheeled into the emergency room of the JFK Medical Center in Atlantis, Florida, at 2 a.m. on 2 October. The chart clipped to his stretcher described him as 'not oriented to person, place, or time'.

Soon enough, Stevens's astonished doctors began to understand why: anthrax was charging through his body, whistling as it worked, shutting down every vital organ, one by one. Anthrax, it is said, does to its victims from the inside what South American flesh-eating ants do from the outside.

But I didn't want to believe that Saddam Hussein, or Osama bin Laden, or any other celebrity killer on the international terror circuit, had used a biological weapon to murder Stevens. The very idea of someone launching an anthrax attack on a Florida supermarket tabloid seemed comic: worthy of one of *The Sun*'s own wacky news items. For the first time in journalistic history, however, the facts were on *The Sun*'s side: it was virtually impossible to catch the inhalation form of anthrax by accident. Cutaneous anthrax, the more common version of the disease, was usually passed on by cattle in Third World countries. Stevens, whose most adventurous activity before his death was a five-day fishing trip to North Carolina, could have spent a decade herding goats in Africa and he would still have been unlikely to catch skin anthrax – never mind the *inhalation* version. But even before the statistical improbability of Stevens's death had had time to sink in, another employee of *The Sun*, a seventy-four-year-old grand-father called Ernesto Blanco, came down with the disease. Blanco, born in Cuba, was initially diagnosed with pneumonia, before doctors at Miami's Cedars Medical Center decided that the fluid in his lungs was caused by inhaled anthrax spores. To me, the only positive aspect of the whole affair was that it was happening more than 1,000 miles south of Manhattan. Then anthrax arrived, refreshed from the Florida sunshine, in the Rockefeller Center, yards from my veal-fattening cubicle. It was ready for work.

New York had already faced spectacular, televised violence; now, it seemed, it was going to face invisible, biological violence. Living in Manhattan felt like living in some distant, war-weary outpost – how I imagined Casablanca might have felt during World War II. The White Horse Tavern, an Irish pub on Hudson Street, became my Rick's Bar. Only a few blocks south, debris from a 2-kiloton blast still smouldered; every day brought colour-coded alerts and closed bridges; and every conversation seemed to end with a suicide-attack scenario. 'What if they, like, just walked into Grand Central Station with an AK-47 and opened fire?' I heard one woman ask at the check-out of D'Agostino, a West Village supermarket.

*The Times*'s bureau on Sixth Avenue, meanwhile, became a fortress. Before entering 1211, I had to show my British passport and put my Starbucks chocolate croissant through an X-ray machine. It was, I suppose, a new kind of normality, but it didn't feel very normal – espe-cially not with the posters for missing World Trade Center workers still gummed to every surface imaginable, including the entrance to 666 Greenwich Street, or, of course, the fire stations in the West Village, their blood-red doorways marked by wreaths, candles and makeshift shrines to dead emergency workers. Then there were the news reports of President Bush ordering the bombing of Taliban forces in Afghanistan, and the hit song 'I Wanna Bomb Osama' (to the tune of 'La Bamba') that was all over morning radio and the internet. In Times Square it was possible to buy a 'Wanted: Dead or Alive' T-shirt with Osama bin Laden's face on it for $20. The War on Terror had even affected the gay boutiques on Christopher Street. One of them had put a pink sign in its window saying, 'We Love Everything the Taliban Hates.' I had a serious conversation with James Bone about buying a kayak to escape Manhattan in the event of another attack. But I knew a kayak wouldn't stop me getting the plague. '*Ring around the rosy*,' I heard a pack of boisterous ten-year-olds chant outside the schoolyard on West 11th Street. '*Pocket full of posies*. ANTHRAX! ANTHRAX! *And we all fall down . . .*' They thought it was hilarious.

Half an hour passed, and nothing happened. Barrow, who had asked me to 'hold tight', hadn't called back. I stared at the television, wondering whether to take the next subway back to the West Village. I started monitoring myself for flu-like symptoms. I wished I had bought some Cipro over the internet. I had been put off, however, by the price: $399 for sixty pills. It also occurred to me that I was at the scene of the first ever bioterror attack on America, and should be writing about it. But how do you write about airborne germs? The drama of invisible violence is psychological, not physical: bioterrorism could end up putting war correspondents out of business.

Not, of course, that I *wanted* to write anything: I wanted to run. On the television, a brave or foolish reporter was standing outside the headquarters of NBC, opposite the news ticker at 1211 Seventh Avenue. 'After everything New York's been through over the past month,' he was saying, 'it's hard to believe the city is now having to cope with a biological terror attack.'

The NBC building, like 1211, is part of the Rockefeller Center, an 11-acre village of concrete, glass and nasty Trump-style gold fixtures, connected by windy underground tunnels, one of which leads to the 49th Street subway station. The centrepiece is Rockefeller Plaza, which features a food court and, during winter, an ice rink and Christmas tree. If one part of the complex became contaminated with

*Bacillus anthracis*, I calculated, it would spread to the others, affecting tens of thousands of workers. One of those those poor bastards would be me.

'Business new-*ews*?'

That was Martin again; I couldn't wait any longer.

'Martin? It's me.'

'Chris. You OK?'

'*No.*'

'Oh dear. What's up?'

'You told me to "hold tight".'

'Bit snowed under, sorry. James Bone's covering the anthrax.'

'Oh, righ—'

'I'll put you over to foreign.'

I heard Chopin, then a familiar posh voice.

'Chr-*is*?' Again the info-seeking dip.

Me: 'Hi. I'm in the Rockefeller Center – where they've found the anthrax. Should I go over to the NBC building?'

I was hoping for a brisk 'No.' Let Bone get infected.

'Good idea,' the voice said. 'Go.'

*Shit.*

Outside, as I leaped between the yellow cabs heading upstream on Sixth Avenue, I thought about a film I had once watched called *The Andromeda Strain*. It was about a US Army satellite, named Scoop VII, that had fallen to earth in the New Mexico desert. The satellite, Army scientists discovered, had become contaminated with a deadly extraterrestrial virus. The plot revolved around the race to find a cure for the virus, before it wiped out humankind. The cast of *The Andromeda Strain*, I recalled, wore white chemical suits throughout the entire film.

I, on the other hand, was wearing blue jeans and a YSL shirt. I wondered how effective they would be at protecting me from killer bacteria. I wished I had a gas mask, or some bloody Cipro tablets. Should I even be going anywhere near NBC? Would I end up being wheeled into St Vincent's Hospital at 2 a.m., a chart above my head reading 'not oriented to person, place, or time'? Would the wind carry the anthrax spores deep into my lungs? I imagined the anthrax bacteria multiplying inside my body. I had read that a thousand anthrax bacilli could grow into *trillions* within three days. By the time they killed you, 30 per cent of your blood weight would be live bacilli. Through a microscope, they would look like teeming worms. Your bodily fluids, meanwhile, would ooze into the gap between your brain and skull, making your face swell into an unrecognizable balloon of putrid, yellowing flesh. That was why anthrax had been described as 'repugnant to the conscience of mankind' by the 1972 Biological Weapons Convention, which banned its use on the battlefield. I pictured my face as an anthrax-inflated balloon. But it was too late: I was under orders from the foreign desk. And that, in my warped mind, was more terrifying than any biological weapon.

In Rockefeller Plaza, bemused tourists were staring up at the gigantic video screen on the side of the NBC building. It was spewing out headlines, including one that read, 'Anthrax in New York: Suspicious Package Found in Rockefeller Center'. Office workers, who clearly knew nothing about the story, looked confused as they strolled out into the gentle autumn sun for lunch. They were greeted with sombre news anchors clutching branded microphones. Sixth Avenue, meanwhile, had become gridlocked with a motorcade of belching satellite trucks.

I approached a man in a grey polyester suit, who was pacing inside NBC's lobby. His eyes widened as I told him about the disease – he hadn't seen the video screen. 'I can't believe that my mother is sitting in Atlanta, probably watching this on television, knowing that her son is in the Rockefeller Center meeting his brother for lunch,' he said, wiping his brow. It was strange, I thought, that the image of his mother watching him at the site of an anthrax attack was more scary than actually *being* at the site of an anthrax attack. I asked for his name, but he waved me away. '*Shit!*' I heard him say to himself, as he fumbled with the flip-top of his mobile phone. '*Anthrax. Shit!*' I lingered for a few seconds. 'You know what the crazy thing is,' I heard him stage-whisper into the phone. 'In the Marines, NBC stands for "nuclear, biological and chemical". Yeah, dude, *no shit*. How about we do lunch in Atlanta?'

I was thinking about how surreal it was to cover a story only a few yards from my own desk when I heard the voice of Rudi Giuliani behind me. I spun on my heels, but couldn't see the New York mayor, who since September 11 had become a global celebrity with his pale, corrugated forehead, pinched features and circular, professor's spectacles. In the world's imagination, Giuliani's brow was forever coated with the fine white dust of Ground Zero. The mayor, I soon realized, was inside the NBC building giving an impromptu press conference. I probably should have been there – not, of course, that I would have dared venture any further into the building. I could hear his voice coming from a speaker somewhere inside one of the satellite trucks. 'What I'm going to do now is from an *excess* of caution,' the mayor's voice echoed. 'One floor of the building is going to be closed down.' Rockefeller Plaza emptied. Even the Japanese tourists understood that something was very, *very* wrong. They, of course, had already experienced their own domestic terror: the 1995 Sarin gas attack on the Tokyo subway that killed 12 and injured another 6,000.

I started speed-walking around the building's perimeter, hunting for someone to interview. Inside a doorway I saw a man in his twenties, wearing baggy Ralph Lauren jeans and smoking a cigarette. His name was Scott Bueller, and he worked for the wardrobe department of NBC's *Saturday Night Live*. A week earlier, Giuliani had been the show's celebrity guest. 'I'm here to give you permission to laugh,' Giuliani had said. 'And if you don't – I'll have you arrested.'

I wondered if we *still* had permission to laugh.

'What d'you think about the anthrax?' I asked Bueller, lighting my own cigarette. As I did so, I was reminded of a comment once made by the late comedian Bill Hicks, after someone told him that smoking would ruin his sense of smell. 'I live in New York City,' Hicks scoffed. 'Why the hell do I want my sense of smell back? Yeah, *great*, I can smell a dead guy!' After September 11, of course, New Yorkers could smell 3,000 dead guys. And jet fuel. And now anthrax, too.

'They're trying to play it down BIG TIME in the building,' Bueller confided, as I scribbled in my spiral-bound reporter's notebook. He seemed relaxed, but I noticed that his hands were shaking. 'They're saying that there's no danger . . . but I don't think anyone's buying it. It's kind of hard on Miss Barrymore, because she's not from New York and she hasn't had to live with this shit.'

My pen slid to a halt in a blue puddle.

'*Miss Barrymore?*' I asked.

'Yeah. She's our guest this week.'

'*Drew Barrymore?*'

Bueller nodded, then sucked hard on his cigarette.

In an instant, I stopped worrying about contracting anthrax. This was a good story: *an A-list Hollywood star was in the NBC building at the time of an anthrax attack.* Somehow it made me feel better that a celebrity was going through the same thing that I was. Surely this would be front page.

'Is she recording a show right now?' I asked.

'No . . . she's rehearsing,' came the slow, deliberate response. 'It's called Saturday Night *Live.* That's because it's, er, *live.*'

I winced, but pressed on.

'How did she react?'

I raised my pen, hoping Bueller wouldn't suddenly decide that talking to me might put his wardrobe career at risk.

'She kinda freaked out.'

*She freaked out!*

'It freaks me out too,' he added. 'I've only been to the mail room once, and it was two weeks ago. Now I'm asking myself: why did I go?'

I hurriedly thanked him, and started running back towards my own mail room, a.k.a. *The Times*'s bureau. I knew what Bueller meant: part of me wished I'd never gone back to 1211 after the World Trade Center attack. What if there was anthrax in the veal-fattening pen, hidden in an envelope addressed to the editor? Perhaps I would end up becoming America's *second* bioterror fatality.

As I was about to cross Sixth Avenue, I noticed another smoker outside the NBC building, this time an older woman with unkempt hair and deep welts where nicotine fumes had freeze-framed her laughter.

'I'm not talking to any fuckin' *reporters,*' she said.

'Aren't you scared?' I asked.

'Oh, honey, *come on,*' she laughed, flicking ash in my direction. 'I'm a smoker. Do I look as though I care what I inhale?'

Only in New York, I thought, would someone standing outside the scene of a confirmed bioterror attack give that response.

Later, I wondered if war journalism was really as bad as I had imagined. Buzzing from the Barrymore scoop, I didn't really feel nervous about anthrax any more. It seemed as though the real world, even the real world in a bio-war zone, felt safer than it looked on dramatically edited twenty-four-hour news footage. Or perhaps I was just losing my war virginity. I called the foreign desk and told them about Barrymore. I listened to more Chopin as they digested the news.

Then 'Chr-*is*?'

'Yes?'

'Thousand words, please, on "I saw anthrax scare celebrity".'

The phone went dead.


I closed my eyes, grimaced, and felt cold plastic enter my right nostril.

'This shouldn't take long,' said Dr Ruth.

'When will I find out if I'm dying?' I asked.

'In twenty-four to forty-eight hours, probably: after we've analysed the cultures from your nasal bacteria. But you have to remember, Christopher, that a negative swab doesn't mean anthrax exposure hasn't occurred.'

'*What?*'

'The test isn't necessarily reliable.'

'Oh.'

'But unless your symptoms become more severe, and less non-specific, I don't see any need for a blood test.'

'Rrr-*ight*.'

'I'm going to put a swab stick in your other nostril now.'

There was a wet, sticky sound.

'Urgh . . .'

'*Done*,' said Dr Ruth. 'You can open your eyes now, Christopher.'

I opened them. Dr Ruth, her leg still in plaster, was looking particularly bedraggled today. She probably saw it as one of the upsides of her job: not having to look good in front of ill people. She certainly didn't have to look good in front of me. Terror had taken its toll on my appearance: I had gained weight from boozing in the White Horse, and my skin was popping and bubbling with stress acne. I was drenched in sweat. I blamed it on Osama bin Laden.

Dr Ruth dropped the swab sticks into a plastic bag, then put the bag into a tub labelled 'Special Handling for Anthrax'.

'So, I've taken a culture from each naris,' she explained. 'If you've inhaled anthrax we *should* see it in the results. Unless, of course, the test fails. But at this stage we probably shouldn't worry too much.'

'Jolly good,' I said, with a frown.

'Don't forget to call tomorrow,' she said, hobbling out of the room.

'Not much chance of that,' I replied.

When I got home, I decided to file a *Times* expenses form. At the top of it I wrote 'ANTHRAX TEST: $100' Then I consulted a separate booklet to find the correct 'cost code' for the item. I considered putting it under 'Postage: 7231', but decided instead on 'Other Office Expense: 7299'. Perhaps I'd get a pay rise, I thought, out of pity. I should have known better, however: editors don't reward journalists for being in danger, on the assumption that they *enjoy* danger because it produces better stories. It was the *Bruce Almighty* syndrome. And I was Bruce.

Time passed, and anthrax refused to go away. It soon became clear that whoever was sending it in the post had something against journalists, as well as politicians and postal workers. Anthrax-infected letters turned up at CBS, ABC, the *New York Times*, the Capitol building in Washington, DC, and random postal facilities up and down the eastern seaboard. The bacterium itself wasn't the cocaine-like white powder I had imagined. Major General John Parker, an army bio-weapons specialist, described the substance sent to NBC as coarse and brown, 'like Purina Dog Chow', a US rival to Pedigree Chum. I almost wished it *did* look like cocaine. It seemed a bit more glamorous than being killed by bloody dog food.

I decided to take practical measures to protect myself. On the advice of Ken Alibek, a former Soviet germ-warfare scientist, whom I saw interviewed on Fox News, I started ironing all my post. This, according to Dr Alibek, would kill any stray anthrax spores. The decontamination procedure didn't go well at first. In fact I ended up setting my phone bill on fire, triggering the elaborate smoke-alarm system at 666 Greenwich Street. Eventually I perfected the technique, putting a damp cloth between the envelope and the iron. This,

Dr Alibek said, would kill even more germs. Unfortunately I couldn't iron the parcels that surrounded me at 1211.

The first anthrax-tainted letters, it emerged, had been posted in Trenton, New Jersey, on 18 September, exactly one week after the World Trade Center's destruction. Another batch, containing higher-quality 'weapons-grade' spores, had been sent on 9 October. Even James Bone, who had remained annoyingly composed during September 11, started to sound worried: they might have had burning buildings when he was a war reporter in Afghanistan, but they certainly didn't have any weaponized anthrax. The fact that Jack Potter, the postmaster general, had held a press conference to announce the creation of an anthrax task force, and to claim that 680 million parcels were being tested every day, was hardly reassuring. The postal workers at 1211 had taken matters into their own hands. Benjamin, the messenger who sat next to me, started showing up for work in a home-made bio-hazard suit, black Goretex boots and kitchen gloves. My Sixth Avenue office began to feel more like a laboratory than a news bureau – with me being the unlucky chimp. Finally I went online to buy Cipro. I again abandoned the idea, however, when I saw the price: sixty pills were now $3,999. That was when I decided to ask Dr Ruth for a test. *The Times* kindly agreed to paid for it.

It all seemed so . . . *unfair*. While Dr Ruth shoved plastic swabs up my nose, my friend Glen was on the deck of the USS *Enterprise*, somewhere in the northern Indian Ocean. He had been sent there by *The Times* to watch American warplanes launch their first attacks on Afghanistan. I imagined Glen, his sunglasses on, white shirt unbuttoned, cream linen jacket flapping in the breeze, taking notes as the F/A-18 Hornets howled overhead. It seemed both glamorous and acceptably safe. Part of me wished I could, for once, be on the *giving* end of an attack.

I should have been more careful what I wished for.

What with the burning skyscrapers at the bottom of my street, the carcinogenic fumes in my apartment, the biological hazard at my office and the adrenalin seeping out of my pores, late October wasn't a great time for me to entertain visitors from England. Nevertheless, my sister and her fiancé had bought tickets to New York long before

September 11, and nothing short of a 50-megaton nuke going off in Times Square was going to make them cancel. I was, in fact, deeply impressed with their bravery. If it had been me, I would have begged Virgin Atlantic to swap my ticket for one to somewhere warm, safe and as far away as possible from lower Manhattan: Hawaii, perhaps. Yet Catherine and Tom were due to land at John F. Kennedy Airport on 20 October, just eight days after anthrax was found in the Rockefeller Center. They would stay a week. Neither of them had ever been to the United States before, and both were looking forward to the trip as their last holiday before getting married.

Since September 11, I had become dangerously fixated with America's hysterical twenty-four-hour news channels – in particular, the scrolling headlines that CNN had started to display at the bottom of the screen – and so I was looking forward to some relief in the form of my sister, a down-to-earth schoolteacher, two years my senior. Of the two of us, Catherine had shown the most early promise. She was incandescently bright, got straight As for everything she did, and also earned money throughout high school with a gruelling hotel job. My idea of a hard day's work, meanwhile, was getting out of bed. Catherine, who is tall and slim with an explosion of dark curls that make her look like a Pre-Raphaelite painting, graduated with a degree in Victorian English literature – the ultimate anti-vocational qualification. Then she moved to London to work for a record company. It didn't take long, however, for my sister to realize that a life of Bollinger and stretched Hummer limos wasn't for her, so she moved back up North to do a 'real' job: teaching. It was in Alnwick, the town where we both went to high school, that she bumped into Tom, the teenage rebel she used to sit next to in maths lessons. He, it turned out, had skipped university and got a job in a fish factory. By the time my sister met him, he was *running* the fish factory. Needless to say, Tom, a physically imposing Geordie who negotiated with North Sea fishermen all day, was way too macho to cancel a trip to New York City for something as trifling as germ warfare.

I was glad they were coming. I didn't, however, enjoy the thought of having to give up my studio apartment, which was kept so fastidiously clean and tidy it was clearly rented by someone with an advanced-stage anxiety disorder. The thought of it being cluttered with three people was too much to handle, so I had arranged to stay at Alana's $2,000-a-month wardrobe next to Grand Central. The biggest downside to Alana's place, apart from its size, was that it was literally built on top of a waste-disposal plant. That meant rubbish trucks regularly dumped 3-ton loads down a circular metal chute that fed into the basement. The noise was just about bearable during the day; at 3 a.m., as I tussled with the sheets, it nearly killed me.

My relationship with Alana had become strained after September 11. Alana, a zealous liberal, seemed more angry about the Bush administration's response to September 11 than about the attacks themselves. I, on the other hand, saw nothing wrong with the war in Afghanistan, the X-ray machine outside 1211, and all the other borderline-paranoid security initiatives. After seeing what Osama bin Laden had done to lower Manhattan and the workers in the World Trade Center – not to mention the fact that the bastard had nearly killed *me* – I *wanted* Bush to 'smoke him out', and I didn't care how cheesy or uncool his cowboy-talk sounded. Perhaps this was just another manifestation of my cowardice. But wasn't it *insane* to carry on as normal, knowing that the September 11 hijackers had used flaws in US security to kill 3,000 people? Alana didn't agree. 'If we change our lifestyles, *it means the terrorists have won*,' she said. But if we didn't change our lifestyles, I thought, and we were attacked again, wouldn't that also mean that they had won? And, unlike our imperceptible loss of liberty under the Patriot Act, it wouldn't be an intellectual, or a metaphorical, victory. It would a stolen Soviet nuke taking out Boston; or a 747 flown into a reactor.

As for anthrax, I wasn't entirely convinced it had anything to do with Osama bin Laden. It was the victims, as well as the way the attacks were carried out, that were suspicious. Would the al-Qaeda chief really choose NBC, or a tawdry Florida tabloid, as his first targets? As revealed on September 11, his attacks were more cinematic than that. He would have released a billion spores of anthrax into the New York subway system, or pumped them into the ventilation ducts of Congress. Anthrax, I feared, was the diabolical crime of an all-American lunatic.

On the morning of Friday 19 October, the day before the family visit, I was in a better mood than usual. The whole anthrax business,

I thought, would soon go away. Dr Ruth's nasal swab had turned out negative, and no one I knew had died. How bad could a few stupid anthrax spores be, anyway? The fact that Catherine and Tom hadn't cancelled their trip made me feel even more confident. On Sixth Avenue, I bought a Starbucks cappuccino, a Danish pastry and an armful of newspapers, then dumped them all on the X-ray conveyor belt outside 1211. After a security guard nodded at my passport, I pushed myself through the revolving doors, picked up my breakfast and reading material on the other side, and headed for the office.

By the time the lift reached the ninth floor, however, I was paralysed. The doors opened. 'You gettin' off here, honey?' sang the black woman behind me. Through one of the glass office doors I could see the white-gloved receptionist staring at me. The lift doors clattered shut. 'No,' I croaked. 'I'm not.' We pinged upward to the twelfth floor, and the black woman squeezed past me.

The doors closed.

I stood by myself, the lift not moving. I was transfixed by the front page of the newspaper in my hands. The overhead fluorescent lamp burned into my flushed forehead. I gulped back a mouthful of salty vomit.

The front page of the *New York Post* featured a picture of a woman I recognized, making an obscene gesture with a bandaged middle finger. The headline above her head said, 'ANTHRAX THIS'. The woman was Johanna Huden, a *New York Post* assistant. She had become infected with anthrax, and was displaying her diseased finger. 'When you work for a newspaper, you're part of the story, but not too close,' she wrote. 'This morning I am the story . . . I'm a victim of germ warfare. Anthrax is in my blood. Thanks, Osama.' I knew what she meant about being too close to the story. The accompanying article said that Huden had caught the disease from a letter posted in New Jersey on 18 September. The letter contained brown gunk, along with the following message: '09–11–01, THIS IS NEXT, TAKE PENACILIN NOW, DEATH TO AMERICA, DEATH TO ISRAEL, ALLAH IS GREAT.' The letter would have sat next to my desk, possibly for days, before being taken upstairs by one of the messengers. Perhaps it was one of the letters I rummaged through every day, looking for my own post. *Perhaps I had anthrax.* And what about the post-room workers who sat next to me? I thought about Bob Stevens. I wanted to cry.

I thumped the 'G' button and closed my eyes as the lift sank downward. I stumbled out into the lobby still clutching the *Post*, my stack of other newspapers, and my Danish pastry and cappuccino. Outside, I glanced up and saw a terrifying headline scrolling across the news ticker: '*POST* TRAUMATIC STRESS? – FOURTH CITY ANTHRAX CASE HITS *NEW YORK POST*!' That's it, I thought: I could never go back to the veal-fattening pen again. If I survived anthrax, I would work from 666 Greenwich Street. I would become a terror telecommuter.

Catherine and Tom touched down just before midnight the following day. I couldn't bring myself to tell them about the attack on the *Post*, the other eleven anthrax cases in the so-called 'media mailing', or the twenty-eight workers in the US Senate who, tests confirmed, had been exposed to the disease. Nor did I mention the nasal swab that Dr Ruth had given me. My sister and her fiancé both looked tired as we drove from JFK Airport back to Manhattan in Alana's battered turquoise Dodge Neon. I could hardly the imagine the culture shock they must have felt as we turned on to Greenwich Street, where ashes were still blowing upwind from the eerie white glow of Ground Zero. In spite of their jet lag, however, Catherine and Tom managed to enjoy a cheeseburger and a couple of glasses of beer in the White Horse before going to bed.

The next morning, Tom was off colour – quite a feat, given that his skin is usually a pale shade of very white. We bought a pricey brunch in the meatpacking district, but he had no appetite. Dismissing his malaise as jet lag, Tom, who prides himself on never getting ill or seeing a doctor, went to bed. By Monday he was still there, moaning, sweating, and coughing up blood and phlegm. Catherine, who had never seen her fiancé so ill, acted as though it was nothing but a normal bout of flu. I contemplated calling Dr Ruth, but decided against it – then looked up the symptoms of pulmonary anthrax on the Center for Disease Control's website.

This is what it said:

Inhalation: Initial symptoms may resemble a common cold. After several days, symptoms may progress to severe breathing problems and shock. Inhalation anthrax is usually fatal. Direct person-to-person spread of anthrax is extremely unlikely to occur.

Then I consulted my notes on Bob Stevens:

The couple were driving to North Carolina when Bob started shivering. His face was flushed. The next day Stevens and his wife drove back to their home in Lantana. He wore a sweater all the way. Mrs Stevens was woken up in the night by her husband vomiting, and she took him to JFK Medical Center. Stevens fell into a coma. Three days later, he died from inhalation anthrax.

At that moment, Tom, his face flushed, hauled himself out of bed, crawled into the bathroom, and vomited. He re-emerged, put on a sweater, and got back into bed. 'Don't worry about me,' he grunted. 'I'm grand.'

No one, of course, mentioned the A-word. Until, that is, Catherine and I went to the Macy's department store on Monday. In the cab on the way back to 666 Greenwich Street, the Muslim driver, who was surrounded by every conceivable kind of patriotic 'USA' merchandise, including a 6-foot Old Glory flag tied to his radio antenna, was listening to a news show. An item about anthrax came on. 'This just in,' said the news reader. 'Yet another *New York Post* employee has contracted anthrax. The male victim, who has not been named, works in the mail room of the tabloid's Sixth Avenue headquarters. A spokeswoman for the *Post* said the worker tested positive for the skin version of the disease after noticing a blister on his finger.' Outside the window of the cab, midtown Manhattan dissolved into a blur. I felt a sharp pain in my lower abdomen. *Surely this could not be happening.*

I looked at Catherine.

My sister looked at me.

We were both thinking the same thing: had spores of anthrax from 1211 somehow infected my future brother-in-law?

*Jesus Christ*: had I killed Tom?

The worst-case scenario was entirely plausible. The day after Tom and Catherine arrived at JFK, Thomas Morris Jr, a fifty-five-year-old parcel handler in Washington, died after failing to convince anyone that he had pulmonary anthrax. The day after that, another postal worker died, this time Joseph Curseen, forty-seven, also based in Washington. Over the same long weekend, another two Postal Service employees were hospitalized with anthrax, and nine others were wheeled into casualty with anthrax-like symptoms. The authorities, in a panic, tested 2,200 people who handled post for a living. The FBI, meanwhile, in an effort to hunt down the bioterrorist, put photographs of his, or her, letters online. But some of the more disturbing aspects of the anthrax attacks would not emerge until November. For example, the fact that a sample taken from the plastic evidence bag containing an *unopened* letter to Senator Patrick Leahy contained at least *two* lethal doses of anthrax. Scientists believed the letter itself contained enough spores to send 100,000 to the crematorium. Then, of course, there were the unsettling cases of victims killed by minuscule traces of anthrax cross-contamination. These included Ottilie Lundgren, a ninety-four-year-old retiree from Oxford, Connecticut, and Kathy Nguyen, sixty-one, an office worker at the Manhattan Eye, Ear and Throat Hospital.

It was probably just as well that I didn't know anything about all this as Tom lay flat out in my bed, his sweat seeping into the mattress. Catherine and I tried hard to pretend it was just another normal flu season. Our efforts to convince Tom to see Dr Ruth were futile. '*Not going . . . bloody doctor . . .*' were the only words we could make out from within the sopping bed sheets.

I spent hours online reading about the latest anthrax theories. The most convincing explanation was that the bioterrorist was a Timothy McVeigh-style right-winger who wanted to scare the American public into enforcing racist anti-immigrant laws. According to this theory, the first batch of letters was sent to *The Sun* and NBC to create public hysteria (and to make a link with September 11, because *The Sun*'s office was near where the hijackers had taken flight lessons). The second batch was probably a reaction to the muted news coverage of the first. After all, most news channels initially blamed Bob Stevens's death on him catching anthrax outdoors. But whoever was sending the killer dog food shouldn't have worried so much. They certainly had the full attention of this particular media representative.

★

By the end of the week, Tom wasn't dead. For the first time in his life, it seemed, he had come down with a hospital-grade upper-respiratory infection, probably brought on by working sixteen-hour days, then spending seven hours in Virgin Atlantic's economy class. Exhausted and disappointed with her ruined holiday, Catherine hauled Tom back to JFK and boarded a plane to London. By the time their Boeing 747 reached Heathrow, half the passengers probably had Tom's hyper-virus. Perhaps some of them thought they had caught pulmonary anthrax in New York.

The second *New York Post* employee to have got anthrax turned out to be Benjamin, the messenger in the cubicle next to mine, who had started appearing at 1211 in a homemade bio-hazard suit. His kitchen gloves, apparently, were not enough to protect him. Luckily, he contracted only cutaneous anthrax. There was also a *third* skin-anthrax victim at the *Post*: Mark Cunningham, an editorial-page editor. All three recovered after taking Cipro. By the end of the year, a total of twenty-two Americans, from Florida to Connecticut, would develop anthrax infections. Five of them – all inhalation victims – would die horribly from the worm-like bacteria. I went back to the veal-fattening pen only once, to find that my desk had been virtually destroyed by a clean-up crew from the Center for Disease Control. The Aussies, who had refused to budge from the ninth floor of 1211, told me that 'the decontaminators' had turned up looking like Apollo 13 astronauts. At least, I thought, the veal-fattening pen might have been vacuumed for the first time in a decade. No one else from *The Times* had been to the office either: James Bone worked from the United Nations building and Nick Wapshott, who had eventually turned up in New York after being diverted on the *QE2* to Boston, preferred to work from home. By December, our bureau at 1211 had been closed.

In the weeks leading up to Christmas I was the lowest I had ever been. Alana and I decided to go ahead with a long weekend in Miami we had planned for late October. At the airport, thousands of cars stood unrented in the car park: it was the first time I really understood the scale of the damage caused to the economy by September 11. Getting through security took hours. The plane journey itself – my first since the trip from London to JFK on 10 September– was awful. For a start, the stink of jet fuel took me right back to Murray Street.

Once on board, there was no food or drink. Everyone was popping Xanax and looking at each other with unapologetic fear and discrimination. Indians and Mexican had a hard time; as for Arabs, they might as well have just driven. The newspapers were full of reports about airline passengers refusing to get on planes if anyone on board looked even vaguely Muslim or Middle Eastern. Alana, of course, was outraged. When the wheels of our Boeing 767 finally smoked on to the runway in Miami – a few yards from one of the flight schools where the September 11 hijackers had learned how to fly the same kind of planes into tall buildings – the entire coach-class cabin broke spontaneously into weepy applause.

Once again, however, I found myself in the wrong place at the wrong time: Hurricane Michelle was blowing in from across the Straits of Florida, having already wreaked havoc in Cuba. Miami went on high storm alert, and Alana and I climbed back on a plane headed in the opposite direction.

Barrow was right: I was cursed. Then, finally, I snapped: at 35,000 feet, somewhere above the eastern seaboard, amid turbulence caused by crosswinds from Hurricane Michelle, post-traumatic stress kicked in. I started having a full-blown panic attack. I had never before been scared of flying, but there I was: gulping in oxygen, sweating and shaking, my head wedged between my knees and the tray table. The delayed stress of September 11 and anthrax hit me harder than I ever could have expected.

Back in New York, I tried hard to convince myself that life would return to normal. But there was more to come: on 12 November, American Airlines flight 587, carrying 260 people, nosedived into Rockaway, a part of Queens where many of the firefighters who died on September 11 had lived. Fear flushed through my body as I watched early reports of the crash on a local news station. *Could things get any worse?* I was dispatched to cover the story, and for the second time in two months I got to smell burning flesh and spilled jet fuel. By the time I reached Rockaway the streets were an asphalt graveyard of black body bags.

The cause of the air crash was not terrorism, however; investigators suspected that the tailfin and rudder of the Airbus A300 had been sheared off when the plane hit turbulence caused by a 747 in front of it.

It was a reminder that life could be still taken by fate, as well as by Osama bin Laden. Two of the victims, Kathleen Lawler, forty-eight, and her twenty-four-year-old son, Christopher, were simply sitting at home in Belle Harbor when a fireball came out of the sky and devoured them.

I desperately wanted to leave New York. I knew I was supposed to love the Big Apple, but I couldn't pretend any more. *I hated it.* It was nothing like the relaxing, sunny business trips to Silicon Valley I had taken while covering the dot-com industry in the late nineties. By spring, I saw a chance to move when Peter Stothard, *The Times's* editor for a decade, announced his retirement. He was replaced by Robert Thomson, managing editor of the American edition of the *Financial Times*. I asked Patience if there was a chance that Thomson would reopen *The Times's* Los Angeles bureau. Patience said yes, but that I was unlikely to get the job. 'Chris, you've got to remember: you're still very young,' she said. 'And, besides, you're a serious financial journalist. Los Angeles is all about celebrity fluff.' A week later, she called back: I was the new Los Angeles correspondent. I wasn't quite sure how it had happened, but I was delighted. Thomson had also decided to reopen the New York bureau, this time in Battery Park, and hire two people to cover Wall Street – essentially ending the culture of lift and view. I wasn't quite sure how it had all happened, but I was delighted. He apparently had wanted someone on the West Coast who could write about the *economics* of celebrity fluff, as well as the celebrity fluff itself.

Alana, on the other hand, was distraught: she hated the idea of giving up the West Village for La-La Land. I suggested going alone and trying a long-distance relationship. After several furious arguments and a brief separation, she decided to come with me. In the end we drove there, picking up my company Jeep in Long Island and pointing it west. California, I imagined, would mark the end of my career as an accidental war correspondent. My two years in New York would be a violent blip on an otherwise peaceful life. I would spend my days lounging by the Beverly Hilton swimming pool, and my evenings at celebrity parties in the Hollywood Hills. I would drink cappuccinos in Shutters of Santa Monica, sink vodka martinis in the Sky Bar, and cruise up and down Sunset Strip with Led Zeppelin crunching out of the Jeep's hi-fi system. There would be no anthrax, and no falling skyscrapers.

Oh yes: in California, I would be a new man.

Coronado Island, California

2002

# 8

## A Terrible Mistake

'Any nervous flyers on board?' asked the pilot.

I wanted to raise my right arm, but it was restrained by a nylon belt that was creating a deep red welt in my flesh.

The pilot's voice was coming from within a pair of heavy black headphones, wrapped around my blue crash helmet. I tried to say something, but my chinstrap was pulled so tight it had immobilized my jaw. The other passengers, I noticed, faced a similar problem. No one responded.

'Out*standing*,' said the pilot. 'Because it sure is gonna to be *reeeal* bumpy up there today. *Whoayeah!* And when we land . . . y'all might think we've crashed. But don't worry, folks, it's only gonna *feel* like that.'

Whoops of distorted laughter filled the headphones.

The pilot coughed, then added, 'Ah'll be pretty darn impressed if none 'you media folk don't get reacquainted with your breakfast.'

More distorted whoops.

I tried to remember what I had eaten for breakfast. I had a horrible feeling it involved eggs. Again I tried to speak.

'Ungh,' was the best I could manage.

I was facing the rear of the aircraft, looking out at the hot tarmac of the runway through an open hatch, my feet planted at shoulder level on the back of the seat in front of me. I could hear nothing apart from the pilot's distant, almost mechanical, voice – he sounded like a stormtrooper from one of the early *Star Wars* films – and the industrial drone of the twin T-56 turboprop engines, which had redefined my understanding of loudness. Nausea tickled my stomach.

'*Okey-doke folks!*' said the pilot, and I felt the battered aircraft, a US Navy C-2A Greyhound, start to jerk forward.

Within the next hour we were due to land on the USS *Constellation*, a 5,000-crew aircraft carrier sailing in wide circles 100 miles off the coast of San Diego. My plan to write about celebrity fluff in Los Angeles had gone badly wrong. The Greyhound would collide with the *Constellation*'s deck at 150 m.p.h. and be yanked to a standstill within two seconds, or 320 feet, by a hook on the tail that snagged an 'arresting cable' stretched across the deck. Sometimes, I had been told, the hook would miss and the plane would skid off the other end of the deck, into the Pacific.

That would explain why I was also wearing a lifejacket.

I emitted a loud groan, rendered silent by the engines.

The Greyhound gathered speed, and the pitch of the turboprops jumped an octave. The hatch slowly closed. Finally, with clatter and a violent wobble, the 28-ton plane heaved itself off the tarmac. I wasn't near any of the aircraft's tiny, porthole-shaped windows, so I stared instead at the exposed ducts and wires inside the cargo bay, making an internal promise never to complain again about Virgin Atlantic's economy class. The headphones gave a cough of radio static.

'OK, kids,' said the pilot. 'Looks like it's gonna be another real nice, sunny Californian day. But it ain't gonna be so nice and sunny where we're going. Hope y'all brought some warm sweaters . . .'

I wondered if I would be OK in a T-shirt: it was all I had packed.

The aircraft banked, groaned, and corrected itself.

The pilot continued: 'Sit back, relax, and I'll check back with y'all when we make our *dee*-scent. Remember folks, this AIN'T like flying American. We'll be landing on a moving runway, in a gusty crosswind. If you feel an impact followed by a bounce, it means we missed the S.O.B. and we'll have to try again. But don't worry, folks: we got THREE tries before the gas runs out.'

I closed my eyes and inhaled jet-fuel vapour: my favourite smell.

I wished I was lying by the pool.

Life in California hadn't gone exactly to plan. Alana and I arrived at our new home in late August, having bumped and rattled 3,000 miles across the country in *The Times*'s Jeep, at first heading south-west through Virginia to Atlanta, then directly west via Oklahoma, Texas, New Mexico and Arizona. Eventually, after two weeks of roadside cheeseburgers, $30 motel rooms and 55 m.p.h. speed limits, we made a scorched dash through the Mojave Desert, passing razor-wired Department of Defense missile ranges and proving grounds, before dropping down into the neon-lit pinball machine of metropolitan Los Angeles. By that time my copy of *Exile on Main Street* had almost melted into the Jeep's CD player.

I had barely watched or listened to the news as we drove cross-country. If I had, I would have known that the CIA was accusing China, France and Syria of selling chemicals, probably intended for long-range-missile fuel, to the Iraqis. I would also have known that, in response to this accusation, Saddam Hussein had suggested talks with a suave, seventy-four-year-old Swede called Hans Blix, the chief United Nations weapons inspector. The UN had turned down the request, asking instead that Blix be allowed to send his inspection team back into the country. The news headlines would also have told me that President Bush had dared the UN to confront the 'grave and gathering' threat of Iraq, or step aside and let the US Marines take care of business. In other words, I would have known that war was inevitable.

But Iraq was the last thing on my mind as we motored west. As far as I was concerned, we were fleeing the terror of anthrax and Ground Zero, and heading back in time to the rich and *safe* country I had visited on my business trips to Silicon Valley. In fact I felt slightly guilty for leaving New York: as though I should have stuck it out and shown solidarity with the Big Apple. I was, after all, running away. No other city on earth, perhaps, could have evoked such a reaction – not even London. We learn from an early age that New York is the Best City in the World, and that to be a New Yorker is something noble and proud. Alana – no more of a New Yorker than I was – felt particularly bad. Leaving was tantamount to desertion.

The guilt was overwhelmed, however, by worry. How would I fare in my new job? And what would Martin Fletcher, *The Times*'s foreign-news editor, think of me? I had, in effect, been thrust upon him by Robert Thomson, for reasons I had yet to fathom.

Since writing my first nib for Barrow, I had covered nothing but business for *The Times*, largely because I found it comfortable, safe, and civilized. No matter how violent or bloody the world became, everything in finance could be expressed in easily quantifiable terms: a beheading in Pakistan became a three-point dip in the Karachi Stock Exchange; a *coup d'état* in Columbia a devaluation in coffee-bean futures. The language of business served the same purpose as military jargon: emotional distance and, by extension, anxiety reduction. When Warren Buffett, the 'Sage of Omaha', gave a speech after September 11, he described a possible nuclear terror attack on New York City as a '$1 trillion event'. By putting a dollar figure on it, Buffett made it less scary: Armageddon became an insurance claim.

To me, the swells and rip tides of the money markets were a logical expression of the illogical human condition – like abstract art. And I preferred the bold colours and straight lines of the suprematist to the random strokes of the real. Of all the news wires at *The Times*, my favourite was 'The Bloomberg': it showed the chaos of the world through a prism of numbers, ratios and equations. When working late shifts in London, I used to stare at the data feeding into The Bloomberg from news bureaux across Asia, Europe and the Americas, and feel steadied, calmed.

There was no doubt about it: business journalists cruised the information superhighway in the back of a stretched, leather-upholstered Jag. In Los Angeles I would be puffing down the hard shoulder on a rusty bicycle. There would be no more comfort or safety in abstract numbers. I would be permanently 'off diary', as my old City tutor Linda Christmas used to say. I would also have an eight-hour time difference to deal with. For the first time in my five years at *The Times*, I would be leaving behind Patience, Barrow and the comfy armchair of the business desk. But how difficult could the West Coast be? Hollywood was, in a way, just a different kind of stock market, with *Variety* box-office figures instead of share prices, celebrity marriages instead of mergers. And the parties, at least, would be a bit livelier. Perhaps I could also try out Cole's lunch tutorial at The Ivy or Morton's, the infamous celebrity troughs on Robertson Boulevard. Not that I knew anyone, apart from Alana, to lunch *with*.

Fletcher, meanwhile, had other things to process in his billion-gigabyte brain. Most urgent: how to cover a war in the Gulf, if or when it started. He was already aware that the Pentagon was talking about 'embedding' reporters with military units during a possible pre-emptive strike against Iraq. He was sceptical, however, of claims that journalists, including foreigners, would be placed directly with troops on the battlefield for the first time since World War II. The military had demonstrated such trust in the press only once before, when Ernie Pyle, along with an elite band of thirty or so other 'conflict correspondents', had landed in Normandy on 7 June 1944. Even in Vietnam, war reporters had not been permanently assigned to front-line units.

None of *The Times*'s 'real' war correspondents, Fletcher reasoned, would believe the Pentagon's claims, or run the risk of becoming glorified PRs for the United States Marines. He also assumed, based on the behaviour of the military during the first Gulf War, that even if war correspondents *were* embedded they would be stuck with units deliberately kept far away from the fighting. There would be nothing worse, in Fletcher's mind, than having Saddam throw mustard gas at the front lines while Anthony Loyd wrote about Portaloo logistics from the rear.

The Pentagon's behaviour in 1991, of course, was a reaction to Vietnam. In that war, reporters were given a high level of access to battlefield operations, largely because of the precedent set by World War II. But journalists used it against the US military, portraying the war as a 'quagmire', with no realistic victory or exit plan. The main culprit was the CBC news anchor Walter Cronkite – 'Uncle Walter' as he was known – who wrapped up a report about the Tet Offensive in 1968 with an editorial stating that the Americans were 'mired in stalemate'. Improvements in technology, meanwhile, made it easier for television news crews to bring horrific images of war back home. After Vietnam, therefore, military commanders tended to regard journalists as hippy-sympathizers, cowards and traitors. As a result, reporters were kept as far away as possible from later conflicts in Grenada and Panama. The gung-ho coverage of 1991, however, which saw Cronkite replaced with the likes of NBC's Arthur Kent (a.k.a. 'the Scud stud'), changed all that. News networks treated the expulsion of the Iraqis from Kuwait City like a cross between a video game and a football match, complete with hyperbolic commentators, 3D graphics, and player statistics. The tone was partly a result of awe at the advances in US weaponry: John Simpson, for example, filed an infamous report for the BBC saying that a Tomahawk missile had just streaked past his hotel window and 'turned left at the traffic lights'.

Fletcher didn't know it, but by 2002 the US military had forgiven the media for Vietnam. Fletcher's solution to the embedding dilemma, however, was to put young, inexperienced reporters in the American scheme, *just in case* they were needed. It would, he thought, serve as a gentle introduction to the world of war reporting – a bit like doing it on work experience. As I sat behind the wheel of the Jeep, whistling along to Mick Jagger and congratulating myself on getting the hell out of Manhattan, I had no idea Fletcher was thinking about embedding *me*.

If I had, I might have headed straight back to New York.

Los Angeles, when we finally arrived, was everything I had hoped for, and everything Alana had dreaded. Skyscrapers melted into single-storey 'strip malls'; business suits were swapped for shorts, polished Ferragamos for flip-flops. In place of Manhattan's diners, with their sticky menus and home-fried potatoes, there were soy-latte stands, oxygen tents and tofu steakhouses. Walking – Alana's favourite exercise – was a social taboo. And the drivers were terrible: producers' wives applying lip-gloss at the wheels of stadium-sized SUVs; octogenarian Ferrari-owners; uninsured immigrants; and drunk actors snorting coke at the reds. *No one* indicated – unless, of course, they indicated in the wrong direction, before pulling a U-turn across seven lanes of traffic. '*Ohmagod!*' the producers' wives squealed, as their 3-ton Chevrolets mounted sedans and bounced over two-seaters. Then there were the Mexicans: the illegal, ubiquitous proletariat, tending to wilted palms, unparked Porsches and untouched appetizers. And all of it was set against the blue monotony of sky, the glare of the billboards, and the rim of smog that lined the horizon like scum on an unwashed sink.

I *loved* Los Angles. Perhaps it was just because Los Angeles wasn't New York. Or perhaps it was because of the weather: a crisp 72 degrees, as reliable as the London drizzle, or the West Village gale. Before I left New York, Glen asked where I was going to live: 'Beach or canyon?' I soon realized it was a theoretical choice: I couldn't afford either. I could live thirty blocks from the ocean in Santa Monica, or in a hilltop home overlooking the San Fernando Valley – within lead-poisoning range of the 101 freeway. Instead, I opted for a West Hollywood apartment much the same as the one I'd left behind in the West Village. Our new home, at 1131 Alta Loma Road, was less stylish than 666 Greenwich Street, what with its gold fixtures, beige carpets, eighties kitchen appliances, and pink-tiled 'wet bar'. But it did have a communal swimming pool, tennis court and, perhaps best of all, hot tub.

After signing a lease on the apartment, I went through the standard foreign correspondent's checklist of Things to Do. I kitted myself out with a landline, mobile phone, desk, computer, printer, high-speed internet connection, *Los Angeles Times* subscription (for lift and view) and espresso machine (for the horribly early deadlines). By September I was ready for work. There was only one thing left on the list: meet the competition. So, with a deep breath, I dialled the number of Oliver Poole, Los Angeles correspondent for the *Daily Telegraph*.

Like most English correspondents abroad, including myself, Poole was a 'bureau chief'. That meant he was the head of a bureau of one, with a budget of his salary (plus the occasional lunch and travel expenses), working from an office halfway between his kitchen and bedroom. Being a bureau chief is psychologically important, however, largely because it sounds good to Americans, with their vast teams of reporters, fact-checkers, copy-editors, commissioning chiefs and sub-editors. It also makes us feel like professionals. Whenever English foreign correspondents get together in hotel bars, they laugh about the 'one-man bureau', just as they chuckle about lift and view. However, no one finds it particularly funny.

After talking briefly to Poole, we arranged to meet the following Friday at Chateau Marmont, the celebrity dormitory in Hollywood where John Belushi died of an overdose, James Dean auditioned for *Rebel Without a Cause*, and Jim Morrison once fell out of a window. (There are very few locations in Hollywood where Jim Morrison *didn't* fall out of a window.) I knew from previous visits to the Chateau that the waiters considered themselves the A List in waiting. A cold burger, or a warm Chardonnay, could take hours to emerge on a large silver platter, accompanied by an even larger tab. Regardless, it seemed like a good venue.

On the phone, Poole made conversation at a relentless pace, in a broken Etonian tenor hoarsened by early deadlines and cigarettes. 'One can get dreadfully paranoid in Los Angeles,' he advised, making surprise use of the royal pronoun. 'It's the distance: 6,000 bloody miles to London, and an eight-hour time shift. The desk forgets you *exist* if you don't call twice a day.' I imagined him to be of cavalry height, with dark, Olympian curls, sea-water eyes, and an all-linen wardrobe. He would arrive at the Chateau in a shabby, antique Bentley, with an actress girl-friend from Martha's Vineyard: she would be making some body money in Hollywood before doing *Hedda Gabler* at the Globe. Glen had already told me that Poole, three years my senior, had been educated at Eton and then Oxford, before taking a job on the *South China Morning Post*. After that came the *Telegraph*. According to Glen, Poole's friends at Eton had included Crown Prince 'Dippy' Dipendra of Nepal, who died in a mysterious gun massacre, along with most of his family, amid a dispute over his bride. Poole even had a title – the Honourable Oliver Poole – because he was the heir to Lord Poole, the London corporate financier and former Downing Street adviser. I had also heard a rumour that Poole owned a yacht, moored at Marina del Ray. (The rumour was true, although the yacht was small, and Poole owned it with a friend.)

I tried hard not to feel intimidated.

When Friday came, I arrived early at the Chateau, accompanied by Alana and some friends I had made while covering my first celebrity-fluff story: the Beverly Hills shoplifting trial of Winona Ryder. (The story had gone well, apart from me arriving late on the first day and body-slamming Winona in the corridor, breaking a strictly enforced rule that no journalist could come within 10 feet of her. To make matters worse, I had reached out to steady myself and nearly grabbed her right breast.) All of us at the Chateau were either reporters or paparazzi. We sat on sofas and armchairs in the high-ceilinged drawing room, watching the breeze ripple through the tall curtains. Every thirty to forty minutes a walking headshot in a waiter's uniform would peer into the candlelit room, then disappear. I made a heroic effort to get drunk – not easy, given the time between refills. There was no sign of Poole anywhere.

At 8 p.m. I checked my watch. Poole was an hour late. I wondered if I was in the right place. Then my mobile started vibrating.

'It's Oliver,' said a glum voice. '*They won't let me in.*'

It was no surprise that Oliver had failed to get past the Chateau's clipboard-wielding hostess, positioned strategically in the Ferrari gridlock of the driveway. In fact Alana and I had snuck in through the back garden. It was also reassuring, however: Poole clearly hadn't arrived in a vintage Bentley. Or with a famous actress girlfriend. 'Don't worry. Sneak round the back,' I advised him. 'There's an unlocked gate that leads into the garden. Meet you there in two minutes.'

I strolled outside, pausing to see if I could trace the outline of Tom Cruise under the heat lamps, then headed for the gate. As I opened it, a young, bespectacled Englishman, wearing ripped Levis, a zip-up fleece and desert boots, scurried out of the darkness. The fringe of his ruffled schoolboy's haircut had curled into an accidental quiff, and around his neck was a handmade chain, the provenance of which appeared to be a Goa street market. The effect was nearly, but not quite, cool. Poole looked like a cross between James Dean and Harry Potter.

'Oliver?'

'Chris. Hi,' he said, offering an inky palm.

'Hey. Where did you park?' I asked.

'Didn't,' he said, speed-walking through the garden. Poole seemed to operate on fast-forward. 'Got the bus. Took *ages*.'

I tried to calculate how long it would take to get from Santa Monica to West Hollywood on Los Angeles public transport. I concluded that Poole must have left his house at about 4 p.m. the previous day.

'Don't you have a car?'

'Bloody crashed it. *Telegraph* won't buy me a new one. Need a beer.'

'Cheers to that,' I said.

'Let's get pissed then. Celebrate your arrival.'

Formalities over, we sat down with the others.

An hour later, a waiter emerged.

It was an enjoyable evening. Of the two of us, Poole seemed the more down-to-earth, ordering 'spag bol' from the Chateau's bar menu and eating it off his lap, while I prodded at an organic tofu salad. It was an odd role reversal, given that I was the one who had gone to a comprehensive school and red-brick university. We shared cigarettes and gossip about reporters we both knew in London. By midnight we had relocated to The Standard, another Sunset Strip hotel. We sat outside, by the soothing glow of the pool, overlooking the infinite, glittering sprawl of Los Angeles. My rival, I concluded, was clearly a talented and energetic, almost hyperactive, reporter. But he didn't appear to be the career-destroying scoop-machine I had feared. And we were very different people, bound to suggest different ideas to our foreign desks. The competition in Hollywood, I reassured myself, was nothing to worry about.

I should, of course, have known better.

'Martin?'

This was me, a few weeks later, on a morning call to Fletcher.

'Yes, *what?*' The 'what' was playful – probably delivered with a handsome, inscrutable smile. I often suspected, however, that there was some genuine annoyance beneath Fletcher's charm.

'When am I going to get something in the paper?'

'You got something in yesterday.'

'It was a nib.'

'It was a LEAD nib. And, besides, long doesn't mean good.'

'I know . . . but, *still* . . . when I worked for Patien—'

'It's the war! It's taking up lots and lots of space. Readers don't want to read celebrity fluff at the moment. They want to know when Bush will invade, or what kind of gas Saddam puts in his mortar shells.'

'What if I did something war-related? From, er, Hollywood.'

'That would be excellent. The *Telegraph* did a lovely piece on soldiers' sperm the other day. What are you offering?'

Soldier's sperm? Shit. *Bloody Poole.*

'Chris?'

'*Yes.* I'll come up with something. Promise.'

'Gd.'

The Greyhound banked again, and this time I dry-heaved. I really shouldn't have ordered the 'full American' from the hotel's breakfast menu. I closed my eyes and wondered why I was on a Navy plane, about to experience a 150 m.p.h. impact with the deck of an American supercarrier. Then I remembered: since arriving in Los Angeles I had got almost nothing in *The Times*. Highlights included a piece about a Slovenian swimming the length of the Mississippi (three paragraphs) and an inaccurate prediction that an Irishman would become the new LAPD chief (four paragraphs). The foreign desk had, as Glen predicted, ignored me. I spent my mornings cruising pointlessly around Beverly Hills, wondering whether I had made a terrible mistake. Alana, meanwhile, had got a management job at a magazine, and was doing well. She still despised Los Angeles, however. And we had no friends.

I got the idea to visit a Navy aircraft carrier after watching a story about the USS *Constellation* on KCAL-9, a local news channel. *Connie*, as the ship is known, was the first American aircraft carrier to attack North Vietnam, and was likely to become one of the first vessels deployed to Gulf War II. When I called the Navy's West Coast headquarters on Coronado Island, near San Diego, I expected to be quickly fobbed off. As it turned out, the opposite happened.

'Hi, I'm calling from the London *Times*,' I said.

'How y'doin' today, sir?' said a friendly female voice.

'Er, great. Thanks.'

'Out*standing*, sir!'

'I was wondering if, perhaps, I would be able to visit the *Constellation*?'

'Yes, sir.'

'Sorry?'

'Yes, I believe you *will* be able to visit, sir. Be here at 0700 hours.'

'*Tomorrow*?'

'Absolutely, sir.'

It turned out I had called at the right time: a group of reporters was set to visit the *Constellation* early the next morning. Someone had dropped out at the last minute, allowing me to take his place. I drove to San Diego that afternoon, stayed overnight, and got to Coronado Island at 8 a.m., just in time to hear 'The Star Spangled Banner' being played over the PA system. I assumed the reporters would be transported to the *Constellation* by boat or helicopter. Instead, I was directed to a car park next to an airstrip, on which a dirty C-2A Greyhound was idling its engines. I wondered how it could be possible for a 28-ton transport plane to land on the 320-foot deck of a warship. Then I noticed the metal hook near the aircraft's tail.

I groaned. Glancing around me, I noticed there were about twenty other dyspeptic journalists, news photographers and television camera operators gathered on the runway. They all looked as though they were regretting their breakfasts. The look became more pronounced as we were each handed headphones, earplugs, goggles, a life jacket and a crash helmet. Then we were shoved on board and strapped tightly into our plastic seats.

Now the Greyhound's engines were shifting pitch. My earwax blistered as we started to lose altitude. Static fizzed and popped through my headset. A distorted scream cut through it: 'BRACE FOR LANDING!'

I was strapped in so tight I couldn't brace anything. So I grimaced instead, and screwed up my eyes. If I survived the landing, I said to myself, I would never feel nervous on a commercial flight again.

'GET READY!'

I wondered what would happen if a British Airways pilot acted like that while preparing to touch down at Heathrow.

The turboprops made a 1,000-decibel groan, and the Greyhound seemed to shake the screws loose from its frame. We swung violently from side to side as we fell out of the sky. I strained to look out of the windows, but couldn't see anything. Our speed increased, and I broke out into a sweat.

*This must be what it feels like to cras—*

Before I could finish the thought, gravity drop-kicked me in my chest, crushing my shoulders into the seat. The force of the deceleration, meanwhile, lifted my buttocks as far as the limited give in the nylon harness would allow. I thought, for a moment, I would perform a fatal backward somersault into the cockpit's instrument panel. Then came a terrible mechanical clatter, followed by giddy, weightless release, and a gravity kick from the other direction, into my back. My neck slumped forward and I tasted tongue and blood. I felt the Greyhound fall, then swing violently upward. The engines were hysterical – kamikaze almost. The plane wobbled, corrected itself, then banked. The arresting cable, it seemed, hadn't arrested us. And now we were low on fuel, in a rainstorm, with two more chances to land.

'*Oops*,' said the pilot.

I wondered how I would release my seat belt if we ended up in the ocean.

Then the plane started to fall again.

We landed about fifteen minutes later, on the third and final attempt. When the Greyhound's hatch reopened, we might as well have been on another planet. Pressurized steam from the ship's engines rose through cracks in the deck, as though the scene was being directed by a pop video director for MTV. The noise of seventy warplanes idling their jet engines on the deck of a 1,069-feet long, 80,000-ton warship rendered all other human activity silent. All I could hear was the blood inside my ears. And the voice inside my head asking me what the hell I was doing.

And so began a two-day Navy junket – and my first experience of the American military. We spent our time on board talking to the crew, watching F/A-18 Hornets leap off the deck like flying reptiles, and eating stodgy food in the officers' mess. We also spent a lot of time sitting around and doing nothing. 'Hurry up and wait,' I learned, is the military's motto. I asked the sailors about Iraq. Some said they blamed Saddam Hussein for September 11 and anthrax. 'After all the pain and suffering he has given us,' a mechanic told me, from a room several hundred feet below *Connie's* deck, 'we're going to go over there and take care of business.'

Surely not, I thought.

A week later, when I was back at home in West Hollywood, Fletcher called. The time was 6.30 a.m. – much earlier than usual.

'Ayres, do you want to go to war?' he asked.

Still half asleep, I struggled to understand the question.

'Yes! Love to!' I blurted.

'Gd. Enjoyed your piece on the *Constellation*, by the way. You might as well go to the Gulf – there won't be much of a market for LA when the war starts. No one wants to read about celebrities any more.'

'*Absolutely*,' I said, feeling dizzy.

'The Americans seem to have some kind of scheme. It's called "embedding". Make sure you get on it, Ayres.'

'Okay.'
'Gd.'
He hung up.
*Oh no.*

This was my plan: if I had to spend the war with the American military, I would do it in the safest place possible – below deck on the USS *Constellation*. As *The Times*'s designated 'embed coordinator', I called the Pentagon and asked for as many slots as they could give us, citing my experience of reporting from aircraft carriers. 'It would be great if we could get some places on, say, the *Constellation*,' I said, 'or a logistics unit.' I nearly added, 'But not, *y'know*, if it's too much trouble.' I secretly hoped that a London newspaper, albeit an influential one, would be considered unimportant, and therefore be given boring positions at the rear. A few weeks later I received an email from the Pentagon. 'Thank you for your interest in embedding,' it said. 'Your embed allocation will be faxed to your section editor soon.'

As the Christmas holidays approached, I tried to forget about war. I was in denial. The invasion would never happen, I reassured myself. I didn't want to believe Alana's theories that President Bush wanted revenge on behalf of his father, or that he had his eye on Iraq's oil reserves. From a coward's perspective, however, Saddam's regime was troubling. As recently as 1997, UN weapons inspectors had found Iraqi briefcases containing *Clostridium perfringens*, the bacterium that causes 'gas gangrene', a disgusting and lethal infection that covers the skin with huge blood blisters, while turning it a bronze colour. Why would Saddam develop such bio-weapons – when most other countries were destroying them – if not to use them? Perhaps he thought he could get away with an attack as long he outsourced it, and blamed it on Osama bin Laden. But why not go further? Why not supersize the attack, and buy a couple of old Soviet nukes from the alleged stockpile of 80,000 warheads poorly guarded by the Russians. Saddam could simply FedEx them to the White House. After all, any instability in the world, as long as it wasn't blamed on Saddam, could give Iraq the opportunity to re-invade one of its wealthy neighbours, such as Kuwait or Iran.

It was a cliché, but the terrorthon of 2001 had changed everything. If Congress could be shut down with a spoonful of bootleg anthrax, and Wall Street be closed for nearly a week by two hijacked airliners, what kind of attack could Saddam bankroll with his oil billions? It was a bowel-loosening thought. And it was clear that sanctions against him weren't working. They were simply allowing Iraq to get sympathy from the Arab world (according to some unverifiable figures, 2 million Iraqis died from the economic sanctions, half of them children) while simultaneously earning him billions from the UN's flawed oil-for-food programme. It seemed to me that President Bush had three options: lift the sanctions, and make Saddam the world's first psychopathic trillionaire; keep the sanctions, along with the alleged seven-figure child fatalities and the hatred of the Arab world; or invade. It was certainly a crappy set of options, and hard to work out which was more terrifying than the other. An invasion was by no means the obvious answer, given that it was almost insanely ambitious, and had no precedent for success (apart, some would argue, from Afghanistan). And if Osama bin Laden and his fundamentalist terror troupe were pissed off *before* September 11, what would they do after an Arab country's sovereignty was violated? War footage, some of it from the embeds, would serve as a free, global al-Qaeda recruitment campaign. Look how the Americans are plundering the Holy Land! Join us in jihad! And the legitimacy of the 1991 coalition against Saddam would be hard, if not impossible, to reproduce.

A war would be a lonely, bloody venture.

I flew back to Wooler for Christmas, while Alana returned to her family in Ohio. The headlines, meanwhile, informed me that a new team of UN weapons inspectors had entered Iraq, and that Turkey had moved 15,000 soldiers to the Iraqi border. The Turks clearly knew exactly what was about to happen. It was hard to enjoy my Christmas pudding, or to wear the silly paper hat I found in my Christmas cracker with much conviction. Never before had I felt that my life was in the hands of political leaders. I would rather have had my life in the hands of a ten-year-old child. Every night, from the womb of my parents' living room, I would watch miserable-looking BBC journalists report from the sandstorms of Kuwait.

'Oh, Christopher, I'm so glad you're in California and not somewhere *horrible* like Iraq,' said my mother on more than one occasion.

My father at one point chipped in, 'You'd have to have a screw loose to go there, wouldn't you, son? Best sticking to Hollywood, eh? A bit more fun than Iraq.'

I got back to Los Angeles in January, just in time for a heat wave. It was as though California was taunting me: showing off the outdoor cafés, open-topped Porsches and palm-tree-lined boulevards I would miss if I were sent to war in the Middle East. I had told Alana all about the embedding scheme, but she refused to believe that *The Times* would send her boyfriend to a battle zone. 'But you're not a war correspondent,' she huffed. 'So *why* would they send you?' I told her that war reporters had to start their careers somewhere. 'But you're not the *type* who would become a war correspondent,' she said. 'It's just so stupid.' I agreed: it *was* stupid. But I also knew it was true. Alana, of course, was immersed in denial: she didn't want to be left alone, for the length of an entire war, in a city she hated. To make matters worse, she was bitterly against an invasion. She even drove to San Francisco to take part in a protest march. 'Regime change begins at home,' said her placard.

By February I was dreading the fax from the Pentagon, or the phone call I would get from Fletcher. When it finally came, I was sitting outside the Coffee Bean and Tea Leaf on Sunset Strip, sipping a non-fat cappuccino. As my mobile phone chirruped and vibrated, causing the metal table to rattle, I looked jealously at the aspiring actors, models and rock stars that surrounded me. For the first time since arriving in Hollywood, I desperately wanted to be one of them. None of them, after all, would ever be asked to join the front lines to keep their jobs.

'*Chrisayres,*' I said, in my most fearless professional voice.

'It's here,' said Glen. 'The *fax.*'

I was glad it wasn't Fletcher. But this was terrible news: part of me had still been hoping the Pentagon would overlook *The Times* entirely. I had fantasized that no one in London would notice until it was too late.

'Please say it's an aircraft carrier,' I said.

'Uh-uh,' said Glen. 'No such luck. And it's TWO places.'

'*What?*'

'I've got one place; you've got the other.'

At least, I thought, this meant I would get a travelling companion. 'Come on, Glen,' I croaked. 'Tell me what units they're with . . .'

'You're not going to like this,' he said.

'Oh no.'

'Indeed,' said Glen. 'Well, the first is with the Air Force.'

That wasn't so bad, I thought. The Air Force, after all, would never put a base anywhere near the front lines. And the embedded position would be at the base. *It would be both glamorous and acceptably safe.*

'And the other?' I asked, feeling slightly more cheeful.

'The Marines. Front lines. On the ground.'

I wondered if the Coffee Bean had a lavatory.

Then I said, *'Jesus Christ!'*

'Yes, you'll probably be needing him,' replied Glen. 'If, of course, that's where Fletcher decides to put you.'

'What do you mean?'

'He hasn't made his mind up yet,' said Glen.

Glen, of course, knew as well as I did where Fletcher would put me. I worked for Fletcher's department; Glen worked for home news. There was no way Fletcher was going to put someone from a rival department with the Marines. We both knew instantly, therefore, what my choices were: accept the embedded place with the Marines, protect my career at *The Times*, and put my life on the line; or turn down the Marines, protect my life, and put my career on the line. There was, of course, another consideration: if I turned down the Marines, I was effectively putting Glen's life at risk. If, that is, he was stupid enough to go, or not brave enough to turn it down. There wasn't much of a chance, however, that I would be brave enough to turn it down either. Ambition and testosterone, it seemed, could overcome fear.

'Hang on,' interrupted Glen, before I had any more time to con-template this existential dilemma. 'I can see Fletcher picking up the phone. He's bound to be calling you. Let me know how it goes.'

He hung up. Within seconds my phone was vibrating again. The caller ID said 'unobtainable'. It had to be Fletcher.

*'Chrisayres,'* I said.

'Good news!' said the clipped, posh baritone from 6,000 miles away. I could feel my jaw tighten: good news to Fletcher could only be bad news to me. 'We've been given two of these "embedded" positions with the Americans,' he said, sounding genuinely delighted. 'One's on the Al Jaber airbase in Kuwait, and the other . . . erm, hold on a second, Chris.' I could hear a scuffling sound, then a garbled murmuring, as Fletcher answered an urgent question from one of the night editors. I closed my eyes and tried to imagine what death would feel like.

'Chr-*is*?' It was Fletcher again.

'Yes?'

'So, congratulations. You're with the Marines: front-line stuff. Well done! Should be very interesting.'

'Yes. Interesting. Very,' I said.

'We also got a place on an Air Force base in Kuwait, but I imagine that'll be quite dull,' added Fletcher, as though he were comparing the routes for a pleasant afternoon hike. I pictured pilots, hundreds of miles from the fighting, enjoying hot coffee, bagels and cigarettes back at the Kuwait base. 'There's a chap called Glen Owen going from home news. He seems pretty happy with that. I assume that's OK with you?' A vivid image of Glen, also enjoying hot coffee, bagels and cigarettes, flashed into my mind. I wished, for a moment, that I was Glen.

'*Chris?* Are you still there?'

I wasn't sure if I *was* really there. Surely this couldn't be happening to me. Surely I couldn't seriously be going to war.

'Won't this be quite, er, *dangerous*?' I ventured, following it with what was meant to be a chuckle. It came out as a squeak.

There was a baffled silence.

'. . . No! Go! Enjoy!' came the surprised reply. 'It'll be a character-forming experience for you, Ayres.'

Then came the aftershock. For a second, Sunset Strip went hyper-real: sound played backwards, and the cars bled into the sunshine. Breathe. *Breathe.* I saw Dr Ruth, with her broken leg. '*It's fight or flight, Christopher,*' she said. '*Animals react to threats with a general discharge of the sympathetic nervous system.*' Then normality clicked back into place. When I stopped hyperventilating, Fletcher was still calmly chatting. He was talking about some kind of course.

'So you've done the course, haven't you?'

I jolted to attention.

'*What course?*'

'The Pentagon course. Military training. How to put on a gas mask. How to avoid beheading. That kind of thing . . .'

'Er, *no.*'

'Oh. Right. Your mate Oliver Poole's done it. Wrote a lovely piece about it in the *Telegraph* this morning. Very interesting.'

'*Poole?*'

'Yes, Poole. He's going in with the American infantry. Good job you got the Marines. Anyway, not to worry. We have our own course here. It's with some chaps from the SAS. You'll need to fly back to England. Get on the internet now and book your ticket. We'll see you next week.'

With that, Fletcher hung up.

The worst conversation of my life over, I gulped back my cappuccino, got up from my seat, and began to walk home on unsteady legs. My breathing was quick and shallow, as though someone were sitting on my chest. As much as I was terrified, however, I also felt slightly elated – heroic, in fact, for agreeing to go to Iraq. I had joined the elite and noble club of John Simpson, Ernie Pyle and Walter Cronkite. Colleagues would be jealous; girls' hearts would beat faster. And perhaps Fletcher was right: perhaps it *would* be a character-forming experience. There was something almost fatherly about Fletcher, and I couldn't imagine him deliberately sending me off to a hideous chemical death. Besides, if Oliver Poole could go to war, so could I.

'Poole is embedded,' I told Glen later.

'I know – saw his name included in the Pentagon emails. It's quite amusing, isn't it? Hollywood Reporters Go to War. Actually, I've heard that Poole's fearless. He can't wait to see some action.'

'Yeah, right.'

'No, seriously. He probably caught the bloodlust at Eton, from Prince Dippy of Nepal. Or from his grandfather: he was a colonel to Field-Marshal Montgomery, y'know. Helped plan D-Day.'

I groaned.

'Oh no,' I said weakly. 'Poole's one of those *war types.*'

'There's a tradition of it at the *Telegraph*,' continued Glen. 'Their man in Afghanistan was particularly impressive. He covered that battle with the Pathan tribesmen in the Swat Valley.'

'The *what* valley?'

'Took him a month to get there. Spent a good week of the journey on a train from Bangalore, in insufferable heat.'

No wonder Poole didn't have a car: *Telegraph* reporters were probably taught to trek through the desert, in their underwear.

'Of course, all of this was quite a while ago,' said Glen.

'When?'

'Eighteen ninety-seven, actually,' said Glen.

'What? What was his name again?'

'Winston Churchill. He went on to be quite famous, apparently. The *Telegraph* paid him only five quid for his effort – the tight bastards. At least that's what it says in the Roy Jenkins biography.'

Over the next few days, more daunting factoids about Poole's family connections kept being relayed to Los Angeles, including the revelation that his stepfather was the former Tory politician Lord Fowler, whose ex-wife was none other than Linda Christmas, my terrifying former City tutor. I half expected Glen to call back with the news that Poole was also related to George W. Bush. And Tony Blair. And the Iraqi royal family. The situation was turning into what Barrow had once called 'the black curse of Ayres'. Why couldn't the *Telegraph* have posted someone shallow and celebrity-obsessed to Los Angeles? Why *Poole*, for God's sake? The best I could hope for was that the Marines would dump me in the rear, so I could blame my lack of heroism on bad luck. Still, comparisons between the two Hollywood correspondents would be inevitable. The media gossips in London would love it. I almost expected Poole to return from Baghdad with full military decorations for bravery.

Now that the worst-case scenario with the embedded scheme had actually transpired, however, I also felt strangely relieved. At least going to war might end my guilt over everything from my grandfather's treatment by the Nazis to the fact that I had deserted New York. I wanted, in a strange way, to lose my war virginity properly. Not, of course, that I had any idea of what was in store for me. I knew nothing about the military. My only experience of it had been standing on the deck of the USS *Constellation*. My inability to visualize it made it worse. War films were my only references, and gore-soaked scenes from *Saving Private Ryan*, *Three Kings* and *Apocalypse Now* flickered in my imagination like a private horror show. I saw Humvees and tank trenches; grenades and M-16s. And I remembered a line by Private Joker, the war correspondent in *Full Metal Jacket*: 'A day without blood is like a day without sunshine.' I had no idea how I would break the news to Alana. I knew, however, that until the moment I boarded a plane with a ticket to Kuwait she wouldn't believe it was happening. My parents were another matter. Perhaps I shouldn't tell them at all.

I was still reeling from the double hit of euphoria and terror when I got home. I sat down heavily at my desk, chewed on the end of a ballpoint, and shook my head in sheer disbelief. I flicked on the television, and listened to a CNN report about British intelligence on Iraq having been copied from the thesis of a Californian student. Then I noticed a fresh sheet of paper, shiny like cheap toilet roll, lying on top of my fax machine. It was dated 10 February, 17.21 GMT. At the top of it was the News International Pension Plan logo. Below, it said, 'Nomination of Beneficiaries Form'. Underneath that were my name and British national-insurance number.

With dread, I skimmed what followed:

> To: News International Pension Trustees Limited
> I understand the Trustee has complete discretion as to the application of the lump sum benefit payable on my death within the terms of the Trust, but I wish the following to be considered as possible recipients:

At the bottom of the page were four columns, for the names and addresses of recipients, along with their dates of birth and their relationship to me. The final column was for the percentage share of my life-insurance policy they would receive if I were shot, blown up, beheaded or gassed by the Iraqis.

I stared at it for a second, shook my head again, then started up my computer and opened Outlook Express so that I could email Glen. I noticed a new message from the Pentagon in my inbox. It had arrived with two bulky Word-file attachments. I double-clicked on them. The first document was entitled 'Smallpox Vaccine'; the second, 'Anthrax Vaccine Series'. They both had the same heading: 'RELEASE, INDEMNIFICATION, AND HOLD HARMLESS AGREEMENT; AND AGREEMENT NOT TO SUE'.

I looked at the text of the email. It said:

> The Department of Defense has agreed to administer anthrax and
> smallpox vaccines to your media employees who will be participating
> in the DoD's embedding programme. These vaccines carry risks
> along with benefits. We emphasize the importance of warning your
> employees who agree to be vaccinated to remain cognizant of any
> change in their health following vaccination and if there is,
> immediately seek medial assistance.

I closed the email.

Three words came into my head: 'Gulf War Syndrome'. I had stupidly assumed that death could come only on the Iraqi battlefield.
Perhaps I wouldn't even survive the inoculations. My nervous system
was delicate enough, without pumping it full of fifty-seven varieties
of poison. To inoculate against a disease, you first have to be given the
disease. Anthrax, my old adversary from New York, would finally be
introduced to my bloodstream, along with smallpox, cholera, typhoid,
tetanus, diphtheria and hepatitis. I imagined the size of the needle:
4 inches in circumference, with a canister the size of an oil barrel,
filled with green liquid.

Churchill apparently used to call his wartime depression the 'black
dog'. And as I sat there, numbed with the fear hormone, I could have
sworn I heard it bark. Oh, how the black dog bayed and howled. I felt
suffocated; helpless. I could have said no to all this. I had brought it
all on myself.

Herefordshire, England

2003

# 9

# Who Runs Lives

The reporter was on his knees. His beard was matted with dribble and watery snot, and his right hand was cuffed to a radiator. Above him were his captors: two young, smiling men. They could have been Columbian, Algerian or Arab. They wore denims and lumberjack shirts, which probably smelled of sweat, percolated coffee and bootleg aftershave. In any other context their hesitant smiles would have been endearing, fit for a mother's mantelpiece. One of the men patted the journalist on the head and tousled his knotted hair. For a second it was possible to imagine some fondness between them. Then the knife appeared. The reporter's eyes died. His muscles lost grip of his flesh. A rag was stuffed into his mouth, and the cuffs were unlocked. The man with the knife frowned with concentration. Now there was steel between the reporter's ring finger and pinky. There was a muffled howl, and the sound of an empty stomach contracting. The journalist's finger was detached with surprising ease, but more blood than expected. The second captor swore as polka dots appeared on his white Nikes. The reporter was again patted, this time more vigorously – as though he were a favourite but misbehaving pet. The butcher held up the lonely digit. He found it amusing. Still laughing, he put it into an envelope. The reporter was hunched and crying.

'Look at 'im,' said a male voice, with a Yorkshire accent, from the front of the darkened room where the reporter had been freeze-framed in his agony. It seemed cruel to keep him there, even though he was made of pixels and projected on to a wall. I wished there was a 'dramatic reconstruction' disclaimer; or another scene, in which the surviving hostage was interviewed on *Oprah*, looking relaxed and happy, with a Venice Beach tan. 'Kidnap Ordeal Made Me Stronger', the screen caption could say. But I feared there was no happy ending. I feared the worst.

The red dot of a laser pen drew a circle round the journalist's dead stare. 'Completely out of it: 'ee's in shock,' said the voice. 'Remember what we talked about yesterday: shock is a state of acute circulatory insufficiency of the blood. In other words, yer 'art can't pump enough blood, at the right pressure, through yer vital organs. Symptoms: apathy; weakness; rapid 'artbeat. In some cases you stay conscious but lose alertness. But I'll be surprised if this fella doesn't pass out. *Watch.*' The video resumed, and the reporter fell heavily on to the worn, stained carpet. I noticed his thin bare legs, covered in a spray of human sewage.

As I tried to control my breathing, I felt something push hard against the back of my plastic chair. '*Skewsme,*' said a muffled female voice, near my left ear. I turned to see a woman – a fellow delegate on the 'Surviving Dangerous Countries' course – dive for the door of the conference room. Her right hand was clamped over her mouth. The door slammed behind her. We heard stilettos on ceramic. There was another slam, this time softer and with a short echo, as the soon-to-be-embedded journalist bolted into the bathroom. I considered following her.

Switches flicked. The overhead lights in the conference room buzzed and flashed, before capturing twenty worried, sweaty faces in unflattering glare. The voice at the front of the room belonged to David Silver, a former Royal Marine and one-time member of the Special Air Services. The elite regiment was based a few miles north, at a former RAF base in Hereford. Silver was in his late forties, and looked as though he had been made from squares: square jawbone, square shoulders, square skull, and neat, square beard. He was dressed in corporate hikewear: desert boots, ironed Rohans, and checked, vented shirt, carefully tucked in. He looked like a lifesize Legoman. Silver's mini-biography, which was fastened to the course's syllabus, said he had spent two years attached to the US Army Rangers, and had once trained the private army of a billionaire sultan. I wondered if he had been one of the SAS commandos in black-hooded jump-suits who stormed the Iranian embassy in London on 5 May 1980. The raid came after Khuzestan terrorists, funded by Saddam Hussein, took twenty-six hostages. All but one of the living hostages were rescued, while five of the six captors were shot dead. The commandos, like real-life 007s, had gone straight to a champagne reception with Margaret Thatcher when it was over. The siege at the embassy later inspired a Hollywood film called *Who Dares Wins*, after the regiment's motto.

Silver attempted a square, mechanical grin.

'Any questions?' he asked.

The room fidgeted.

On one side of me was David Sharrock, *The Times*'s Madrid correspondent, and on the other Richard Mills, a *Times* photographer from Northern Ireland. Opposite was a Dutch television news crew. The rest of the Surviving Dangerous Countries delegates were junior producers from the BBC and *Tonight With Trevor McDonald*, plus a Swiss radio journalist. It was an overweight, hungover and nicotine-addicted room. There was a salty, sweaty taste in the air. I felt nauseous.

Finally, someone pointed at the image of the weeping, fingerless reporter and said, '*Is that gonna happen to us?*'

Silver laughed. It was a barracks laugh – as cold as a wet day in Wales.

'Let's 'ope not,' he said.

There was more fidgeting. Everyone wanted a cigarette, or a drink, or both. There was a bar only yards away, in the lounge.

'Look,' said Silver. 'Let's not pretend. After September 11, everything changed. Westerners are now seen as targets. Members of the media – especially journalists from America or Britain – are seen as ambassadors of their countries. If you think you've got immunity, forget it. Back in the day, people didn't *deliberately* target the media. Even in Vietnam. Or Gulf War I. *They do now*. Look what happened to that fella from the *Wall Street Journal*, Danny Pearl.'

I imagined how much worse the video of Pearl's death would have looked than the amateur amputation we had just witnessed. The tape of Pearl's murder, entitled 'The Slaughter of the Spy-Journalist, the Jew Daniel Pearl', was released on 21 February 2002. It was three minutes and thirty-six seconds long. In it, pictures of dead Muslims, and footage of President Bush shaking hands with the Israeli Prime Minister, Ariel Sharon, were displayed alongside a jumpy reel of Pearl's murder. The worst moment came precisely one minute and fifty-five seconds into the video, when the reporter's throat was shown sliced open (an apparent technical error by the captors had prevented the act from being filmed). Afterwards, Pearl's head was detached, and held up by the scalp, while a list of the captors' demands, including the release of prisoners in Guantanamo Bay, was superimposed on top. The terrorists, who called themselves the National Movement for the Restoration of Pakistani Sovereignty, had sent their demands to the *Wall Street Journal* from the email address kidnapperguy@ hotmail. com. The captors' final email said, 'If America will not meet our demands, we will kill Daniel. This cycle will continue [until] no American journalist could enter Pakistan.' Pearl's decapitated body was found three months later, in a shallow grave outside Karachi. At the time of Pearl's murder, his wife, Marianne, was pregnant with their first child.

I suddenly felt very cold. Silver was still talking.

'Take out yer booklets,' he said, 'and look at the stats: 347 journalists killed worldwide in the past ten years. That's *five times* more reporters than were killed in World War II. In 1994 alone, twenty journalists were kidnapped – by militants, criminals, guerrillas, government forces or whatever – and executed. That's why we're 'ere: to help you reduce the risks, while still getting yer stories.'

Silver pointed to the reporter still in agony on the projection screen. It was like a holiday snap from hell. 'This poor fella up here, I think, survived,' he said. 'Someone must have paid the ransom when they got 'is pinky in the post. But you can imagine the psychological damage. And if yer gonna do this "embedded" thing with the Americans, it's something worth thinking about. If the Iraqis get hold of you, they won't be that interested in a ransom. Or yer little finger.'

'Portland Place, please. Langham Hilton.'

This was me, in a London cab, a few days earlier. The date was Saturday 15 February 2003, and I had just staggered off a flight from Los Angeles International Airport to London Heathrow, on my way to meet Fletcher's 'chaps from the SAS'. The chaps, it turned out, ran a school for war reporters from a luxury hotel near Ross-on-Wye, in Herefordshire, and were best known for a five-day course entitled

Surviving Dangerous Countries. Fletcher had booked me on it. The syllabus said that on Monday we would learn about 'target awareness', and on Tuesday about 'controlling bleeding'. The former would 'demonstrate why people become targets', while the latter would 'explain the causes and types of bleeding'. The message seemed clear: journalists stupid enough to embed themselves with the Marines would become walking targets, *who bled*. I feared the Surviving Dangerous Countries course would convince me to avoid dangerous countries, never mind survive them. At least leaving Los Angeles had been easy: Alana was away on a business trip.

According to office gossip, the SAS course had cost *The Times* $4,000. There was also a rumour that *The Times* saved 40 per cent on Lloyd's of London insurance for journalists who took it, with the policy covering claims of up to $1 million. This, however, was not true. I later learned that News International had its own blanket policy that covered all reporters on the battlefield.

Fletcher had placed his war correspondents on a map of the Middle East like a high-roller at a roulette table. Anthony Loyd was in northern Iraq with the Kurds; Janine di Giovanni was in Baghdad; and another *Times* veteran, Stephen Farrell, would be posted near the Iraq–Jordan border. My fellow course delegate David Sharrock, a veteran of the first Gulf War, would follow the British troops into the southern port town of Basra. Ayres and Owen, meanwhile, were wild gambles on the one-armed bandit. The odds of a decent story: a million to one.

During the eleven-hour flight from Los Angeles, I had listened to a depressing Nick Cave CD, and read the even more depressing Valentine's Day edition of the *Los Angeles Times*. It informed me that Hans Blix had declared Iraq's 'al-Samoud 2' missiles to be in breech of UN resolution 687, because they had a maximum range of 180 km, instead of the allowed 150 km. I wondered why Saddam didn't just come clean with his weapons. Perhaps he didn't think President Bush was serious. I almost wanted to go to Baghdad and tell him myself: *he's serious*.

'You 'avin a laugh?' asked the cabbie.
'Sorry?'
'Portland Place? *Today?*'

'Er, yeah.'

There was a short silence. I wondered what was wrong with Portland Place, but was too jet-lagged to ask. I was dizzy with worry, cosmic radiation, coach-class miniatures and chemical food. So I looked out of the window instead, and watched a British Army soldier, in jungle fatigues, clomp his boots by an outdoor ashtray. He was clutching what looked like a sub-machine gun. I couldn't remember seeing soldiers at Heathrow before. At that moment a column of armoured vehicles, complete with caterpillar treads and gun turrets, grunted into the short-term parking area, slowed down, then carried on, towards a roundabout with a model Concorde on top of it. I remembered reading in the *Los Angeles Times* that Eid ul-Adha, or the Feast of the Sacrifice, an important Islamic holiday, was this week.

'Blimey,' I said, to no one.

'I'll do it, but it'll cost yer,' said the driver, finally. A thick forefinger reached for the meter. The back of the cab smelled of vomit and diesel. We jerked forward into the camouflaged traffic. All I could see of the cabbie was a red Arsenal scarf, a thinning turf of grey hair, and a tattooed forearm.

It felt good to back in England.

'What's the problem with Portland Place?' I asked eventually.

'What? Other than the ONE MILLION *wankers* marching through central London, protesting against the war?'

He said 'war' as though it were spelled 'woe-aghr'.

'You're kidding me.'

'I wish. A million of the buggers. Biggest protest march since the 1840s, according to Five Live. Gridlock, innit?'

He turned up the volume of his radio. 'Listen,' he said.

'. . . actress Vanessa Redgrave . . . is one of the marchers,' said the news reader. Redgrave came on. 'The world is against this war,' she declared. 'No one doubts Saddam Hussein is a brutal dictator, but war is the most ghastly way to try to bring change.' I heard chanting and cheers.

'So you support the invasion?' I shouted, leaning in close to the plastic screen that separated driver and passenger.

'What? *Nah*. Bloody stupid idea. Blair must have been born yesterday. That George Dubya is leading 'im up the garden path,

I reckon. I've got a nephew in the Royal Marines, though, so you've got to support the boys, 'aven't yer? Poor buggers. This one won't be over in five bloody days.'

'Right,' I said.

'Mind you,' continued the cabbie, 'after what 'appened in New York, with them twin towers, makes you think, dunnit? Last thing we need is old Mohammed sitting in a field in Berkshire, firing rockets at EasyJet.' He pointed to a tank parked on the hard shoulder of the M4, under the Heathrow flight path. 'Sometimes I wonder if these Army boys know something we don't.'

He laughed, which seemed to cause problems deep within his lungs. The laugh ended as a violent, eye-watering cough.

'Anyway, where've yer come from today?' he asked, when he finally recovered. 'Been on 'oliday, 'ave you?'

I told him everything. I didn't mean to, but I couldn't stop myself. At one point I thought I was going to have to use the metal tissue box that had been thoughtfully screwed to the cab's rear window ledge. In the end we got to Portland Place in fifteen minutes – a world record. The roads were empty. No one, it seemed, had dared face the predicted gridlock in central London.

'That'll be fifty-four thirty,' said the cabbie, as we pulled up to the Hilton. 'Thought you was looking at a ton – easy.'

I shuffled backwards out of the cab, dragging my luggage in front of me.

'*Cheers*,' I said, as I stood on the pavement and passed him four crisp notes through the window. 'Here's sixty-five.'

The cab driver's face was plump and mottled, but dadish. He bent down to make eye contact through the passenger window.

'Take care of yourself, son, wontcha?' he said, with a nod.

'I'll try,' I replied.

The taxi gave a diesel snarl and began to make a U-turn across Portland Place. There was an oily clack as its doors locked automatically. I saw the driver's lips move. '*Silly bugger*,' I could have sworn he said.

In the bleached hotel room, with its panoramic view of plumbing and masonry, I washed off the sweat of a night in economy class, slumped on to the double bed, and attempted to calm myself by reading an issue of *Car* magazine. Unable to concentrate, I prodded the television awake. It showed me a column of well-dressed anti-war protesters marching through London, hoisting placards that read, 'NO WAR FOR OIL', 'MAKE TEA NOT WAR', and just 'NO'. They didn't look like the usual hippy peaceniks. There was barely a pair of Dr Martens, or a woollen beanie, to be seen. They looked like *Times* readers, in fact. The television told me there had also been demonstrations in New York, Berlin, Paris and Athens, with a total of 5 million protesters worldwide. Then it cut to Tony Blair, who was giving a defiant speech in Glasgow to the Labour Party. '*There will be no march for the victims of Saddam,*' he declared, '*no protests about the thousands of children that die needlessly every year under his rule; no righteous anger over the torture chambers which, if he is left in power, will be in left in being.*' I didn't know whom I found more convincing: the peace marchers or the Prime Minister. The truth, however, was that I was too selfishly preoccupied with being sent to Iraq to worry about the justification for the invasion. My instinct was to support it. If I was going to be gassed by Saddam in the desert, I at least wanted it to be for a good cause. But I admit it: part of me was happy that someone was trying to stop it happening.

'What d'you make of the protesters?' I asked Glen, later that evening, over a salad at Vingt Quatre, a posh diner on Fulham Road.

'My mum was one of them,' he said.

'Your *mother* marched?'

'For selfish reasons, probably. Doesn't want her son to go to war.'

'You're going to an aircraft base.'

'Still technically war,' he said, pointing his fork at me. 'And Scud missiles, as you know, Chris, can land anywhere.'

'I'm sure my mum would've done the same. If she knew I was going.'

Glen glanced up from his £20 plate of lettuce. Behind him I could see Chelsea blondes with their banker boyfriends.

'You haven't told her?' he asked.

'Nah. Waiting for a good time.'

We munched in silence for a few seconds, then Glen said, 'It doesn't feel quite right, does it? The war, I mean.'

'Part of me thinks it's justified,' I said, with a frown. 'And part of me thinks it's one of stupidest ideas I've ever heard.'

'At least in '91 we had Stormin' Norman,' said Glen, 'and the Saudis on side. But he's a complete bastard, Saddam. Makes you feel quite bellicose, really. Especially when you see what he did to the Kurds . . .'

Our concentration returned to the overpriced food. I remembered reading about the shells of mustard gas that fell on the Kurdish city of Halabja on 16 March 1988. The gas apparently smelled like fertilizer, or rotten garlic. Those who breathed too deeply ended up going blind, while their skin bubbled and blistered. Survivors arguably got a worse deal than those killed by immediate asphyxiation: they suffered brain damage, leukaemia, infertility and disfigurement.

Then I said, 'He's going to use chemical weapons, isn't he?'

'Without a doubt,' said Glen.

I pushed my plate away. It smelled like garlic.

The SAS course turned out to be a bit of a blow to morale. I had no idea there were so many things that could kill you, injure you, maim you, or otherwise ruin your day on a battlefield: heavy artillery, light artillery, tanks, machine guns, handguns, sub-machine guns, landmines that explode upward, landmines that explode downward, landmines that jump out of their craters and explode *in front of your balls*, and, of course, snipers. I had completely forgotten about snipers. But apparently we'd be hearing a lot from them in Baghdad, if we ever got there. And we hadn't even started on chemical or biological weapons. It was a wonder, I thought, that soldiers even bothered to turn up for wars. There didn't seem to be much point.

We were shown footage of dead people, nearly dead people, beheaded people, alive people who were soon to be dead people, and gruesomely injured people. We were advised to carry a zip-lock bag in our backpacks, for severed fingers or toes. I wondered if we should also carry freezer-sized bags, for larger appendages. A good deal of time was spent learning how to tie and loosen tourniquets, to stop the gush of blood from limbless joints. I practised applying a tourniquet to myself, but nearly passed out when my leg went numb. The appendage I was most worried about losing, however, was my head. But tourniquets don't work on the neck.

The climax of the course was 'field training'. It involved our flabby press battalion, commanded by a clearly bored David Silver, taking a pleasant walk through the frosted countryside, eating Mars bars, and fumbling with maps. When we got back to the hotel, I took Silver aside and asked if he thought it was a good idea to be embedded. 'Wouldn't be too keen on it meeself,' he said. 'Seems to me, if Saddam's got chemicals, 'ee's gonna use 'em, int 'ee? But, to be honest, I can't see the Yanks lettin' you lot anywhere near the action. No offence, but you'll just slow 'em down. And if you *do* end up with a front-line unit, I can't imagine the Americans will be very 'appy about it.' There were three ways, I concluded, to look at Silver's analysis: as good news, because it meant I would probably be kept away from the fighting; as bad news, because if I *was* allowed near the fighting, the Marines would resent me for slowing them down; or as very bad news, because the prospect of chemical warfare in Iraq was too scary even for Silver. And Silver had been in the bloody SAS.

No one on the Surviving Dangerous Countries course seemed to believe that embeds would face any serious danger. Surely, I thought, *The Times*, the BBC and Granada Television couldn't have *all* misjudged the situation. If embeds really did end up at the front, I thought, the British and American public would be lucky if they recognized a single correspondent – all of them would be under the age of thirty and, if I was anything to go by, cowering in foxholes.

The online edition of the *New York Times*, which I checked every morning from my hotel room, told a different story about the embeds. 'In many ways, this is going to be historic,' the paper quoted a US Defense Department spokesman as saying. He added that more than 500 reporters, 100 of them from international organizations, including the Arabic-language al Jazeera cable channel and Russia's Itar-Tass news agency, had signed up. Even *Men's Health* had a embed, as did *People* magazine and *Rolling Stone*, still known for its hippy, pot-smoking sympathies during Vietnam. I wondered what on earth *Men's Health* would write about: war was the antithesis of men's health. The embedding scheme was the biggest media mobilization of all time, the *Times* said, requiring a massive logistical operation of its own. The Defense Department spokesman explained that embeds would not be allowed to carry weapons, and would not have to pay

for their transport, food or accommodation. 'There's no cost for the
six feet of ground they'll lie on and the rations, although they may not
like them,' he said. *Six feet of ground?* Wouldn't we get a bunk bed?

The only full-time war correspondents on the SAS course were the
Dutch crew. The chief reporter, Gottfried, was a heavy, saturnine
figure, with a carcinogenic suntan and worry lines as deep as the
Grand Canyon, hardened by the fumes from his forty-a-day Marlboro
habit. He reeked of death and tobacco. Gottfried had witnessed some
of the most depraved acts of humankind, in all the world's major
terror-tourist destinations, including Kosovo, Rwanda, Liberia,
Chechnya and the Sudan. He looked as though he hadn't got a decent
night's sleep since 1974.

'So what's it like?' I asked him, over a pint of warm Boddingtons
in the hotel bar one evening. 'Going to war, I mean.'

He looked at me with black eyes. I expected to hear tales of adventure, heroism, bad rations, and the honesty of soldiers.

'I lost my wife,' he said, emptying his glass with a single wrist movement. 'And my children. I lost my children, too.'

'. . . they died?'

'She left me. My wife *left* me, and she took the kids. I was gone for
six months of the year covering the wars. She couldn't wait any longer,
Christoffel. I don't blame her. Why wait for Gottfried? Gottfried talks
only of hell.'

I began to feel immense pity for the giant Dutchman, whose elaborate television hairdo seemed at odds with his face. For a moment I
thought he might cry. But his tear ducts had dried up long ago.

'It's a great job, of course,' he told me. 'But a dangerous one. And
a lonely one, also. You have a wife at home?'

*A great job?* Being Bono was a great job. Being Gottfried? Surely
not.

'Girlfriend,' I replied.

Gottfried laughed. It was a harrowing sound – gentle, like weeping.

'My advice to you, Christoffel: get rid of your beautiful woman
now, before it starts. It won't work. *It never does.*'

We are all born fearless. Perhaps we lose it as we get older and realize
the value, and the responsibility, of love. When I was a choirboy at

St Mary's church in Wooler, forced every Sunday into a white vest-ment and a frilly ruff collar, I was sure I wanted to be a man of action. The vicar once asked me, in front of the entire church, what I wanted to do when I grew up. The answer was obvious, because I had just seen *Who Dares Wins* on Betamax. 'I'm going to be in the SAS,' I replied, quite seriously. The carrot-haired boy, with his milky, freckled face and scaffolded teeth, couldn't understand why the con-gregation laughed so hard, for so long.

I was never particularly brave. When I was a toddler, my mother stayed at home to look after me. She would bake bread, and read me stories about Snoopy and Willo the Wisp. When I was old enough to go to school, my father was there to keep an eye on me: he was, after all, the head teacher, who walked down the corridors on his hands. My mother eventually got a teaching job at the same school, meaning I was near both parents twenty-four hours a day. Perhaps it was this idyllic childhood that stopped me toughening up. But there were downsides. The head teacher's son is never a popular kid, and by the time acne and adolescence had ruined me, at the age of thir-teen, I was sullen and silent company. I emerged from the worst of it three or four years later, with a terrible haircut and even worse taste in music. I was determined to move to London in search of some kind of compensatory fame and wealth. It was only when I finally left Wooler, however, that I realized how lucky I had been: some-times I wondered if my parents were the only happily married couple left in England.

I told my mum about Iraq the day I left London for the Surviving Dangerous Countries course. Passengers standing next to me at Paddington station heard the following one-sided conversation.

'Mum, I'm being sent to, er, *Kuwait* for a while.'

'KUWAIT. It's very safe.'

'I'm going to be, write about . . . I'm going to spend some time at a military base. It's very safe. Really, *very* safe.'

'It's for the wa—'

'I know I'm not a war correspondent.'

'Like Kate Adie, yes.'

'I know I'm not the type.'

'Because no one wants to read about celebrities at the moment.'

'Well, y'know, Mum, war correspondents have to start their careers somewhere.'

'Yes, it's near Iraq.'

'Yes, I know he used chemical weapons on the Kurds.'

'I'm in England. Doing a course with the SAS.'

'I *am* taking this seriously.'

'OK, I'll talk to my father.'

The conversation reminded me of an ethical problem I had once studied in a philosophy class at Hull. It concerned a young Frenchman who, during World War II, was forced to choose between joining the Allied forces in England or staying at home and looking after his sick mother. The man desperately wanted to fight the Nazis, but felt an overwhelming guilt at abandoning his beloved mum, who begged him to stay. The dilemma, posed by Jean-Paul Sartre, had no solution. According to Sartre, it simply proved the anguish of man, and the absence of God. 'Everything is permissible if God does not exist,' wrote Sartre, 'and as a result man is forlorn.' He was a cheerful soul, old Sartre. On the positive side, he argued that man was free. The freedom part made it worse, though. It reminded me that I didn't *have* to go to Iraq. I was, as Sartre said, in anguish. Come to think of it, I also felt pretty damn forlorn.

There was no way, of course, that I could tell my parents about what I feared the embedding scheme might involve. So I told them what we both wanted to hear: I would go to Kuwait, live at a military base, and perhaps go on 'day trips' into Iraq, after it had been safely invaded by the Americans. But then I did something really unforgivable: I asked my father's opinion on whether I should go. 'Yes, son, I think you should go,' he said, hesitantly. '*The Times* wouldn't put you in any danger. And it sounds like a great honour. You must be doing well, son. Best of luck.' My father's bogus approval made me feel better, for a while. But I knew he would have given me different advice if he'd known the Pentagon's real plan for the embeds. I also knew that if I died in Iraq my poor old man would never forgive himself.

On my way back to California after the course, I called Alana from Heathrow. It was early in Los Angeles, but I knew she would be up, still jet-lagged from her business trip.

'How was it?' she asked, trying to sound enthusiastic.

'Oh, y'know, pretty useful. I think.'

'Jeez, I can't believe you *did* all that,' she said.

I paused for a second.

'All *what*?'

'Oh, I had a look online. Your friend Oliver wrote about going on one of these military courses. Must have been gruelling . . .'

'Poole?'

'Y'know, Oliver. From the *Telegraph*. The good-looking one. We met him once in Chateau Marmont, I think.'

'I know exactly who he is,' I said, a bit too quickly, through a clenched jaw. 'What kind of things did *he* do?'

'Oh, the same stuff you did, probably. The 5-mile tactical march with the 50 lb rucksack; being shot at with live rounds; applying facial camouflage; chemical decontamination; jumping from helic—'

'It wasn't the same course,' I interrupted. 'He did the Pentagon course. He did it at Fort Dix, New Jersey.'

'I know, Chris. But it's the same thing, right? Did they teach you how to self-inject the nerve gas antidote?'

'No.'

'What about how to "dead-reckon"?'

'Look. It's not the sam—'

'Did you create a field latrine with a shovel, wooden planks and baby wipes?'

*What the hell was a field latrine?*

'No,' I croaked. 'Look—'

'Tourniquets?'

'YES! We did tourniquets.' In my relief, I almost told her about the near-fainting incident, but caught myself in time.

'Cool,' said Alana. 'Missed you.'

'Yeah, missed you too.'

'It's hard to imagine you putting on a gas mask. Oliver said he had to get it over his head and seal it in nine seconds.'

It was then, in a moment of exquisite torment, that I realized the most important thing about the Surviving Dangerous Countries course: we hadn't learned a *single* thing about chemical or biological weapons. My blood turned to iced panic. 'Hang on, Alana,'

I mumbled, as I fought my hand luggage, pulling out the glossy brochure with my itinerary on it. I found the section entitled 'Nuclear, Biological and Chemical'. This, I learned, was a separate course, to be held the following week in London. 'Of particular importance to those embedding with the American military,' it said. By next week, however, I would be in Los Angeles, making final preparations for Iraq. I couldn't believe it: I had taken the wrong bloody course.

'Is everything OK?' I heard Alana say.

# IO

# The List

There were thunderstorms over Greenland. The Boeing 747, like a great basking shark, tumbled and twitched as its pilots sweated over glowing instruments. Through my rain-splashed window, I stared at the wing as it bounced in a downdraft. We banked starboard and lost altitude quickly. Transatlantic flight remains one of humankind's most unnatural acts: 524 people, breathing a ton of pressurized air, falling 10,000 feet at 567 m.p.h., as they travel backwards in time. No wonder the kids of the seventies, the war virgins, are so strung-out on Zoloft and Xanax: our lives are built on technology, and stalked by fear of technology failing.

So how did I feel, as I sat in the cheapest seat of the American Airlines jumbo, downing miniatures with my back to the stench and gargle of the chemical loo? I was pretty worried about the gas mask situation, that was for sure. And I felt terrible about conning my father into giving me approval to go to war. Strangely, however, the thunderstorms weren't bothering me. My flight on the Navy Greyhound had shown me the real meaning of turbulence: *this was nothing*. Perhaps, I thought, I wouldn't be scared of anything if I survived Iraq. Perhaps, after being denied comfort and technology, and forced to sleep rough in the desert, I'd be cured for ever of anxiety. Or perhaps I'd come back like one of the 'mental cases' in the World War I poem by Wilfred Owen: 'purgatorial shadows, / Drooping tongues from jaws that slob their relish, / Baring teeth that leer like skulls' teeth wicked'.

Shortly after becoming an official embed, I got a call from Nick Wapshott in New York. 'Congratulations, young Ayres,' he crooned. 'Marching off to war, eh? You'll come back a changed man. Everyone always does.' As long as I came back breathing – and with no absent, much-loved limbs – I didn't really care. My fragile mental health had already survived September 11 and a biological attack on my office. Now it was Saddam's turn to try to unhinge me.

In the taxi home from the airport, I marvelled at the hot breeze, the blue slab of sky, and the spiky desert foliage. Once again, California was teasing: showing off what I would miss if I went to war. It had been *snowing* in Ross-on-Wye, with a Welsh-prima-donna gale blustering in from the west. As for the weather in Iraq – it was hardly worth thinking about. I imagined the Gulf forecast: a fog of war expected from the south; high pressure in Baghdad; a chance of a poisoned cloud blowing in from the north; invaders and embeds advised to stay indoors.

I clambered out of the taxi at 1131 Alta Loma Road and offered a nod of recognition to the Mexican doormen – the foreign legion sentries who guard every West Hollywood apartment complex. If the Mexicans ever decide they want California back, the Americans are in trouble: the Latinos pretty much run the place already. They have a head start, unlike the Americans in Iraq. I once read that there wasn't a single US spy in Baghdad. Why would anyone risk it? Not even James Bond could smirk his way through one of Saddam's tongue-pulling sessions.

After dragging my bags through the canyon of SUVs in the garage, I passed the swimming pool and tennis court, and took the steps up to my apartment. I shook my head. *What the hell was I doing?* Why was I giving this up for Iraq? I considered my options for the month of March: swimming pool or death. But I was still grasping at the hope that the invasion wouldn't happen. I had heard on the news that the Turks were getting stroppy, and refusing to allow President Bush to offload military equipment at the port of Iskenderun. If the Americans couldn't advance into Iraq from the north, that would leave Kuwait as the only friendly country from which they could attack. And surely no military commander in his right mind would invade a country the size of France from just one direction. Finally, at 4.23 p.m., I clattered through the front door of my apartment, heaving my bags behind me.

Alana wasn't home. I inspected the fridge for alcohol: it was empty. I debated whether to take a quick shower or check my emails. I decided on the latter. My computer gave an indignant bleep and began clacking and whirring as it powered up. At that moment, the front door was flung open and Alana appeared, her hair ironed and shiny from an expensive primping in Beverly Hills. She was carrying groceries – a dozen bags of supermarket ballast from Trader Joe's.

For a second we looked at each other in silence.

Then Alana said, 'I bought orange juice! And coffee!'

Her face was a study in relief: that her ridiculous boyfriend, with his ridiculous job, had come back home; and that her week of solitary confinement in Los Angeles was finally over. She couldn't stop smiling.

'Hi,' I replied, feeling slightly awkward after our separation. I was pleased to see her, too. But it was a complicated pleasure, because Alana made everything so much harder, so much more dramatic. War is the opposite of love, after all. And Alana was a reminder that I was trading one for the other.

The details of what happened next have been lost. My memory, with its reporter's talent for minutiae, fails me. Only the pathos remains. We must have embraced; kissed, almost certainly. I know that the shopping bags, with their warm loaves, damp leaves and pungent vegetables, were ignored: abandoned on the floor, leaking and rustling beside my desk. Eventually I must have sat down in front of the computer. It was then I saw the email from Glen, highlighted in a bold font. 'Here we go . . .' was the ominous subject line. It had been sent at 18.12 GMT, when I was somewhere over Greenland. I double clicked. What followed was bad news – the worst news. The email had been forwarded from the Pentagon. 'Instructions for Embedded Media,' it began. 'All embedded media representatives must report to the Coalition Press Center, located at the Hilton Kuwait Resort, at 7 a.m., Zulu Time, on March 5.'

*It was happening.*

This gave me all of ten days to prepare for war. Given that I had no Kuwaiti visa, no flak jacket, no helmet and no supplies – and no inoculations – I would have to turn around and head straight back to London, and from there on to Kuwait. I was looking at 8,300 miles, or twenty hours, of hard economy. I cursed again at missing the gas-mask course. Then I thought of Oliver Poole, who was probably already on the Iraqi border. I pictured him, in desert fatigues and chemical-proof spacesuit, shadow boxing and jogging on the spot. The infantry probably loved him.

'*Oh no,*' I said, as my blood turned sour. 'I have to go back.'

'What?' said Alana, quietly.

'The war. It's really happening. March the fifth. I have go back. I have to get to Kuwait. The *bloody* war! I can't believe it.'

'No,' she said. 'Don't be ridiculous.'

'I'm sorry. I'm so sorry.'

'No,' said Alana, again.

It took a lot to make Alana cry. This, however, was more than enough. She sat among the unpacked grocery bags, her thwarted attempt at a normal life, shivering and sobbing as tears spoiled her make-up. 'What am I going to do with all these groceries?' she asked, and for a moment she looked like a little girl left alone on her birthday by a cruel stepfather. I thought of Gottfried and his failed marriage. '*She couldn't wait any longer, Christoffel,*' I heard him say. '*I don't blame her. Why wait for Gottfried? Gottfried talks only of hell.*'

I'm ashamed to say that part of me felt annoyed at Alana – it was *me* that was being sent to war, not her. And she didn't seem to understand the strange contradiction that could make her boyfriend both a neat-freak hypochondriac *and* a war reporter. Then again, I didn't understand it either.

I realized, of course, that I was being selfish. I didn't have to go to the Gulf. I didn't have to leave my girlfriend alone in the city she hated (and to which I had selfishly dragged her). I didn't have to bullshit my own father, potentially destroying him with guilt if I died on the battlefield. I didn't have to do any of this. But I was scared: scared of losing my new career as a foreign correspondent; scared of someone else taking my place and doing well; and scared of squandering an opportunity that many reporters worked their whole lives to get. It was essentially a form of cowardice that was pushing me to Iraq. I thought of Jean-Paul Sartre's dilemma of the young Frenchman and his sick mother. Perhaps there was no right or wrong in this situation. Man is free to do what he wants; there is no God; as a result, man is forlorn.

At some point I joined Alana on the floor. I was probably crying too. 'What kind of a job is this?' I think I asked. War reporting is supposed to be macho. But there was nothing macho in this. Nothing macho at all.

Later, the self-pity over with, I noticed the file attached to the Pentagon's email. It was a list of things to buy for Marine embeds. This was how it started:

| *ITEMS TO BE WORN* | *QUANTITY* |
|---|---|
| KEVLAR HELMET W/CHIN STRAP | 1 |
| MOPP SUIT (W/GLOVES CARRIED IN RT CARGO POCKET) | 1 |

It went on for two pages. Some items were obvious ('Undershirt, 1'), others worrying ('Boots, Mark Left Boot with Blood Type/Social Security Number, 1 pair'). Many items were simply baffling. What, for example, was a 'MOPP suit', and why did we need *gloves* in the desert? I also didn't like the sound of the 'M291 Chemical Decon. Kit in M-40 Carrier', or, for that matter, the 'M-40 Series Field Protective Mask w/Filter'. The second section of the list, entitled 'Items in Backpack', was worse than the first: what the hell was an 'Entrenching Tool w/Carrier'? And why did I need a 'Bivvy Sack', or a 'Camelback', or 'Canteens w/Covers and NBC Caps'? What were NBC caps? Were they for cameramen? For a second I wondered if the Pentagon had mistakenly sent me the foreign-language version of the list. Then another thought struck me: *where would I buy all this stuff in West Hollywood?*

It was then that I noticed the most terrifying item in the entire document. It was number four from the top, under the 'Items to be Worn' section. I looked again, but there was no mistake. 'Underwear, 1 pair,' it said. Yes – I was being sent to war, in one of the hottest countries on earth, for weeks, if not months, and I was expected to take *one pair* of underwear with me. For a moment I felt pity for the unlucky garment that would be chosen to accompany me to Iraq. By the time we reached Baghdad, I concluded, it would be a biological weapon in its own right.

By Monday afternoon I had booked a ticket to Kuwait via London. I would leave Los Angeles on Saturday 1 March. The foreign desk, feeling sorry for me, had let me fly 'premium economy' on Virgin Atlantic. I had also made an appointment with the visa department of the Kuwait embassy, for 9 a.m. the following Monday. 'What's the purpose of your visit to our country?' the official had asked, through a nearly impenetrable Arab accent. I almost said, 'Pre-emptive invasion,' but thought better of being a smart-arse. No one, I suspect, likes a smart-arse in a Gulf emirate. 'Business,' I declared instead. Fletcher, meanwhile, arranged for me to get an armful of inoculations at the News International medical centre, which was opposite *The Times*. He also said I could pick up a flak jacket, a Kevlar helmet and an Arab-made Thuraya satellite phone when I came into the office. The only thing I had to do before leaving Los Angeles was buy the items on the Pentagon's list – and pack them. But where could I buy a MOPP suit? I decided to start with a camping shop. Unfortunately, I knew of only one: The North Face, which, if I remembered correctly, was on Rodeo Drive.

I climbed into the Jeep, and headed west.

My war, it seemed, would start in Beverly Hills.

I stood in front of a full-length mirror, wearing a canary-yellow, down-stuffed Gortex jacket, with a fur-trimmed hood. Behind me was a 20-foot indoor waterfall made entirely from glass, with a North Face logo etched into it. The rest of the shop had been contrived to look like the inside of a cave: intrepid Beverly Hills shoppers were greeted with a wall of fake volcanic rock beyond the front door. It wasn't so much a shop as a Hollywood film set: a miniature retail Disneyland. Outside, on the street, there were more props: Range Rovers and Hummers; Tahoes and Expeditions. These days we experience the outdoors through our consumer purchases. Apart from me, of course. Apart from the idiot embed, drafting himself into the Marines.

'Yo – that's *bad-ass*,' said a tall black man, who was flicking through a nearby rack with gold-flecked fingers. I looked down at the $399 price tag on the jacket. 'Yes, it's very nice,' I concluded. 'But I'm not *quite* sure it suits my purposes.' I furtively pulled the Pentagon's list out of my back pocket: 'Gortex Jacket, 1,' it said. In brackets, it advised, 'Muted Desert Colours'. I glanced up at the giant, fluorescent yellow Michelin man in the mirror. He didn't look very muted. If yellow is the colour of sand, I wondered, does that make yellow a desert colour? Then I felt a slap on my back. It was my fellow shopper. 'Ain't no purpose if you ain't lookin' good,' he advised. 'With that jacket, you'll be beatin' off the ladies with a stick.'

He had a point. In Iraq, however, I feared the stick would belong to the Marines, and that the jacket, not to mention *me*, would be on the wrong end of it. I took the coat off and put it back on the rack. Beverly Hills, I feared, wasn't the ideal place to prepare for war. After all, the last time the 90210 Zip code had seen any fighting was in 1847, when the Mexicans were cornered by the Americans at the Cahuenga Capitulation. There hadn't been much need for combat supplies since. Lamborghini parts and luxury dog spas, yes; gas masks and MOPP suits, no.

My trip to The North Face wasn't entirely wasted, however. I managed to find an arctic sleeping bag, some hiking trousers, and a khaki vented shirt. I even bought a jacket, opting for a black Gortex shell with a zip-in windproof fleece instead of the puffy yellow one that made me look like Ali G. Of the seventy-three items on the Pentagon's list, I had crossed off four. Whatever a MOPP suit was, The North Face didn't have one. 'A *what* suit?' asked the butch female sales assistant. 'You want something for *mopping*?' I shook my head. 'Don't worry about it,' I said. For some reason I was too embarrassed to tell her about the whole embedding thing. This being Beverly Hills, I feared I might get an anti-war or anti-Bush lecture. And I wasn't in the mood. 'I'll just pay for these,' I said, dumping an armful of aggressively branded merchandise on the counter. Before I signed the credit card receipt, I asked if she knew of any other camping-gear suppliers. She told me to try 'Xtreme 19' on Sunset Boulevard.

I felt apprehensive as I walked back to the Jeep: Xtreme 19 sounded a lot more serious than The North Face, and I didn't want to be exposed as a camping fraud. In fact I was a camping virgin: I had never slept rough, or toasted a marshmallow over an open fire, in my entire life. What's more, I had never *wanted* to. I like carpets, central heating and goose-down duvets. Sod the outdoors.

As the Jeep bumped into the Xtreme 19 car park, I practised my game face. As a reporter, I was used to faking knowledge on any number of subjects. Surely, I thought, I could do it with camping. I went to pieces, however, when I saw the kayaks and backpacks in the window display. They gave me a flashback to the Cub Scouts, which my mother had forced me to join when I was a boy. I had hated Sir Robert Baden-Powell's organization with a passion from the second I was manhandled into a stupid brown-and-green uniform, complete its yellow neckerchief fastened with a red 'woggle'. Even as a ten-year-old, in 1985, I knew a woggle could never be cool. I wanted to look like David Hasselhoff. Why couldn't they give me a black leather jacket, a Pontiac Firebird and a pair of aviator shades? Every Friday my fellow Cub Scouts seemed to have amassed a new set of sew-on buttons in reward for their knot-tying skills, cycling proficiency or ability to jump over logs. I personally couldn't see the point. The Cub Scout leaders took an immediate dislike to the puny ginger kid who kept asking if he could opt out of pledging his duty to God, because he was an atheist. He distracted the other children, they said, and affected Scout morale. That was because I wanted to be at home, doing something constructive, like eating ice cream, or watching *The Muppet Show*. Eventually my mother gave up. Her son, it seemed, was not interested in the great British outdoors, the discipline and cama-raderie of a pseudo-paramilitary organization, or, for that matter, the Cub Scout Law. In her darker moments my mum must have won-dered if her son was destined to become a loser. I doubt she ever thought there was much risk of him joining the US Marines.

The door to Xtreme 19 swung open with a strangled buzz. In front of me was an alien landscape of camping equipment, mountain bikes and cardboard cut-out rocks. Outdoorsy people browsed the mer-chandise. Exotic birdsong played over the PA system. The place stank of athlete's foot, crotch powder and butane gas. *This was more like it*, I thought, looking around. The male and female staff members were indistinguishable: both wore Gortex boots, baggy sweaters and lip balm. I felt an sudden and almost overwhelming urge to drive to the nearest fashionable bar, order a martini, and light a cigarette. I fought it, and took a deep breath. Having learned my lesson from The North Face, I decided to come clean with the shop assistant. I would tell him all about Iraq, hand over the list, and let him do the rest.

'How y'doin'?' said a friendly male voice. 'Need help?'

I took a long look at the Xtreme 19 employee who was about to make the biggest sales commission of his career. Brock was my height, with a knoll of earthy brown, neglected hair, which kept his forehead in heavy shade. At the end of his folded arms were farmer's hands, raw with rock grazes and bramble pricks. Dirt was crusted under his broken fingernails. Judging by his flush of post-adolescent acne, he was in his early twenties and a sophomore at Cal-State or UCLA. He spoke with a stoner's drawl, but was in good condition under his shapeless hikewear: he clearly spent more time scaling mountains than smoking weed in his dorm.

'I have a shopping list,' I said.

'Big trip comin' up,' he replied, with a nod but no question mark.

'Yeah, a big one. A very big one.'

'Cool.'

I wondered if outdoorsy people could sense their own kind. I wondered if Brock already knew I was a camping amateur.

He took the list and stared at it for what felt like an hour.

Finally he coughed and said, 'Dude, what the hell are y'gonna do with all this? Invade Mexico?' He looked up.

'Iraq,' I said. 'Not Mexico.'

Brock made a whistling noise, like a World War II shell. He was now staring at me through his dense overgrowth of his hair. This English guy can't be in the Marines, he was thinking. He's *way* too much of a pussy.

'I'm a reporter,' I explained. 'London *Times*. I'm being embedded.'

'All right,' said Brock, nodding slowly. Somewhere, his logic gears were grinding and smoking.

'*London* Times?' he asked.

'Based here,' I clarified. 'I write about, er, Hollywood. And stuff, y'know?'

'And they're sending *you* to . . . Iraq?'

'Yeah. They are.'

Brock nodded again. Under that mound of hair I could have sworn there was a raised eyebrow. He seemed paralysed. Then he said, 'I mean, no offence: you don't look the type. Doesn't the London *Times* have, like, war correspondents? Don't they need you to cover the Oscars, or something?'

'Yes, we do have war correspondents,' I said, through a sigh. 'But it's going to be a big story, so they need a lot of people covering it. War reporters have to start their careers somewhere, y'know.'

I felt as thought I was talking to Alana, or my mother.

Brock nodded again. He was beginning to irritate me. 'Cool,' he said, again. 'Not that, y'know, I think killing Iraqis so that rich guys can drive big-assed SUVs is, like, a good idea. But, whatever, man. Let's get started.' Then Brock froze again. 'Whoah,' he said, looking down at the Pentagon's list.

I waited for the inevitable.

'Dude, what the *hell* is a MOPP suit?'

It was a long afternoon. After initially assuming some background knowledge, Brock gave up and started to openly patronize me. I was grateful. A canteen, I learned, is something you drink water out of – apparently they don't have Coke machines up mountains, or in war zones. A camelback, meanwhile, is a kind of canteen: it looks like a hot-water bottle, and you strap it to your back and drink from it with a plastic tube. After studying the Pentagon's list, Brock recommended a backpack with 7,000 cubic inches of storage space, with a separate compartment for my North Face sleeping bag, and straps to attach my inflatable mattress and ground cover. When Brock took it off the wall display, it was almost as tall as me. Then he handed me a bivvy sack, which turned out to be a waterproof Gortex cover for my sleeping bag. 'By the looks of this list, you're gonna be sleeping in shit every damn night,' he said. By the time we were finished, the shop's staff had locked the front door and started shutting off the lights. I looked outside: the customer car park was almost empty.

In the end, it took three staff members to help me carry my purchases to the cash register. I had hiking boots, hiking boot laces, spare hiking boot laces, hiking socks, hiking foot powder, thermal underwear, a portable shaving mirror, a short-wave radio (to pick up the BBC World Service), a sewing kit, and three different kinds of floppy sun hat, all of which looked ridiculous. I even had a two-man tent, picked out by Brock, and a combat-proof case for my laptop computer. At one point I flirted with the idea of buying a mountain bike and a kayak. The only things Brock couldn't help me with were the MOPP suit and all the other technical-sounding equipment on the Pentagon's embed list. I concluded I could probably live without 'NBC Caps' or an 'M291 Chemical Decon. Kit in M-40 Carrier'. The

MOPP suit, however, was number two on the list of 'Items to be Worn'. It *had* to be important.

Perhaps I could get one in Harvey Nicks, I thought.

'That'll be, let's see, $5,132.16 please,' said Brock. I gave him my Barclaycard, which was immediately declined. I tried American Express: it worked, but only after I had spoken to a fraud officer in Memphis. 'I'm sorry, Mr Ayres,' he said, 'but your purchases at North Face and Xtreme 19 appear to have triggered our "unusual spending behaviour" fraud detection system. Have you ever bought goods from an outdoor store before, Mr Ayres?' I told him that I hadn't, as Brock and his colleagues looked at each other with laughter in their eyes.

Finally, at 7.41 p.m., I left the empty, shuttered shop. It was a relief to taste the toxic smog of the Los Angeles traffic.

'Be careful, man,' said Brock, as he gave me an ironic salute.

It struck me as absurd advice. How could I be careful in a war zone? The only way to be careful was not to go. Perhaps that's what Brock meant. The cab driver in London, I remembered, had ended our conversation on a similar note. 'Take care of yourself, son, wontcha?' he had said.

'I'll try,' I said to Brock, as I loaded my bags into the Jeep.

'Hey,' said Brock, from the doorway. I turned to look at him. 'Is it really going to happen?' he asked. 'The war, I mean?'

I paused. Then I said, 'Brock, if it's got the stage where someone like me is buying a tent from someone like you, I think we can assume it's going to happen. To be honest, I don't think there's any doubt at all.'

'Right,' said Brock. He looked depressed.

'Cheerio,' I said, slamming the Jeep's tailgate. For the first time, I realized, I actually believed it: *I was going to war.*

It wasn't until Friday night, hours before my flight back to London, that I decided to practise erecting the tent. I thought it might avoid some embarrassment later on, in front of the Marines. So, with a six-pack of Heineken beside me, I ripped open the box containing my 'Two-Man Xtreme 19 Mountain Adventure Pod'. For the next hour I fumbled with metal rods and waterproof canvas, swearing periodically. Eventually, feeling so pumped up with male hormones I could have beaten a drum, I had constructed a small, space-age dome in my living room. It was then, however, that I realized the problem. Brock had sold me a tent in the same canary yellow colour as the North Face jacket I had tried on in Beverly Hills. Admittedly, it wasn't *all* yellow: it had a two-tone colour scheme, with dark, military green on the lower half. The yellow half, however, was bright enough to cause temporary blindness. I stood up and scratched my head. It was then I noticed another problem: the tent had a fluorescent red cross on its roof, so that it could be identified from the air by mountain rescue teams. 'Brock, you *fuckwit*,' I muttered. I looked at Alana. She seemed on the verge of laughter, or tears – I wasn't sure which. 'Did you *know* it was this colour?' she asked. I took another look at the luminous battlefield liability in front of me. If I put it up anywhere near the Marines, I thought, I would get court-martialled or shot – if, that is, I didn't get hit by an incoming Scud first. I imagined a huge yellow blob appearing on an Iraqi radar screen, and a Republican Guard intelligence officer pointing excitedly. But it was too late now. Xtreme 19 had closed an hour ago, and I had to fly to London the next day. 'The tent is coming with me,' I declared. 'I'm not sleeping on the floor.'

I looked again at Alana.

'Darling,' she said, softly. 'It's yellow, and it's got a bull's-eye on top.'

'I don't care,' I replied. 'I'm packing it.'

Kuwait City, Kuwait
2003

# 11

# The Last Starbucks before Baghdad

If war is hell, someone had forgotten to tell the staff of the JW Marriott Hotel in Kuwait City. On the evening of Wednesday 5 March. I was lying, or rather floating, on a king-size mattress which felt as though it had been stuffed with the hair of 1,000 virgins. To my left, on the mahogany bedside table, was a bowl piled with fruit so fresh it had probably been picked that morning. To my right was a pot of Earl Grey, wisps of fragrant steam twirling from its spout. And on the 42-inch television in front of me was Britney Spears, censored so that only her face was showing. 'My loneliness is killing me,' she confided. '*Hit me baby, one more time.*'

I had just emerged from the 'rainfall' shower room, and was wrapped in one of the hotel's white, Egyptian-cotton dressing gowns. It had a 'JW' logo on the right breast, underneath which was the Marriott's slogan: 'The biggest smile in Kuwait'. As I lay on the bed, I studied the heavy, gold-embossed room-service menu. I was facing a dilemma: should I go for the dozen Gulf prawns with lobster tail, crab and caviar; or a 12-ounce filet of Wagyu-Kobe beef, flown in (first class, I presumed) from Japan. I considered ordering both, before remembering that Martin Fletcher had to sign off on all my Iraq-related expenses. There was a good chance, however, that I would be dead or hospitalized before Fletcher got the bill. So what the hell.

My first full day of war reporting had gone better than expected. It started at 10 a.m. with a breakfast buffet in Café Royal, one of the four restaurants in the five-star Marriott's glittering, million-dollar lobby. I hadn't brought any smart clothing to Kuwait, so I turned up to the restaurant in hiking trousers (with zips below the knees to turn them into shorts), Gortex boots and a black, long-sleeved T-shirt. The front-desk staff – elegant, Persian-looking women in black Chanel with gold jewellery – performed a synchronized eye-roll as I walked past them.

At the buffet, I piled my plate with imported Scottish salmon, Greek olives, Italian ham and Swiss cheese. Kuwait's domestic farming industry, it seemed, didn't play a big part in local cuisine – hardly surprising, given that most of the country's 11,072 square miles of land is covered with hot gravel. After emptying my plate, I went back for more, serving myself some bacon and eggs with mushrooms, tomatoes and toast. I nearly embarked on a third mission to the steam table, but stopped myself: I could hardly return from the war *fatter* than when I left California.

The café's clientele, I noticed, was an uneasy mixture of war correspondents, Pakistani waiters and Arabs in billowing dishdasha robes. The locals kept their platinum Nokias on the tables – Chelsea-style – and conducted conversations with their hands, offering brief glimpses of diamond-encrusted Breitlings and Rolexes. Every so often they looked warily at their Western visitors. It must be strange, I thought, to have 150,000 foreign soldiers in your New Jersey-sized country, along with a 500-strong invading force of media representatives.

The 315-room Marriott had become the unofficial headquarters for embedded journalists from the wealthier media outlets. On separate tables opposite me sat Oliver North, the villain of the Iran-Contra Affair of the 1980s, who had become a reporter for Fox News, and Geraldo Rivera, his moustachioed television-network colleague. (Rivera was still smarting from a 2001 broadcast during which he appeared to be at the scene of a friendly-fire incident in Afghanistan – infact, he was 50 miles away, it was later claimed. Rivera's stint as an embed in Iraq would be equally volatile.) Upstairs, meanwhile, was a public television lounge, where American and British journalists consumed gallons of tea, nibbled Walkers shortbread, and swapped jokes about the French. 'Why do the French have tree-lined boulevards?' a cameraman had asked me the previous day, shortly after I checked in. I offered a shrug. '*Because the Germans like to march in the shade,*' came the punchline.

I ended up sitting alone in Café Royal, under a window, sipping a low-fat cappuccino and reading the English-language *Kuwait Times*, which made the *Wall Street Journal* seem like *Playboy*. Above my head was a mural-sized portrait of a smiling Arab with a Blackadder-style moustache and a goatee. He was wearing a classic white 'gutra' head-dress, with a skullcap underneath and a double circle of purple rope on top. I assumed this was the Kuwaiti Emir, Sheikh Jaber al-Ahmad al-Sabah, who had fled to Saudi Arabia when the Iraqis invaded at 2 a.m. on 2 August 1990. The al-Sabah dynasty, I remembered reading, had been in charge of Kuwait for more than 250 years. I also recalled that the Emir's favourite way to end political problems was to dissolve parliament.

I felt fine, apart from an almost hallucinatory bout of eleven-hour jet lag and a swollen, throbbing right arm, which had been shot full of vaccines – including the first injection of the three-stage anthrax inoculation – at the News International medical centre in London. As feared, the anthrax needle had looked like a hydraulic pump – and it had felt like a ballpoint pen as it punctured my skin. The experience was made more traumatic by the thick wad of forms I had signed before the jab, which declared that I wouldn't sue if I came down with anything resembling Gulf War Syndrome. I had no intention of visiting an American military hospital in Kuwait to get the other two anthrax shots before the war. As for the smallpox vaccine, I had decided to avoid it entirely after reading online that patients could experience 'an accidental spreading of the vaccinia virus caused by touching the vaccination site'. By the time I got to the part about it 'usually occurring on the genitals or face, where it can damage sight', I had made my mind up. Being sent to war was bad enough, without having to deal with a smallpox-infected penis. Or, for that matter, blindness.

There was only one other thing ruining my otherwise comfortable visit to Kuwait: fear. In particular, fear of the immediate future. The overwhelming luxury of the Marriott, with its designer mini-mall, sushi bar, colonial-style tea lounge and American steakhouse, made the thought of going out into the desert even worse. I remembered what Brock had told me in Xtreme 19: '*By the looks of this list, you're gonna be sleeping in shit every damn night.*' I tried to fight the adrenalin with Earl Grey and Marlboro Lights. But they seemed only to make it worse.

I called *The Times* at midday, Kuwait time, even though it was still early in London. I didn't have anything better to do. It was also a good excuse to test the satellite phone Fletcher had given me in London. Before dialling, I had to extend the chunky antenna and point it out of the window, as the phone tried to locate the Thuraya satellite. When it locked on, I felt like a secret agent.

The phone rang in long, distorted electronic beeps, a sure sign the call was going to cost a fortune. Someone in London had told me the international satellite rate was $10 per minute, but I didn't want to listen.

'Foreign new-*ews?*' said a familiar nasal voice.

I looked at the screen of the Thuraya to make sure I'd dialled correctly: I had.

'Martin . . . *Barrow?*' I asked.

'Your lucky day,' said Barrow. His sarcasm, it seemed, was powerful enough to withstand a return journey into space.

'Don't you work for *business?*'

'Not any more,' Barrow revealed. 'Couldn't bear to be without you, Chris. I'm a distinguished member of *The Times*'s foreign staff now: I'm a card-carrying *intellectual*. Yesterday we debated the small print of the Kyoto Treaty for a full forty-five minutes. So what are you doing in Kuwait City, Chris? Knowing your luck, there'll be a *war* or something. Did you see lots of people running in the opposite direction when you landed at the airport? Do they know about the curse?'

Barrow was laughing so hard he temporarily lost the ability to talk. I held the receiver away from my ear for a second.

'I see you haven't lost your sense of humour,' I said. In some warped way, Barrow was actually making me feel better.

Finally, he calmed down. 'So what are you offering today?' he asked, meaning war-related news stories.

Nothing, as it turned out. *The Kuwait Times* didn't provide much lift-and-view material. As for the al-Jazeera news channel, I couldn't understand a word of it because it was in Arabic. Besides, it seemed only to broadcast pictures of dead Palestinians. So I offered to rewrite a few stories from the wire services – which I could get via Yahoo! on a twenty-minute delay, using the computers in the Marriott's business centre. Barrow wasn't interested. After all, the foreign desk already had a 'proper' war reporter working from Kuwait: Daniel McGrory, who in 1999 had co-authored a book about Iraq's nuclear ambitions, called

*Brighter Than the Baghdad Sun.* It was clear I was a back-up plan: a substitute, kicking my heels on the bench. This, however, was re-assuring: Fletcher clearly hadn't changed his mind about embedding. He still regarded it as an elaborate publicity stunt. Later, when I bumped into McGrory in the hotel lobby, he did his best to be polite, but I got the impression he shared Fletcher's view. (McGrory has since told me this wasn't the case: he simply didn't want to be with the military. As the American humorist and occasional war correspondent P. J. O'Rourke said, 'One of the few benefits of being a journalist is that you're not in the Army. The whole idea of putting you in the Army and not giving you a gun – gee, no thanks.' O'Rourke compared embeds to the 'dumber kind' of conscientious objectors in Vietnam.)

With nothing to write and nothing to do, I decided to pretend I was in Los Angeles. So I made an afternoon appointment with the Marriott's penthouse-level health spa and fitness centre. Then I went shopping.

If this was war, I could live with it.

My 8,300-mile journey from Los Angeles to Kuwait, via London, hadn't gone smoothly. It all went wrong when I visited *The Times's* office in London to pick up my satellite phone, first-aid kit, flak jacket and helmet. The problem was luggage space. I had openly flouted the Pentagon's rules and packed twenty pairs of Calvin Klein boxer shorts, in the hope that my stint in Iraq would last less than a fortnight. I had also packed my electric toothbrush, a badger-hair shaving brush, shaving foam, several rolls of double-quilted toilet roll, and dozens of tubes of factor-40 sunblock and other essential ointments, along with a selection of fashionable yet outdoorsy combat outfits. 'Have the Marines ever met a metrosexual?' Alana had asked me at one point, holding up a tube of $15 Clinique oil-free moisturizer. I gave a humourless grunt, inaudible from deep within the black cavern of the rucksack, where I was trying to re-create my West Hollywood bath-room cabinet. I tried to dismiss the nagging thought that my girlfriend was probably better suited to life on the front lines than me.

Eventually I managed to close the drawstrings at the top of the backpack, but only after I'd transferred my bright-yellow Two-Man Xtreme 19 Mountain Adventure Pod to a separate bag. Weight was also, admittedly, a problem. I couldn't actually *lift* my rucksack, but I could drag it across the floor – as well as my tent bag, laptop case and A4-sized waterproof travel wallet – for a few agonizing seconds at a time, using a bent, shuffling movement. The thought briefly entered my head that I might actually have to *march* with all this stuff, but I quickly dismissed it: surely no one marches in modern warfare. I imagined leaving my gear at a desert Marine base and taking short, safe trips to the front lines in an Apache attack helicopter.

By the time I got to London, I knew I'd made a catastrophic packing error. I didn't realize I would have to carry *another* bag for my flak jacket and helmet – unless, of course, I wanted to wear them on the plane. To make matters worse, the flak jacket, being made from bullet-proof Kevlar, was slightly heavier than a Ford Focus. Body armour, it seemed, hadn't changed that much since the Gilbertese Islanders in the South Pacific used to clad themselves with protective vests made from coconut hulls. The Kevlar helmet wasn't much lighter – it also didn't fit me properly, sitting awkwardly above my receding hairline, creating a deep, red, circular imprint on the rim of my skull. When I took it off, I looked like the victim of a failed lobotomy. The first-aid kit, meanwhile, was a miniature hospital ward in its own right. It even came with a dozen horse-sized, self-injectable canisters of nerve-gas antidote.

Before I left the office to get my injections, one of the foreign desk's office assistants shoved a thick, cream-coloured envelope into my hand. I opened it, and saw an immaculate bundle of new $100 bills.

'What's *this*?' I asked, taken aback.

'It's $5,000,' said the young, blonde assistant. 'An advance against expenses.'

'What for?'

'Bits and bobs,' she replied with a brief, shrill laugh. 'You know, if you get into any, er, trouble. That kind of thing . . .'

I stared at the envelope. Then it dawned on me: it was ransom money. *The Times* thought I would get *kidnapped*.

'Is this for kidn—' I began to ask, but she was gone.

I put the envelope in my back pocket.

My luggage-related problems worsened when I emerged from the News International medical centre after my vaccinations. My right arm had a circular pattern of bleeding puncture marks in it, and felt as thought it had just been pumped full of every Third World disease known to man – which, in a way, it had been. I could barely carry my passport, never mind 300 lb of combat equipment. Somehow I managed to get my gear into the back of a taxi, which drove me to the Kuwait embassy to collect my visa. As the cab grunted down Kensington High Street, I spotted a shop called The London Luggage Company. I suddenly had a brilliant idea. 'Pull up here for a second,' I told the driver, and jumped out. I re-emerged a few minutes later carrying a Chinese-made metal dolly, featuring a folding frame, an elastic strap, and four rickety castors. It was perfect for my luggage. I just hoped it was combat-proof.

Before dawn the next morning – 4 March – I took a taxi from my hotel to Heathrow Airport, picking up Glen at his flat in Notting Hill on the way. Glen, who also had to report for duty at the Hilton Kuwait Resort, sauntered out of his front door carrying two compact, light-weight bags. He was wearing blue jeans, an open-collared shirt and a cream linen jacket. With his oak tan, angular features and Hugh Grant hair (still intact, six years after City University), he looked like the classic intrepid English foreign correspondent. I wondered if I had gone too far by following the Pentagon's list to the letter. Perhaps, I thought, I should have made more of an effort to look cool. In the airport, we watched CNN footage of an Iraqi bulldozer crushing three more al-Samoud missiles, bringing the total number destroyed to nineteen. The UN, the television shouted, had asked for 100 missiles to be put out of action. 'Despite whatever limited head-fakes Iraq has engaged in, they continue to fundamentally not disarm,' I heard a White House spokesman comment. I wondered if Saddam had already fled.

I spent the first part of the Kuwait Airways flight staring at the electronic map on the miniature television screen in front of me. It showed our flight path to the Persian Gulf, which involved taking a huge detour around Iraq, which was still being patrolled by American and British fighter jets enforcing the 'no-fly' zone. I wondered if there was a chance of being shot down by a stray missile. I tried to ignore my stomach, which was doing a good impression of a tumble-drier filled with acid. Then the in-flight meal arrived: it was curry, served with peanuts.

Glen and I finished our meals in silence. Neither of us could quite grasp the consequences of what we were doing.

'Brought anything good to read?' asked Glen eventually.

'Oh, lots,' I said, reaching for my hand luggage. 'I've stuck to the war theme, to put me in the right frame of mind. I have *The Quiet American*; Norman Schwarzkopf's autobiography; *Bravo Two Zero*; and *Endgame*, written by that former chief UN weapons inspector bloke. Oh, and I've also got the Lonely Planet guide to the Middle East. There's no Rough Guide to Iraq, apparently.'

'Christ,' said Glen. 'I brought P. G. Wodehouse. I thought Jeeves might keep my spirits up when the war starts.'

'*Jeeves?*' I asked.

'It's good for the soul,' replied Glen, testily.

I reconsidered my reading list. Perhaps it was a bit on the heavy side. Graham Greene's *The Quiet American* was depressing the hell out of me. It was, after all, about a war-weary, opium-addicted and borderline-suicidal *Times* correspondent in Indo-China, who keeps putting himself in mortal danger only to get just a single paragraph, if that, printed in the paper. I had reached the part where the hero's girlfriend (his marriage had failed) leaves him for a rich American.

Unable to face another miserable chapter, I pulled out my copy of the Lonely Planet guide and thumbed my way to the eighteen-page section on Kuwait. I started reading a paragraph entitled 'Dangers & Annoyances'.

I stopped after coming across a phrase I didn't understand.

'What's "wadi-bashing"?' I asked.

'Off-roading,' said Glen. 'You're going to be bashing a lot of wadis with the Marines, I imagine. Why do you ask?'

I winced, then read the paragraph out loud: '*Because of the difficulty in detecting landmines, wadi-bashing is a very dangerous sport in Kuwait and you ought to think long and hard before indulging . . . People who keep track of these things emphasize that stuff still blows up every month . . .*'

Glen laughed, then shrugged.

I remembered the SAS class on landmine injuries: most of it had involved learning how to perform battlefield amputations. That was when I nearly passed out trying to secure a tourniquet on my own leg.

Suddenly I became aware of something behind me. I turned to see a fellow passenger looking over my shoulder. He was in his thirties, with a Midwestern belly and a sleeping mask pulled up over his forehead, giving him an unflattering quiff of thick, dirty brown hair. He was blinking wearily.

'Are you guys embedded?' he asked, through a yawn that smelled of curry.

'Yeah,' we said in unison.

'Me too,' he replied. 'Jake Hansen, cameraman, ABC News.' He offered a sweaty hand over the back of the seat. Glen and I took it in turns to shake it. Neither of us were really in the mood to socialize.

'Hey guys,' said Jake, excitedly. 'Have you seen this?' he passed over what looked like a mascara pen with its lid on.

'What is it?' I asked, studying it. Then I gave it to Glen.

'It's a lipstick cam,' said Jake, proudly. 'Look: *it's tiny.*' He snatched it from Glen, then held it up to his forehead, over his blindfold. 'We stick it to the top of a Marine's helmet, like this, and watch 'em shoot,' he said. '*How cool is that?* The folks at home get a front-row seat on the front lines!'

It was, indeed, an incredible piece of technology.

'Are you sure the Marines are going to let you do that?' I asked. 'And how d'you know you'll be going to the front?'

'Are you kidding?' said Jake. He whipped a sheet of paper from his laptop case. 'Did you read this?' he asked, showing me the title. It said, 'Public Affairs Guidance on Embedding Media during Possible Future Operations'. I shook my head. With a chewed fingernail, Jake pointed to an underlined section. Then he read, '*Commanders will ensure the media are provided with every opportunity to observe actual combat operations. The personal safety of correspondents is not a reason to exclude them from combat areas.*' He paused for dramatic effect. Then he smiled.

'It's going to be *hardcore*,' he said.

We climbed off the plane in a daze, and got stuck immediately in an immigration queue. The airport officials looked deeply unhappy about the white people swaggering into their country – Kuwait, after all, doesn't issue tourist visas, and only 37 per cent of its population are actual citizens. The rest, mostly from the Indian subcontinent and Asia, are there on work visas. Kuwait used to be home to thousands of Palestinians, but they sided with the Iraqis in 1990, and wisely decided to consult their travel agents after the war. After an hour, and a brief interrogation, we were allowed into the country. It didn't take long for my rucksack and flak jacket to appear on the baggage carousel – the Kuwait Airways jet had been almost empty, after all. My metal dolly was awkward to assemble, but worked none the less. I was delighted it had survived the journey so far. As we left the wing-shaped terminal, I noticed scores of Kuwaiti families heading in the other direction. It seemed like the sensible thing to do. We stopped briefly to get ripped off at an airport bureau de change. Then we made our way to the taxi rank.

Ten minutes later we were approaching the city at 95 m.p.h. on a California-style desert highway, complete with floodlit billboards displaying Western brand names and Arabic slogans. The taxi driver's overtaking technique was to almost nudge the bumper of the car in front, while leaning on the horn, flicking his headlights on to full beam, and swerving out towards the central reservation. As he did this, a riot of Middle Eastern percussion and a crazy, strangled wind instrument blared out of the AM radio. I cracked open my window and felt the dragon's breath of the desert on my face. Then I saw it: the country's most famous landmark, the Kuwait Towers, poking out of the horizon. The towers are three enormous, upturned spikes, two of which bulge in the middle as though liquid has been injected into them and got stuck halfway. They were designed by a Swedish architectural firm in the late 1970s, but could easily have come from the brush of Salvador Dali. The bulges, the cab driver told us in mangled English, hold the city's 4.5-million-gallon supply of drinking water.

All I could think about, however, was the Iraqis crashing over the border in 1990 and claiming this alien world as their own – before looting the place and trashing it when they couldn't get their way. Saddam's forces set more than 600 oil wells ablaze as they retreated, an environmental catastophe that took nine months to contain. The scale of his ambition was astonishing.

I wondered if Saddam would lob a few Scuds at the Kuwait Towers when the coalition forces invaded. I imaged 4.5 million gallons of purified drinking water drowning the city.

'This is *mental*,' I said to Glen.

He grinned, and nodded in agreement. We were both thinking the same thing: that, in spite of the fear, the bowel pain and the crap pay, there is sometimes no better job on earth than being a foreign correspondent. There I was, with $5,000 in cash, a satellite phone and a dozen canisters of nerve-gas antidote in my bag, speeding into a deserted foreign city on the brink of Armageddon. At that giddy, fleeting moment, I told myself that it was worth it. And that if I died as a result of this stupid, ill-thought-out embedding scheme, at least I had *lived* in my twenty-seven years.

The feeling didn't last.

When we reached the hotel, there was good news: a notice on a whiteboard in the lobby informed us that our initiation as embeds had been delayed indefinitely, and we no longer had to report for duty at 7 a.m. the next morning. Perhaps, I thought, President Bush was losing his nerve. Perhaps, without Turkey on side, an invasion would be impossible. Or maybe it was just the weather: time was pressing on, and the spring storm season was approaching, as was the summer heat.

That night, Glen and I had dinner at the Marriott's Terrace Grill. A local family was throwing a birthday party, and a karaoke system had been set up at the back of the dining room. We sat at a dazzling white tablecloth and nibbled on celery and raw carrots as a teenage girl in a black cloak and hijab headscarf performed an atonal rendition of a Kylie Minogue song. Eventually a Pakistani waiter appeared, and we both ordered beers. It felt appropriate to celebrate. The waiter returned a few minutes later with a silver tray, on top of which were two bottles of Budweiser, dripping with icy condensation. He poured them carefully into the crystal glasses on our table. 'Cheers,' I said, raising my drink, before taking a long, thirsty gulp. I grimaced. Something was wrong. I looked at the bottle. 'The beer's off,' I declared.

'No it's not,' said Glen, from behind his enormous menu. 'It's non-alcoholic. Beer's illegal in Kuwait. Thought you knew.'

'What?' I spat, looking at the bottle with disgust. I felt like a child at a fairground who'd just dropped his stick of candyfloss.

'Don't worry,' said Glen. 'This stuff still gives you a hangover. So at least you can feel like Hemingway in the morning.'

It was only when I saw the Marriott in daylight, after my epic two-course breakfast in Café Royal, that I realized Kuwait was preparing seriously for war. The building was protected by a wall of brown sand-bags and concrete, as well as a platoon of Kuwaiti soldiers, who had installed an airport-style X-ray machine in front of the revolving door. They smiled sarcastically – the way teenagers with semi-automatic weapons do – as I walked past. My plan was to visit two of Kuwait's American-style shopping centres: the Marina Mall and Souq Sharq, on the Kuwaiti seafront. I would head back to the hotel for a swim and a massage that afternoon.

'Taxi?' asked the middle-aged Pakistani bellboy.

It was windy, and I could barely see the other side of the street through a stinging cloud of dust blown in from the desert.

I gave a bilingual nod. Moments later, a white Ford Taurus – straight out of the American suburbs – crept up beside me. The driver, a distinguished-looking Kuwaiti with a heavy moustache and two-tone hair, grinned and nodded at me through the passenger window. I found it a bit unnerving.

'Hussein will look after you,' said the bellboy, with a sing-song accent.

'*Hussein?*' I said, sliding warily on to the worn leather of the back seat. I feared this was some kind of awful practical joke. The door clonked shut behind me, and the Taurus began to inch forward on its big, wobbly American suspension. Hussein, I noticed, was staring at me in his rearview mirror. I wanted to beg him not to kidnap me. I wondered if the bellboy was in on the plot. I patted my pockets for the $5,000 envelope, before remembering I'd left it at the hotel.

'Hi,' I ventured. 'I'm a journalist. I'm a journalist for the London *Times*, a British newspaper. *I'm here to cover the war.*'

The taxi driver grinned and nodded. We edged out of the hotel valet-parking area and on to the busy two-lane highway. Every other vehicle was a US military Humvee, with a machine-gunner poking out of the roof. I could feel the slow drumbeat of a headache inside my frontal lobe. Glen was right: the bloody non-alcoholic beer had given me a hangover. And quite a nasty one, too.

'*Sahaffi?*' asked Hussein.

I had no idea what he meant.

'Yeah, very happy,' I said, hoping that would be the end of it.

'*La tapar, ana sahaffi!*' he continued, and started to laugh riotously. I wished I'd learned some Arabic before leaving Los Angeles. (I later discovered that *sahaffi* means 'journalist'; *La tapar, ana sahaffi* means 'Don't shoot, I'm a journalist.' It's extremely ill-advised to travel without learning such basic phrases.)

'My name's Chris,' I said, slightly irritably, in an effort to steer the conversation back into English. 'Nice to meet you.'

The driver turned to look me in the eye. Then he grinned and produced a business card from under his armrest. At the top was a blue logo in English, which said 'Al Kuds Taxi Service, 24-hours'. Underneath was confirmation that the bellboy hadn't been joking. 'Salman Hussein – Chauffeur,' it said.


As I looked out of the taxi's window, Kuwait's lottery-style oil wealth was obvious: the skyscrapers, hotels and mini-malls all looked as though they'd been FedExed overnight from Texas, then dumped in the sand. It was also clear from the patchy infrastructure: it seemed as though the Kuwaitis hadn't had time to join up the hastily constructed buildings. Pavements stopped and started at random, making way for the occasional open sewer. A lunchtime stroll would probably get quite unpleasant without a pair of galoshes. The city's dilapidated souks, meanwhile, looked older than the Old Testament, but were stacked full of the latest in Silicon Valley gadgetry, from Xboxes to 42-inch plasma screens. In spite of the wealth, however, the scars of the Iraqi invasion were still visible: every so often the Taurus cruised past the blackened foundations of an office building, mottled with bullet holes and tank craters.

Hussein dropped me off at the Marina Mall first. He asked for 15 dinars, which seemed reasonable, so I paid him 20, largely out of relief at having arrived safely. Once inside, I experienced profound culture shock as I watched a young Kuwaiti woman lift up her veil so she could take a bite out of a quarter-pounder Big Mac. At the Virgin Megastore there was a gigantic banner that said, '*If it's not banned, we've got it!*' I wondered if the Kuwaiti authorities had read Sir Richard

Branson's autobiography – which contains anecdotes about the Virgin founder's wife-swapping and the Rolling Stones' Keith Richards running naked from his studio at gunpoint – before giving the Megastore a licence. I doubted it.

The English-speaking Kuwaitis I talked to were convinced that, because I was a *sahaffi*, I knew exactly when the invasion would start. They became visibly irritated when I told them I knew nothing. They hated Saddam Hussein, they said, but the war was bad for business, so they wished the Americans would hurry up and get it over with. I was taken aback by their pragmatism.

Bored, I bought a CD from the Arabic section of the Virgin Megastore and called Hussein to ask him to pick me up. Souq Sharq, however, turned out to be much the same, only with more fast-food outlets. Hussein's fare, meanwhile, seemed to increase every time I opened the back door. It cost 25 dinars to get to Souq Sharq, even though the journey seemed shorter than the last one.

By the time I got back to hotel – in time for the daily 'turn-down' service and the chocolate truffles left on my pillow – I had laid waste to a 50-dinar note. Before ducking through the X-ray machine at the revolving door, I asked the bellboy if he knew the dinar–dollar exchange rate. 'I believe the dinar is worth about $3.30, sir,' he said, with a deferential smile and a slight bow. That meant I had spent about $170 on cab fares. *Shit!* Once again I dreaded the expenses claim I would have to send to Fletcher. Either taxi fares were extraordinarily high in Kuwait (unlikely, given that a gallon of petrol cost about 77 cents) or I had been given the full tourist work-over by Salman Hussein. The bellboy noticed my look of anguish. 'Is everything OK, sir? Did Hussein look after you?' he asked. I gave a desultory nod, and headed inside. Back in my room, I found the entry on taxis in the Lonely Planet guide. 'Kuwaiti taxis have no meters,' it said. 'Negotiate a fare at the beginning of the trip.'

Days passed. Hussein got richer. I became a regular at the Marriott's penthouse health spa. I put on weight. On the roof of the hotel, television news networks set up cameras to watch for incoming Scuds. The desert haunted me. At night, storms decorated my hotel-room window with sand. One some mornings the only view from my room was an eerie orange glow, the sand having rendered the sun useless. I wondered how the Marines could fight a war in such conditions. I became a veteran of the alcohol-free hangover. I kept the television tuned to MTV. The headlines, however, were unavoidable: '*Saddam destroys another two al-Samoud missiles; UN soldiers guarding the 200-mile-long "demilitarized zone" between Kuwait and Iraq complain that American Marines keep cutting holes in their fence; the Pope calls on Catholics to commemorate Ash Wednesday by fasting and praying for peace; Colin Powell accuses Saddam of ordering the production of more al-Samouds; and, in Washington, Iraqi exiles say Western anti-war protesters are "ignorant and misinformed".*'

Finally, almost a week after arriving in Kuwait, the notice I had been dreading appeared in the lobby: 'All embeds must report for duty at the Hilton Kuwait Resort at 7 a.m. on Tuesday, March 11.' On Monday, Glen and I moved to another hotel, the Golden Tulip at Messilah Beach, because our reservations at the Marriott had expired and the hotel was full. The hoteliers of Kuwait would all probably retire after the invasion, I thought. My five-night room bill at the Marriott had come to nearly $2,500. The Golden Tulip was to the west of the city, with gardens that sloped down to the shores of the Persian Gulf. The hotel was still undergoing reconstruction after the Iraqis had razed it in 1990. It even had an information board, positioned in front of a half-demolished wall next to the swimming pool, showing what the place had looked like immediately after the war. 'The Iraqis did this,' it said. The hotel's tennis court, however, had survived – albeit with a few bullet holes in the tarmac surface. And so, on our last day of freedom, Glen and I thwacked out a couple of amateur sets to the soundtrack of a call to prayer which echoed out of speakers bolted to the telegraph poles.

I needed all the prayer I could get.

'It happens,' said the burly female Army instructor, with a sigh. 'If you're in the suit a long time, you're going to do it. *No question.*' She used a thick, manly palm to wipe the sweat from her forehead, and made a tough-luck face. I could see saddlebags of sweat under the armpits of her T-shirt. I squirmed on my folding plastic chair, pulled my brown Nike baseball cap lower over my face, and glanced around at my fellow media embeds. We were all wearing the same expression: that of children playing a fun but forbidden game – a game that could get us all killed.

It was hot out on the tennis court of the Hilton Kuwait Resort – hotter than California; probably hotter than Venus on a hot day. In fact the Hilton looked as though it belonged on another planet. Whoever had built the place, with its 134 rooms, 4 presidential suits, 80 beachside chalets and 62 private apartments, was a big fan of 1950s space-age modernism. The building was long and flat, and constructed almost entirely out of concrete rectangles and blue-tinted glass. Its size was inhuman; the hotel was more than 90 per cent full, but it felt deserted.

We had been led out on to the clay court to learn how to use our gas masks and chemical suits – a relief, given that I'd missed the 'NBC' course in London. The instructor's claim – that 'It happens' – was in response to a query from an ageing Canadian with a foie-gras belly and a beard that sprouted like white moss over both his chins. 'Excuse the question, ma'am,' he'd rasped. 'But what happens if we shit in our chemical suits during an attack?' It was clearly a question that the instructor – barely out of her twenties, with a wide, oval face and a boyish bowl of black hair – had thought about at length. 'It will degrade your suit's ability to perform, sir,' she said. 'It's water-resistant, but not water*proof*. You shouldn't urinate inside it, but you're going to be sweating so much you won't have to. As for *defecation* . . . Well, sir, you never know how your body's gonna react to being slimed.'

The phrase 'being slimed' made me think of *Ghostbusters*, the film in which Dr Peter Venkman, played by Bill Murray, gets gunked by a ghost called Slimer. I had to hand it to the military's euphemism department: it made the thought of being gassed a lot easier to stomach. It certainly beat Wilfred Owen's description of a gas-attack victim in 'Dulce et Decorum Est': 'yelling out and stumbling, / And flound'ring like a man in fire or lime . . . / . . . the white eyes writhing in his face'.

The day – 11 March – had started at 6.30 a.m., when Glen and I left the Golden Tulip in Hussein's taxi. Glen initially refused to get in the car, claiming that Hussein had ripped him off consistently ever since he'd arrived in Kuwait. Eventually, however, a fare was negotiated, the Taurus was loaded with our luggage, and we headed to the Hilton. The traffic outside the hotel was so bad that we decided to get out and walk the last few yards: it seemed like a good idea, until the wheels of my metal dolly got stuck in a patch of gravel, bending the frame. It survived, however, making it beyond the sandbags and concrete anti-tank barriers to the military checkpoint, where a Kuwaiti soldier went through every item in my rucksack. 'Is this *yours*?' he asked, holding up my electric toothbrush. Behind me, I heard sniggering.

Glen and I had to report to different sections of the hotel, so we parted in the lobby with an unsentimental 'See you later.' A handshake would have been too weird. I wondered if I would ever see Glen again.

The Hilton felt unreal: a vision caused by dehydration and too many days in the desert. Completed in 2002, it was a $100-million shrine to the oil economy, sitting in 61 acres of grounds, on a mile-long private beach front – one of the longest on the Arabian Peninsula. On a clear day, with a pair of binoculars, you could see Iran over the molten Gulf. Today, however, there was a sand storm blowing, and sunbathing would have been as much fun as a bath with a metal sponge. Not, of course, that anyone wanted to fry themselves on the sun deck anyway. This was primarily a place of business. And now it was also a place of war, where the Coalition Press Center had taken over an entire floor of one wing, and where Halliburton con-tractors were already working on their GDP-sized room bills. They were there, like the embeds, for a transaction of a different kind: the hostile takeover of the Republic of Iraq.

At the hotel, I hurried up and waited. I didn't receive my official 'embedded media' press pass – featuring a scowling passport photo-graph of me taken at a souk opposite the Marriott – until late morning. In the press centre, embeds mingled awkwardly, like fresh-ers on the first day of university. While I waited, I ordered breakfast at Teatro, one of the Hilton's several restaurants, and smoked about a hundred cigarettes. I sat with Mike Wilson, a nervous, bespectacled reporter of my age, who worked for the *New York Times*. He had already been assigned to an artillery unit; it sounded less hellish than the infantry, but not much. The truth was that I had no real idea what either would entail. I was never one of those teenage boys who played war games on computers, or who read books about Napoleonic campaigns. 'This war's making me fat,' complained Mike, as he edged a half-pound Angus burger into his mouth. 'When I get back to the newsroom, they're gonna think I went to the Mid-East to fight a frickin' chocolate pudding.' Teatro's clientele was an even stranger mix than the Marriott's: Marines in desert fatigues and hip-mounted gas masks sat next to Arab couples with young children. I couldn't work out if the Arabs were there for business or pleasure. If it was the latter, they didn't seem to be having much fun.

At about 2 p.m. we were ushered into a conference room with a digital video projector and big leather chairs, designed for overweight oil executives. I quickly learned that I shouldn't have worried about buying the technical-sounding items on the Pentagon's list: the Marines would provide us with a MOPP suit, which was essentially a Marine uniform with a chemical-proof lining, a gas mask (the mysteriously titled 'M-40 Series Field Protective Mask w/Filter'), and a bag of other equipment, including chemical boots, gloves and a decontamination kit. 'We're assuming that every incoming Scud is biological or chemical,' said the Marine public-affairs officer, to a silent room. I shivered in the sub-zero air conditioning. 'The *good* news is that we don't think Saddam has nukes.' After being reminded of the 'ground rules' – in short, that everything was 'on the record', apart from precise information about the location of troops – we were shown outside to a row of tables where cheerful Marines were handing out our standard-issue equipment. It meant carrying yet more luggage.

By the time I reached the end of the last table, I was clutching a heavy-duty plastic bag containing a MOPP suit, a gas mask, a decontamination kit, a chemical-resistant water canteen, rubber boots, gloves, and two medical packs which included twenty-one tablets of the nerve-agent antidote pyridostigmine bromide and three 'auto-injectors' – one each of atropine, pralidoxime chloride and diazepam (the 'happy-death' juice). The labels said they should be 'administered by a buddy to soldiers incapacitated by nerve agent poisoning'. Along with the canisters *The Times* had given me, I now had enough liquid narcotics to fuel a Glaswegian rave. If I survived the war, I could probably sell the lot in Brixton and retire on the proceeds. I attempted to lighten my bags by wearing my gas-mask holster and chemical-proof canteen, which came with a green nylon belt. Without my trusty dolly, however, I would have been in trouble. I prayed for it to survive the war. I also prayed I would be travelling in a vehicle, not on foot.

In the queue for the NBC equipment, I stood next to a blonde female photographer whom I recognised as being a part-time paparazzo from the Hollywood party circuit. She was casually eating a chocolate croissant, licking her fingers after each bite, as she threw the items into her plastic bag. 'Isn't this *fun*,' she giggled, with a flirty smile. I began to wonder if I were going insane.

A few minutes later I was standing on the tennis court in 100-degree heat wearing a gas mask, a chemical suit, a hood, wellies and gloves. I felt like some kind of cyborg from the twenty-fifth century – a reportinator, perhaps. The wellies were so big they could be pulled over my hiking boots. Inside the mask, the only thing I could hear was my own breath – it came in shallow, panicked gulps – and the muffled shouting of the Army instructor. My baseball cap was lying on the floor, and the sun was frying the top of my skull in its own oil. I tried to concentrate on not passing out.

The instructor, Lieutenant Tiffany Powers, was the kind of girl you wouldn't bet against in a bar fight. She had a rugby player's complexion, and knuckles the size of beer-bottle tops. Her face was set in an expression that dared you to shock her. It was a dare that countless soldiers had probably failed.

Earlier, Powers had shown us how to use our gas-mask holster like a Wild West gun sling. She whipped the mask out, pressed it to her face, exhaled, then breathed in with her hand slapped over the filter, creating a seal. All this happened within nine seconds. Then she took off the mask and said, 'Let's see who has the fastest draw in the Mid-East.' There was a pause. Then she shouted, 'GAS! GAS! GAS!' After a full minute of inept fumbling, I looked around to make sure everyone else was doing as badly as me. They weren't. In fact everyone, including the Canadian, was fully masked up. I felt as though I were back in the Cub Scouts, failing my reef-knot class. With my fellow embeds watching, I eventually got the rubber straps of my mask over my head. Then I snapped them into place and yanked them tight. Something, however, had gone horribly wrong, and the straps acted like a catapult, flinging the mask on to the floor. Powers doubled-up, her muscular forearms covering her face. For a moment I thought she was pretending to be a mustard-gas victim. Then I realized she was laughing. She was laughing so violently, in fact, that she almost lost her lunch.

'This guy', she said, red-faced and pointing at me, 'is one *very* dead media representative. But well done to the rest of you.'

I made a second attempt to don the gas mask, with more success. My stubble, however, seemed to interfere with the seal. It was then I remembered reading somewhere that embeds had to remain clean-shaven. It made sense now. I was glad I'd brought my Mach 3 razors and badger-hair shaving brush.

By now I felt as though I'd lost 10 lb in body weight through sweating alone. Inside my mask, I could feel beads of salt water drip on to my nose. I instinctively lifted a gloved hand to scratch it. The mask, of course, made it impossible. I felt dizzy. I needed a drink of water. *Badly*. I started to panic.

'Now we're going to learn how to rehydrate in a chemical environment,' said Powers. She lifted up an NBC-proof water canteen, pulled out a plastic drinking tube, and fitted it to a sealed attachment on her gas mask. It looked easy enough. In practice, however, I found it impossible to handle the canteen with my gloves, and I couldn't find the sealed attachment on my mask. I ended up pulling off the mask in frustration, unscrewing the canteen, and taking a swig.

I gave Powers a defiant look.

'Tut, tut,' she said, waving a thick finger. 'Dead again.'

After what seemed like hours, we were allowed to take off our suffocating MOPP suits. As I looked at my pale skin, trembling under my drenched T-shirt, I wondered how long I would survive once the invasion started.

The tutorial resumed.

'MOPP stands for Mission-Oriented Protective Posture,' shouted Powers. 'There are *four* MOPP levels. One, just the suit. Two, the suit and boots. Three, the suit, boots and the gas mask. And four, the whole miserable ensemble, including the rubber gloves and the hood. Your suit has an activated-charcoal lining and is good for forty-five days and six washes. Does everyone understand that?'

She looked at me, while the group gave a collective grunt. I felt blood rush to my face, which was red anyway from the heat.

'*Good*,' said Powers. 'When we cross the line of departure we'll be at MOPP level two. If the Iraqis decide to attack Kuwait, the MOPP level will be higher. If we get slimed by Mr Hussein, it'll go up to four. Once contaminated, your suit is good for only twenty-four hours. After that, the suits will be bagged up and buried. As soon as we detect an attack, we'll relieve your unit from duty.'

I imagined spending twenty-four hours in a soiled MOPP suit, in 100-degree heat, with only one canteen of drinking water. And I wondered how much of the gas-mask routine was simply for psychological reassurance. Still, I liked the sound of the 'line of departure' – presumably the Kuwait–Iraq border – because it sounded like a sporting term: something, perhaps, from an American football game. Combat jargon, it seemed, was already having a sedative effect on me.

Powers continued, 'Inside your gas-mask carrier you'll find a decontamination kit, which includes these charcoal towelettes.' She held up what looked like a clump of dirty baby wipes. 'If your skin is exposed to a chemical agent,' she said, 'you can use the towelettes to remove the contaminant. Remember, pat the charcoal on to your skin, do *not* rub it in. Also, remember you have a selection of nerve-gas antidotes in your auto-injectors: if you have been incapacitated, a buddy will inject you. Simply push the canister into a meaty part of the thigh or the buttock and wait for the needle to pop right out. I'm not going to demonstrate, because the last time I did it the goddam needle activated and I ended up being medevaced.' I winced at the thought of one of Powers's thighs being penetrated by an atropine injector. 'After you've used the towelettes and auto-injectors,' she went on, 'we should be able to get an operational decon. unit out to you, which will remove any other liquid contamination and hose you down with water until you're stripped to your mask and gloves. That's when we'll assess battlefield casualties, both ambulatory and non-ambulatory.'

She gave me an accusatory look.

'After today's performance,' she said, '*this* gentleman would definitely fall into the category of *non*-ambulatory. Questions?'

The tennis court fell silent. I felt woozy in the sun. Wind tousled the palm trees. Then the blonde photographer put up her hand.

'If we're attacked, will we be able to *see* the chemical agent?' she asked.

Powers pursed her lips. 'If there are large puddles of nerve agent around you,' she said, 'that means the fucking thing went off right next to you, and you're probably not going to be alive anyway.'

The photographer nodded studiously.

'So I wouldn't worry about it,' said Powers. 'Next.'

Now it was the Canadian's turn. I braced for another scatological inquiry.

'How do we know if there's *been* a chemical attack?' he asked.

'Well,' said Powers, 'one way to know is if someone yells, "GAS! GAS! GAS!" Another is if someone shouts, "LIGHTNING!", which means a Scud attack, or "SNOWSTORM!", which means indirect fire. We'll assume ALL these attacks are chemical in nature. There's also an NBC klaxon, and there's a visual signal, which is the touching of shoulders. Either that, or you'll just start dancing the funky chicken. That's when you *definitely* know you've been hit.'

Powers did a horrible, jerky dance to make her point.

'Is there anything else we should know?' asked the photographer.

'Well, if it's very windy, like it is today, that works in our favour,' she said. 'The nerve agent will just blow away. If it's cold, on the other hand, a blister agent will last longer, so that works against us . . .'

I raised my hand, feeling like a disgraced schoolboy.

'Yes?' snapped Powers.

'What's the weather been likely lately?' I asked.

'Pretty cold,' she replied.

Back inside the soothing chill of the press centre, there was a commotion near one of the whiteboards. I saw Mike from the *New York Times* standing nearby. 'What's going on?' I asked. He pointed to the jostling embeds. 'They've assigned everyone's places,' he said. 'You should go and take a look.' After the ordeal of the chemical tutorial,

I was expecting the worst. I pushed my way to the front of the crowd and scanned the noticeboard for my name. I soon found it.

This is what it said:

*2nd Battalion/11th Marines – Artillery*
London Times, Int'l Newspaper: Ayres, Christopher R.
Boston Globe, US Newspaper: Nelson, Scott
BBC, Int'l TV: Willis, David R.
BBC, Int'l TV: Hiney, Mark A.
BBC, Int'l TV: Beale, Mark

I was relieved: I wasn't with the infantry. I was also glad to be with some fellow Brits, from the BBC. Underneath the whiteboard was a note telling '2/11 embeds' to report to the outdoor terrace of the Blue Elephant, a Thai-food restaurant in the Hilton with an extensive 'mocktail' menu. My contact there was Captain Jim Hotspur, the public-affairs officer who had given the 2 p.m. lecture.

I was the first to arrive. The captain, who was at least 6 foot 2, with a flushed tan and high-laced desert boots, was waiting.

We nodded hello.

'Do you wear eyeglasses?' he asked, unexpectedly.

'Contacts,' I said.

'That's a negative,' said Hotspur, shaking his head and aiming his eyes at me. 'We strongly recommend against the use of contacts. They're impossible to keep clean out in the field. Wear your eyeglasses.'

'OK,' I said. I felt like a recalcitrant private at a court martial.

'Did you order prescription-lens inserts for your gas mask?' asked Hotspur.

*Shit.* I shook my head slowly, fearing the consequences.

Hotspur gave an exasperated snort.

'You'll be blind in your gas mask,' he said, chewing his lower lip with frustration. Then he added, 'But it's better, I suppose, than you gouging your own eyes out when your contacts get slimed.'

I began to suffer another Cub Scout flashback.

'Show me your boots,' said the captain.

I lifted up my right foot, and he examined it. I had scrawled my social-security number on to the sole with a marker pen.

'I can see your social-security number, but where's your blood type?'

'I don't, er, *know* my blood type,' I admitted. It was one of the few things I had forgotten to do before leaving Los Angeles.

Hotspur looked as though he were trying very hard not to pick me up and throw me through the Blue Elephant's screen doors.

'Let's hope you don't get injured, then,' he said, slapping me on the back.

Then he said, 'Let me see your passport.'

I produced it. I didn't expect this to go well either.

Hotspur was shaking his sunburnt head again. I was starting to get worried about the loaded 9-mm pistol strapped to his chest.

'Your visa's only valid for thirty days,' he pointed out. 'That might not be long enough.' He slipped the passport into his trouser pocket and said, 'I'll keep hold of it. We'll apply for a Kuwait residency permit and get your passport back out to you in the field. Should only take a few weeks.'

*A few weeks?* I had hoped to be home in a fortnight.

Hotspur began to stride away on muscular, camouflaged legs.

'Captain,' I called out.

He turned to face me, walking backwards.

'How *dangerous* is this going to be?'

'Don't worry,' he said, with a straight face. 'People think artillery is boring. But we kill more people than anyone else.'

It was done. There was no way out. Even my passport was gone. I hauled my dolly, with its heavy load of war-reporting equipment, to the east side of the vast, deserted Hilton car park, where an unmarked white bus was waiting. It would drive us north, to the other Kuwait: the land of unexploded landmines, tank trenches and camel-herding Bedouin, where 150,000 troops from a foreign superpower were living in camps named after New York, New Jersey, Pennsylvania and Virginia. Soon I would also live in one of those camps. Soon I would become a Marine.

It was only when I stopped and turned that I saw it: a desert mirage, to the far right of the hotel, partly hidden by a row of dancing palms. It was unmistakable – the crowned siren, her long hair falling over naked breasts. She was peering seductively out of a dark green circle decorated with two stars and white lettering. It made me think of happier times: of safe, sunny mornings sitting on Sunset Boulevard with the *Los Angeles Times*. I pictured Alana, saying goodbye at the airport. I thought of my parents. I dropped my bags and ran. I could make it to the other side of the car park and back. *The bus wouldn't leave without me.* There was still time before the war began. There was still time for my last Starbucks before Baghdad.

# 12

## 'The Worst Camping Trip of Your Life'

I immediately regretted getting on the bus. I wished the damn Starbucks had swallowed me into a wormhole and spat me out somewhere on a beach in Malibu. I felt as though I'd been suckered: by the Marines; by Fletcher; by the Kuwaitis; even by the other embeds. What the *hell* was I doing here? The reality of the chemical drill on the Hilton tennis court was only just beginning to sink in. The Marines, it seemed, were preparing for the worst. That made me wonder about the real reason for the embedding scheme. President Bush hadn't shown much concern for world opinion so far in his campaign against Iraq, so why was he now lavishing so much money and attention on journalists – especially *foreign* ones? One of the embeds at the gas-mask tutorial had been from Agence France-Presse, for God's sake. As if Bush cared about *him*. After the tutorial, I'd asked Lieutenant Powers for her theory on embedding. 'If Saddam uses chemicals, no one's gonna believe it unless they see it on CNN or read it in the newspapers,' she told me. 'They'll only believe it when it comes from *you* guys.' But how could we tell anyone about it if we were too busy coughing up our lungs?

The bus headed north for about an hour on Kuwait's pristine, four-lane Highway 80, otherwise known as the 'Highway of Death' after the US Air Force bombed the Iraqi convoys fleeing towards Basra in 1991. After passing a billboard near Mutlaa Ridge that said 'God Bless US Troops', the bus swerved off the tarmac and on to a rocky dirt track. Soon we came across a signpost, made from a wooden ammunition crate, which read, 'Camp Matilda: 10 miles'. This, apparently, was where we would spend our first night as honorary Marines. I unleashed an internal tirade at myself: You're doing this because you're too scared to say no; you're going to die for a stupid news story;

you're going to ruin your parents' lives; you're going to ruin Alana's life; you're being used as bait to prove a political point. Another voice, which sounded worryingly like Fletcher's, defended me against myself: *Other* journalists have been to war and survived; it'll be a character-forming experience; the Americans won't let you anywhere near the front lines; the Iraqis will surrender immediately; Saddam's chemical arsenal is all a gigantic bluff; *it'll be something to tell your grandchildren.*

I scoffed at the last line: I had already been told this by several friends.

'How am I going to *have* any grandchildren if I'm *dead*,' I said out loud, lost in thought. Luckily the diesel grunt of the engine drowned it out, and only the Canadian, who was sitting next to me, looked up.

'Did you say something,' he asked, through a warm garlic breeze.

'No,' I growled.

I stared at the luggage rack in front of me. I noticed that one of the embeds had brought with him an Old Glory flag – on a collapsible pole – to stick in the Iraqi mud. So much for us being 'independent observers'. I started to whistle Tom Wait's 'Waltzing Matilda', for lack of anything better to do.

How was I supposed to feel at this point? Glad that Saddam was going to get his come-uppance, and excited by the professional challenge ahead? Or should I have felt moral outrage at the imperial violence about to be visited on Iraq, and proud of my role in exposing the horror of twenty-first-century warfare?

To be honest, I didn't feel any of those things.

All I felt was overwhelming concern about my personal safety. And, of course, a tug of guilt for my selfishness.

To my right, a man was smiling at me. I recognized him as a reporter for National Public Radio. '*Hey*,' he stage whispered. '*Ever get the feeling we're cheerleaders on the team bus?*' He continued smiling.

I nodded, and continued sipping the dregs of my cappuccino.

Eventually we arrived at Camp Matilda, a city of 'hooches' in a hot gravel wasteland. The hooches were yellow Bedouin-style tents put up by Kuwaiti contractors. The name came from a combination of the words 'hut' and '*uchi*' – Japanese for 'interior'. Each hooch was about the size of a tennis court and looked as though it belonged at a circus – a terrible, military circus, where the lions eat the clowns. The embeds – I counted ninety-five, including myself – were led inside one of them and offered an unappetizing selection of what the Marines called 'chow': bruised fruit, boxes of breakfast cereal, stale white bread, and a warm liquid that tasted like 20 gallons of water mixed with 1 spoonful of freeze-dried Nescafé. As feared, the contrast with the Marriott's room service menu was brutal.

We were invited to sit on white plastic chairs. Then came another miserable chemical drill. I got the feeling the Marines were now shouting 'GAS! GAS! GAS!' for kicks. Still, I needed all the practice I could get. After my conversation with Captain Hotspur, I had taken out my contact lenses and was wearing my rectangular, wire-framed Dolce & Gabbana glasses. I couldn't work out a way to take them off, while putting my gas mask on, in anything less than forty-five heart-pounding seconds. I had now been told about half a dozen times that I was 'totally fucked up'.

At some point, Hotspur strode into the room holding a clipboard. He looked at my glasses, squinted, then nodded approvingly. I could see my maroon British passport still poking out of the top of his trouser pocket.

'OK, folks,' he said. 'The NBC training's over. We have an important visitor for you now. You might want to take notes.'

The embeds stopped short in the middle of their MOPP-suit anecdotes. For a brief, giddy second I expected President Bush to jump out from behind a tent pole. Instead, I turned to see an older man in a stiff uniform push through the tent's opening. His grey hair had been shaved into a crewcut of mathematical precision, and there were two silver stars on his lapel. He made his way around the chairs with all the speed and purpose of a man with an invasion to organize.

'Please welcome Major General James N. Mattis, commander of the 1st Marine Division,' said Hotspur.

Mattis was by now standing at ease in front of the sweating reporters. If it wasn't for his 'digital cammies' – the latest style of pixelated camouflage – he would have looked almost grandfatherly. The general didn't so much have bags under his eyes as two heavy, matching black suitcases.

He offered us a busy smile. Then he said, 'If you're crazy enough to be here, ladies and gentlemen, you're welcome.'

*Great*, I thought: even the two-star general thinks we're idiots. I wondered if he knew what the Republican Guard had in store for us over the border. I wondered if he had already estimated media casualties.

'At times,' he continued, 'you will *hate* being with us. You will stink like a billy goat. The comforts of life will all go downhill from here, folks. In short, this will be like the worst camping trip of your life. And, if we cross the line of departure together, you'll be taking the same chances as us.'

I wondered what the general would do if he knew it was the *first* camping trip of my life, never mind the worst.

I took a sip of the vile coffee.

We were being embedded, said the general, to witness the heroism of the Marines, and to prove that America's military could be 'opened up to the scrutiny of the world'. If it wasn't for a war photographer, Mattis told us, there would be no monument to the Marines who raised the flag above the Japanese island of Iwo Jima on 23 February 1945. The scene was captured by Joe Rosenthal, an Associated Press combat photographer; he won a Pulitzer Prize for it.

'Unsung,' the general quoted, 'the noblest deed will die.' He caught my eye. 'And we're going to do a noble deed here.'

I felt an elbow between my ribs.

'Is that Pindar?' whispered the embed sitting next to me, his pen aloft.

'No,' I said, slightly baffled. 'It's Major General Mattis.'

The embed scowled at me.

'I *meant* the Greek poet,' he hissed. 'The noblest deed, etc.'

He raised his eyes to the canvas ceiling, which was billowing in the wind.

'Oh, right,' I said. 'I've no idea.'

The embed gave me a look that said, 'Clearly'.

I looked up to see Hotspur watching me and fingering his gun.

'We have no fight with Muslims,' the general was saying – 'I have Muslims in my own ranks. We have *no problem* with the Iraqi people. There will be an abundance of innocent people on the battlefield. Last time, if we saw a guy with a gun we shot him. Now, moving up into

Mesopotamia will require a lot more discrimination.' He folded his camouflaged arms. 'The whole concept of a clean open desert, with two armies coming together, is completely gone,' he said. 'We'd much rather go *around* a city if we can, even if the main road goes right through it.'

I wondered if this was Mattis's plan or the Secretary of Defense's. I wondered if in a few years' time we would all find out that Mattis privately thought this plan was insane. It certainly sounded insane to me. *A war without taking cities?* Wasn't that like playing Monopoly without buying properties?

'We can move very, very quickly,' said the general. 'These boys were brought up in southern California. They're fast on the freeways.'

A couple of embeds laughed. I wondered how much death I would see in Iraq. I wondered what the charred bodies would look like.

'OK, time's up,' said Hotspur. 'Any questions?'

The Canadian's hand was first to rise.

'Are we gonna get slimed, sir?'

'Chemical warfare is going to kill more Iraqis than Americans, given the poor protective gear they have,' said the general. 'If you're a *real* man, you can fight without that crap. But if Saddam wants to use it, we can do that too. I'm not in the least bit concerned about whippin' the Iraqis.'

I wondered if Saddam would be in the least bit concerned about whether the general considered him a 'real' man.

The wind rattled the poles that held up the hooch.

The general looked at his watch. 'These Marines are very young men,' he told us. 'But it's going to be their Battle of Guadalcanal when they go in. We've come out here to do a noble deed.'

I scrawled in my notebook, 'Guadalcanal??'

The embed beside me put up his hand.

'What about the weather?' he asked. 'Won't it make it harder to fight?'

'Absolutely not,' shrugged the general, as another gust assaulted the hooch. 'We're an all-weather fighting force.'

With that, the General nodded thank you and left.

Later I called Alana on my satellite phone. It was 9 a.m. on the West Coast. I asked her to look up the Battle of Guadalcanal on the internet. There was a $10-per-minute pause as she went downstairs and loaded up the Google home page. I heard her fingers clatter on the computer keyboard in my office, 8,500 miles away. I wished I was back in California. '*One of the most important battles of World War II,*' she read out loud from an online encyclopedia. '*The 1st Marine Division landed east of the Tenaru River on Guadalcanal island in the South Pacific. The Japanese defeat was so bad the commander committed hara-kiri.*' She made an 'eew' sound as she pictured the disgraced Japanese warrior committing suicide by ritual disembowelment.

'How long did the battle last?' I asked.

Alana paused. I began to feel uneasy.

'Six months,' she said, before realizing what it meant.

*Six months!*

'Christ!' I said. 'Mattis probably thinks that's how long it'll take to invade Iraq. How many American casualties were there?'

Alana paused again.

'Just *tell me*,' I snapped.

'It says 6,000.'

There was an awkward silence.

I wondered if the general had mentioned Guadalcanal on purpose – to prepare the embeds for a mass slaughter. The thought made me nauseous. I contemplated taking a swig out of my diazepam auto-injector.

'What else did the general tell you?' asked Alana.

'He said that after we cross the line of departure into Iraq we'll take the same chances the Marines will.'

Alana's chilly laugh beamed its way from Los Angeles into space and then back to my handset in the Kuwaiti desert.

'Yeah, right,' she said – 'apart from the fact the Marines have guns and training, and you have neither.'

I'd never thought about it that way before.

'Sorry,' said Alana. 'Didn't mean to make you feel bad.'

But she was right. Even the general himself agreed: this assignment was madness. But there was no stopping it now.

It was a long, miserable night. After the general's talk, we were led to another hooch on the other side of Camp Matilda, which would be our sleeping quarters. I claimed a tiny patch of space on the chipboard floor and began to unpack my sleeping bag and unroll my Xtreme 19 ground mat, which turned out to be Day-Glo orange. 'Cheers, Brock,' I muttered, as the embeds around me tutted and shook their heads. Everyone else's equipment seemed more professional than mine. As I prepared my makeshift bed, I realized I hadn't used a sleeping bag since 1987 – on a youth hostel trip with the Cub Scouts. I began to fantasize about the Marriott.

The hooch was lit by fluorescent strip lights, which were bolted on to metal bars that ran horizontally under the canvas ceiling. I didn't know any of the other embeds, and I wasn't in the mood to start making friends. Nor, it seemed, was anyone else. For a tent full of ninety-five journalists, it was extraordinarily quiet. By now it was 9 p.m., but it felt later. The sun had given up on Kuwait hours ago.

The heat and stress of the day had given me a toxic body odour, and I wanted to freshen up. So I picked up my $100 super-absorbent camping towel, my electric toothbrush, my face wash and my double-quilted toilet roll, and set out in search of the bathroom. After about twenty minutes of wandering I found a portable shower cabin with a row of white ceramic washbasins in it. The overhead lights were blinding. I didn't dare look in the cracked, soap-splattered mirror. The taps produced only a slow drip of cold, dirty water. Above them was a handwritten sign that said, 'DO NOT DRINK'. The outdoor toilets – porta-johns, as the Marines called them – were much worse. They were unlit and stank of fresh human faeces, which lay in a pool of urine and chemical solvent a few inches under the soaked horseshoe of the seat. There must have been a few hundred pounds of waste down there. Luckily I had a miniature key-fob torch, which gave me some idea of where to aim. The only way I could stand the smell was to light a cigarette and keep it wedged between my lips. Afterwards I used a cheap antiseptic handwash, with no water, to sterilize my hands. If truth was the first casualty of war, I thought, personal hygiene was a close second.

On the way back I got hopelessly lost. The hooches looked identical in the gloom. The camp, meanwhile, vibrated to the bass soundtrack of helicopter blades, Humvee engines and diesel generators. I had to keep reminding myself that I wasn't on a film set. Every so often I lifted a random tent flap to be confronted by a hoochful of nineteen-year-old Marines, their faces aglow from DVDs playing silently on their laptops. The men, it seemed, would rather lose themselves in Hollywood entertainment than socialize with each other. Eventually I found the media tent, with the 1st Marine Division's press corps passed out inside it. Tomorrow, Captain Hotspur had told me, I would be driven to Living Service Area 5 – a.k.a. Camp Grizzly – about 30 miles south of the Iraqi border. There I would finally meet my unit: the 2nd Battalion, 11th Marines. I wondered if they would be pleased to see me. I doubted it. I imagined the embedded scheme the opposite way around – having a Marine live in my office and stand over my shoulder as I interviewed sources and wrote news stories. It would be unbearable. I climbed into my sleeping bag, zipped it up, and waited for sleep to arrive. It didn't. By sunrise I was still awake, with 'Waltzing Matilda' still echoing in my head.

'Hey, media dude, you should do a story about me sometime.'

This was the first Marine I met at Camp Grizzly. He was young, white and sunburnt, like a Texan farmer's son. It was the next day, and I'd just arrived on the back of a 7-ton truck, along with another embed called Scott Nelson, a *Boston Globe* reporter, also assigned to the 2/11 Marines. It had taken me several minutes to unload my bags, and I was sweating and woozy from the noon sun. The last thing I wanted to do was write a story about anyone.

'Oh, right, of course,' I said. 'Can we do an interview later?'

'No,' he said, shaking his head. I noticed him ball his fists with frustration. 'That's not what you're supposed to say.'

Then he repeated, at a dunce's pace, 'You . . . should . . . do . . . a story about *me* sometime.' He gave me an expectant look – like a dog waiting for a stick to chase. I wondered what the hell was wrong with him.

'OK,' I said, trying to resolve the issue. 'I *definitely* will.' I could feel the sun on the back of my neck, like a branding iron.

'Jesus CHRIST!' grunted the Marine. 'Ain't you never seen *Full Metal Jacket*?'

I began to feel as though I'd just failed a crucial initiation test.

'Er, yeah . . . but a long time ago,' I stammered.

Blood made its way urgently to my face.

'Well, remember the scene when they're in the helicopter and the gunner is shootin' the women and children and shit, and the gunner says to Private Joker, "*You should do a story about me sometime.*"'

'Oh yeah,' I nodded, my memory as blank as a new computer disc. I wasn't even sure if I *had* seen *Full Metal Jacket*.

The Marine's fists balled again.

He tried to prompt me, 'And then Joker says . . .?'

I wanted to go home.

The Marine wasn't giving up. He exhaled. Again, he prompted, 'Joker says to the gunner, "*Why should we do a story about you?*"'

There was a long, hot silence. The Marine's blue eyes, like pilot lights, continued to set me ablaze. Then I realized what I had to do. He wanted me to play the part of Private Joker, the fictitious war reporter.

'Why should we do a story about you?' I asked, triumphantly.

The knot in the Marine's brow unravelled. He beamed at the chance to deliver the next line. I almost passed out with relief.

'BECAUSE I'M SO FUCKING GOOD!' he shouted. Then he turned on his heels and high-fived a buddy behind him.

The two of them bellowed with laughter.

'*Shit* yeah!' said the Marine. 'I've *always* wanted to say that to a media dude.'

If the first ten minutes of my time at Camp Grizzly were bad, the next ten were even worse. After dumping my bags in one of the hooches, I strolled back outside to find something to do. But there was nothing to do. I noticed four Marines sitting on ration boxes in the tent's 5 inches of shade. All of them wore white painter's masks, to stop sand getting into their lungs. 'D'you mind if I join you?' I asked. They seemed to welcome the novelty of my company. One of the men gave me his box to sit on. When I crouched down, however, I felt a strange sensation. Then I realized, with growing anguish, what it was: a tube of oil-free Neutrogena sunblock had just exploded in my right pocket. I looked down, slowly. A dark, wet stain was making its way across the crotch of my North Face hiking trousers.

I tried my best to ignore the stain. And, in an impressive display of military discipline, the Marines didn't say a word. Instead, they handed me a tan-coloured ration pack – otherwise known as an MRE, or 'meal, ready-to-eat' – and invited me to try it. Each MRE, the Marines warned me, contained about 1,250 calories. If you ate three meals a day, it added up to 3,750 calories.

'That shit's gonna give you a fat ass, unless you're out diggin' fox-holes in the sand all day,' advised one of the men. On his left jacket pocket was written 'US MARINES', and on the other 'TRUX'.

Inside the MRE was a random assortment of menu items, each one packaged in the same slippery tan plastic. I had chicken with Thai sauce, pilaf rice, peanut butter, crackers, M&Ms, and a sachet of cappuccino powder. There was also an 'accessory pack', which contained a miniature bottle of Tabasco sauce, matches, salt, chewing gum, and a single toilet tissue. Trux showed me how to heat up the chicken by putting it inside a bag of dry chemicals – a 'flameless heater' – and adding water. After folding the top of the bag and leaning it at 45 degrees, it began to pop and fizzle, as if by magic. A few minutes later, hot steam was wafting out of it.

'The MRE is a marvel of modern technology,' said an older Marine with a silver cross on his lapel. I guessed he was one of the 2nd Battalion's chaplains. 'It's waterproof, wind-proof, vermin-proof and camel-proof – and it can survive a 100 foot fall without a parachute. You can even leave an MRE out in the stinking heat for three years and it won't go bad. Ain't that incredible?'

I nodded, scooping my plastic fork into a sachet of steaming gunk.

'As far as I can tell, there's only *one* downside,' the chaplain continued.

The chicken was now in my mouth. I chewed tentatively.

'That is, it tastes like *horseshit*,' he concluded.

I continued chewing. 'It's not actually *that* bad,' I said. The Marines had clearly overestimated the quality of British food.

They looked slightly crestfallen.

'Let's wait and see what you think in a few days,' said the chaplain. It sounded like a threat.

The Marines told me they'd been at Camp Grizzly since January. Many of them had been deployed straight from a base on Okinawa island in Japan. It had been months since they'd seen their families or, more importantly, their girlfriends. The MREs, it was claimed, were pumped full of chemicals to reduce the men's sex drive, but I doubted it. The only effect the rations had on me was to induce a constipation so stubborn I feared I would never use my bowels again. My normal routine involved at least two evacuations per day, partly a result of war-related nerves. Now there was nothing: just a nagging sensation of growing heavier with every meal.

Camp Grizzly, I learned, was home to the 11th Regiment, which was made up entirely of artillery battalions – these being composed of monstrous, truck-towed howitzer guns and mobile headquarters units, where mapping experts, radar operators, engineers and meteorologists worked out where the rounds would land. The headquarters units could also track incoming Iraqi mortars by radar, and return fire with dismembering accuracy within a few minutes. During the invasion, the 11th Regiment artillery battalions would be loaned out to infantry units, providing them with an onslaught of cover as they advanced on foot and in tanks. If there was anything positive about all this, it was that I wasn't with the infantry, and that the 2/11 Marines were 'mechanized', meaning I wouldn't have to carry my bags anywhere.

Together, the 11th Regiment and the infantry were known as Regimental Combat Team 5 (RCT-5), which was made up of 7,503 troops and more than 2,000 vehicles. I found it hard to comprehend the scale of the American presence in northern Kuwait. RCT-5 alone had nearly four times as many residents as Wooler, my home town. One of the more bookish artillerymen had pointed out to me that the total number of coalition troops in Kuwait – at least 150,000 – was the equivalent of the entire fighting-age male population of Manhattan. In a matter of weeks, the Americans had built one of the world's largest cities in the desert – a sprawling Deathtropolis, where every last resident was a trained killer. Still, 150,000 – which rose to about 250,000 if you included all the forces stationed in the Middle East – was less than half the number of coalition troops deployed in the first Gulf war. And I wondered if it was enough, especially given that they were advancing from only one direction.

I spent the rest of my first day at Camp Grizzly walking around the hooches in a sun-frazzled daze. Outside one of them, a Marine had built garden furniture out of ammunition crates. He'd also put up road sign, pointing north, which said, 'Baghdad, 325 miles'. Every so often an inquisitive Marine would stop and ask me what kind of stories I would write, and why the 11th Regiment couldn't have had a female embed (a 'fembed' as they were known), or 'the dude from *Rolling Stone*'. They wanted the latter, I suspected, because they thought he might have some drugs. They were also keen to congratulate me on Tony Blair's 'balls', or tell me jokes about the French. 'How do you defend Paris?' asked one. I told him I didn't know. 'Neither does anyone else,' came the punchline – 'it's never been tried before . . .'

That afternoon I was told grudgingly by a captain that I had been made an 'honorary major'. This meant nothing other than that I could use the cold, Navy-style showers once a day, instead of every four days. (I later found out that one embed, Charlie LeDuff from the *New York Times*, had tested the limits of his honorary rank by handing out 'field promotions'. They weren't upheld.)

At 9 p.m. I repeated my Camp Matilda bathroom routine, hung my camping towel out to dry, then climbed into my sleeping bag. I was surprised by how painfully cold the desert became at night. My sleeping bag felt about as warm as rolled-up newspaper. I wished I'd brought blankets, or a pillow.

I was woken at 2 a.m. by a gale of apocalyptic fury – as if the gods themselves were throwing a tantrum about the coming invasion. Someone flicked on the lights in the hooch, but nothing was visible amid a thick orange mist of sand. 'This is Iraq's El Niño,' a Marine explained, his PE instructor's voice barely carrying over the wind. 'It's called the southern wind change and it happens every spring. This year it's early. *We should have fucking invaded in February.*' At 3 a.m., some of the Marines formed a human chain to walk the 100 yards to the camp's porta-johns. When they got there, however, they found that most of them had been blown over. I pitied the Marine who would have to clean up the lake of sewage in the morning.

By sunrise, everything in the hooch looked as though it had aged by 1,000 years. My blue Sony Viao laptop had become yellow, with ditches of wet sand between the keys. Every item of clothing in my rucksack looked as though it had been left overnight on a beach, while the pages of my notebooks had turned the colour of parchment.

Worst of all, when I walked outside, my $100 super-absorbent camping towel, which I'd hung on one of the hooch's support ropes, had disappeared. It had probably crossed the line of departure before me. I sighed at the thought of drying my face with underwear for the rest of the war.

Life at Camp Grizzly was an excruciating combination of boredom and fear, interrupted only by rations and Scud alerts – each one forcing us to go to MOPP level four in the oppressive heat. The only way to get my gas mask on in nine seconds was to throw my glasses into the sand. Once the mask was on, I could see nothing – just as Captain Hotspur had warned. Blinded, and with my spectacles uncomfortably close to my steel-capped boots, my only option was to remain frozen on the spot until the all-clear was called. Then I would get down on my knees, my body still tight with adrenalin, and pat the ground in an effort to find where my glasses had landed. The panic of losing them was almost greater than the panic of the chemical alert itself. Not, of course, that I liked wearing them. The fashionable metal frames felt white hot in the sun, burning my already sunburnt temples. The glare from the lenses, meanwhile, gave me a spike of pain in my frontal lobe. I was glad I'd bought a pair of Bono-style fly goggles at the Kuwait Hilton, after a last-minute bolt of inspiration. The goggles were big enough to fit over my glasses, blacking out the sun and pro-tecting my eyes against the relentless wind. The downside, however, was they made me look like Bono.

Gradually I picked up Marine jargon. I learned that 'the head' was the lavatory, with a 'head call' being a miserable trek out to one of the porta-johns (positioned as far away as possible from the hooches, for obvious reasons). My actual head, bizarrely, was my 'grape'. The Marines, meanwhile, called each other 'Devil Dog' – or just 'Dawg' for short – after the Germans' nickname for them during World War I (the German translation was *Teufelhunde*). Morale was boosted by bellowing 'Ooh-rah!' or 'Semper Fi!' at any opportunity. The latter was a shortened version of the Marine Corps's motto, 'Semper Fidelis', meaning 'Always Faithful'.

I dealt with the tedium of the long, hot days by using the kidnap survival technique that David Silver had taught me on the SAS course in Herefordshire. I split each hour into segments, creating routines for each one. Every time I successfully completed a routine – brushing my teeth, for example, or taking a cold shower – I considered it a small victory for Ayres morale.

Every morning I'd walk to the 'chow hall', where I'd eat a plateful of hard, green scrambled egg (MREs were for lunch) and talk to my fellow embeds – Nelson from the *Boston Globe* and David Willis from the BBC. Willis had turned up to the camp in a desert-coloured Land Rover Discovery, of which I was intensely jealous. He had with him a cameraman and a bodyguard. I wondered why Fletcher hadn't given *me* a bodyguard. Willis and Nelson looked almost as incongruous at Camp Grizzly as I did. We all had fair hair, pale skin and bad eyesight. It was as though the Marines had looked at a selection of passport photographs and deliberately picked out the wimpiest-looking reporters, for the sheer comedy value. When Willis went on camera, however, he would take off his spectacles, don an Afghan scarf, and lower his voice by an octave. All this gave him the presence of a kind of ginger Lawrence of Arabia. Off-camera, Willis refused to take Camp Grizzly too seriously. In fact, if it hadn't been for his rowdy, back-slapping laughter I might have gone insane.

The rest of the morning would be spent snoozing on the chaplain's fold-down camping chair. Then I'd listen to the BBC World Service on my short-wave radio, call the office, open an MRE, and, in the afternoon, try to write a story. I could send text files to London by plugging my satellite phone into my laptop and loading up a software program called Copymaster. The process felt antiquated – like something from a 1980s science fiction film. A blue box would open on my desktop, with DOS-style text scrolling down inside it. After I'd logged on, a message would pop-up saying, 'Welcome to Wapping. Waiting to connect.' After an agonizing, $250 wait I would finally be told me how many words had been sent to London. Sometimes Copymaster would simply hang up, beep, and tell me that the 'Attempt failed'. Then my laptop would freeze, forcing me to reboot. I hoped that wouldn't happen in Iraq.

There was very little to write *about*, apart from the sand storms, or the lost camels that would occasionally tiptoe grumpily between the hooches and the gun trucks. I wondered how many of the poor beasts had been turned into exotic steak by stray artillery rounds. Their owners, the nomadic Bedouin tribesmen, must have been furious. The only other newsworthy event came when the Marines were handed two pocket-sized laminated cards, the first outlining the rules of the 1929 and 1949 Geneva Conventions, and the second offering a phonetic pronunciation guide to basic Arabic phrases. On the first card, in bold type, was written, '*Marines do not attack medical personnel, equipment or facilities; Marines do not harm those who surrender; Marines do not kill or torture prisoners.*' It was the second card, however, that provoked the most interest. The Marines were particularly pleased with the unlikely phrase 'And Upon You Be Peace' (Wass-alamu Alay-kum) and the translation of 'What's Up?', which appeared as 'Shoe-*koo*, McKoo?' For hours after the cards arrived, Camp Grizzly echoed with Marines bellowing it at each other, then high-fiving.

Every so often I would try to think of a way to get medevaced out of Camp Grizzly before the war began. I considered deliberately losing my glasses, breaking my wrist, or simply taking one of the Marines' rifles and shooting myself in the foot. I even contemplated sabotaging my laptop or satellite phone. I was convinced, however, that anything other than being hit directly with a weapon of mass destruction would be considered wimping out by Fletcher. It was too late now for lame excuses. To save my career, I had to spend at least a few days under enemy fire in Iraq. Only then, perhaps, could I try to work out a way to go home.

Before going to Kuwait, I hadn't been much of smoker. Nicotine, however, was the only drug available at Camp Grizzly, and I suspected I would need more of it once the war started. So, on a whim, I asked the BBC cameraman to buy me a pack of 200 Marlboro Lights on his next trip to Kuwait City. He brought back 400. After every Scud alert, I'd rip off my gas mask, locate my glasses, then immediately light up, sucking the carcinogenic fumes, along with all the airborne mud and filth, deep into my lungs. And I'd pray that Saddam wouldn't use chemicals.

The main source of entertainment in my hooch was Joe Trux, the first lieutenant I'd met on my first day at Camp Grizzly. With his smart East Coast accent, French fiancée and exhaustive knowledge of

English trip-hop, Trux struck me as an unlikely warrior. In fact, I often wondered what kind of trauma had inspired him to sign up for boot camp. When I was first introduced to him I'd assumed he was my age or younger. It was only when he pulled off his floppy camouflaged sun hat, to reveal a bald skull shaved down to the pink flaking skin, that he suddenly looked much older. 'What happened to Portishead, man?' he asked me once. 'Are they making another album? Did you hear *Dummy*? That was out*standing*, wasn't it?' Before arriving at Camp Grizzly, Trux said, he'd been on extended leave in Europe. Now, like everyone else, he spent his days sitting around and waiting for his chance to kill.

Trux's first big wheeze had been to build a Monopoly board out of the brown cardboard boxes in which the MREs were packed. With a felt-tip pen, he branded it the 'RCT-5 Monopoly: 2003 Kuwait Edition'. Mayfair, inevitably, was replaced with Baghdad, while Park Lane became France. (This made me wonder how the poor sod from Agence France-Presse was faring in the camp opposite.) Instead of being sent to jail, players were directed to Camp Grizzly. Trux had even gone to the effort of writing out 'Chance' and 'Community Chest' cards.

The Chance cards included the following:

1. Clean the shitter. Miss a turn.
2. You are guilty of negligent discharge (accidentally firing an M-16). Go back five steps.
3. M&Ms in MRE. Collect $10.
4. Media rep falls into foxhole. Collect $500.

I was slightly concerned that No. 4 was rewarded with cash. Trux reassured me, however, that it was a joke. The only other entertainment at Camp Grizzly came from fake news, most of which was blamed on the Marine Corps's internal online news service. The biggest commotion was caused by a report that Osama bin Laden had been captured. For hours, cheering could be heard around the camp. Marines slapped each other on the back and yelled, 'Shoe-*koo*, McKoo!' Then came news of Julia Roberts's death in a road accident, and a gory account of Britney Spears's facial disfigurement, also at the wheel of a car. My short-wave radio, however, had an unpopular habit of contradicting these sensational headlines. Trux, therefore, felt personally obliged to come up with another scheme to entertain the unhappy campers.

Eventually he had an idea.

'Hey, guys,' he said in the hooch one morning.

'Shoe-*koo*, McKoo?' replied several voices simultaneously.

'How about a talent contest?'

There were murmurs of encouragement.

'Imagine it: Camp Grizzly's first ever *annual* talent show,' said Trux. 'We could turn one of the 10-tons into a stage . . .'

This got the Marines excited. Logistics and dates were discussed.

'All we need now', said Trux, 'are some performers.'

The men looked at other with blank faces.

Then they looked at me.

The day before the talent show – almost a full week after I'd first arrived at Camp Grizzly – the colonel in charge of the 11th Regiment turned up in a military convoy to give the Marines a pep talk from the back of a 7-ton truck. As the sun sank into the horizon behind him, and the wind blew up a tornado of dust from the desert floor, all I could make out was his uniformed silhouette.

'There's very good chance we'll get the word to go in the next couple of days,' he said, through the tin rattle of a loudhailer. 'On Monday or Tuesday night, the President is expected to make an address to the nation, so make sure you've got everything you need to go all the way to Baghdad.' The men ooh-rahed. 'The indications we're getting from over the border is that there's not much motivation for a fight,' he continued. 'Last week, a bunch of Iraqis came up to the Brits and tried to surrender, but the Brits said, "It's not time yet." '

The men laughed at the thought of the Iraqi army's 51st Mechanized Division trying to lay down their weapons before the fight even began. If the story were true, I thought, the men would probably have been executed as traitors by now. The colonel cupped a hand over his eyes and surveyed the crowd. 'Your average Iraqi,' he said, 'when he sees a Marine with night-vision goggles and an M-16 rolling past his house in an armoured Humvee, is gonna think he's having a close encounter of the third kind. Don't do anything to alienate the people up there: treat 'em with dignity and respect.' He paused, as if savouring the moment. Then he said, 'We're gonna go to Baghdad, fight the Republican Guard, take care of them, replace Saddam, and put stability operations in place. *Then we're gonna come back home.*'

The men cheered, whooped and Semper Fied as the colonel jumped down from back of the truck. He waved and climbed inside the cab, and the convoy clattered off to the next camp. I hated Camp Grizzly more than I had ever hated any other place on earth. So why was the thought of leaving so unbearable?

That night, under the billowing circus-top of the hooch, I shivered in my sleeping bag and listened to the Marines talk among themselves. The lights were off, but one of the men – the corporal who had wanted me to re-enact *Full Metal Jacket* on my first day – was reading a letter by torchlight. Others were watching DVDs. The mood seemed different: more subdued. No one was saying much.

Then the corporal announced, 'Man, this letter's depressing the hell out of me. Even my goddam brother's against the war.'

The roof of the tent flapped in the wind, like a flag at full mast.

'*No shit,*' came a muffled reply.

The corporal continued: 'My brother's the kind of guy who usually says, "Let's just kill the motherfuckers." '

He paused, allowing the men to consider this important background fact. Then he said, 'What's our job here to do *anyway?*'

No one, it seemed, wanted to have this conversation. They were all trying to forget about the desert outside.

Then Trux said, 'Our job is to kill the enemy.'

The corporal didn't seem to be listening.

'Man, it's gonna be just like Vietnam,' he complained. 'When we get home, we're gonna have folks throw stuff at us.'

With a heavy sigh, he switched off his torch.

In the darkness, sleeping bags rustled uncomfortably. Outside, Iraq's El Niño was now whistling tunelessly.

Then the muffled voice said, '*Nobody gonna throw nothin' at me.*'

'Good evening, er, *ladies* and gentlemen,' said the shy, bespectacled gunnery sergeant, squinting under a solitary floodlight. His Noël

Coward impression, not convincing at the best of times, was faltering with stage fright. 'Here's a little number I tossed off recently in the Caribbean,' he continued. 'It's called "The Penis Song".' A hundred or so heavily armed Marines peered up at the makeshift stage, which doubled as the back of a 10-ton flat-bed tank transporter, and gave a raucous cheer. The reflection of the floodlight in the sand made their faces glow dirty orange.

Above and around us was nothing – a cavern of black, empty desert. It was cold, and the air smelled of sand, tobacco and porta-johns. The gunnery sergeant – 'Gunny' for short – was gripping a microphone which was plugged into a PA system designed for giving orders to Iraqi prisoners of war. To his left, a metal cage creaked in the wind. Inside it perched Speckled Ali, the 11th Regiment's 'NBC pigeon'. Ali was looking good – cheerful, almost. That meant the gas alert of five minutes ago was just a drill. We would live, at least until the end of the talent show.

I wondered what would happen if Ali came down with bird flu. Would the entire regiment be medevaced to a quarantine facility? For a brief, exhilarating moment, I contemplated poisoning Ali's bird feed.

The Marines remained fixated on the stage.

Gunny cleared his throat, spat out a gobful of yellow dust, then began:

> Isn't it awfully nice to have a penis?
> Isn't it frightfully good to have a dong?

I recognized the ditty as a Monty Python spoof from *The Meaning of Life*. The rest of the audience wasn't as appreciative. Gunny had barely reached the third line before the Marines started to unsling their M-16s and cock them with loud *ka-clacks*. At first it was funny. Then it started to get unnerving. On stage, to the right of Gunny, Trux made a 'Shush' motion. Above his head was a home-made banner, fashioned from brown ration boxes, which read, 'THE IRAQI REPUBLICAN GUARD IS PROUD TO SPONSOR THIS EVENT.' Next to it Trux had tried to create an italicized Republican Guard motto. '*We Suck Again*,' it boasted.

A blast of wind sprayed the stage with sand and dirt. Gunny paused to empty another mouthful of slime and adjust his rifle's shoulder strap. The first lieutenant wiped his eyes. I heard cursing over the low grumble of a diesel generator. Gunny's right hand was now holding down the Velcro flap on his gas-mask holster. He gripped his NBC-proof water canteen with the other.

This, I thought, would be a great time for another Scud alert.

Gunny was determined to press on:

> So three cheers for your willy or John Thomas,
> Hooray for your one-eyed trouser snake . . .

The crowd couldn't take it any more. 'YOU FUCKIN' SUCK,' shouted a private from the crowd. There was more *ka-clacking*. Gunny persevered, until he reached the last line. 'The Penis Song', mercifully, was only two verses long. When he was finally done, he gave a bow, which turned into a duck to avoid a hurled ration of peanut butter. Trux caught it, then held it up to his chest, as though he were a model in a television commercial. 'Let's give a BIG thanks to our *other* sponsor of this evening,' he shouted, snatching the microphone from Gunny. '*Delicious* "MRE" peanut butter spread!' The crowd roared and stomped its feet as Trux, getting into the spirit of things, began to tap dance in his desert boots and chemical suit.

I marvelled at Trux's ability to prepare such a varied programme, featuring everything from a guitar duo to a rap/dance troupe, in such a short space of time. So far we'd heard a twenty-two-year-old intelligence officer sing in a Michael Jackson falsetto, a short-tempered Midwestern sergeant recite love poetry, and, of course, Gunny's rendition of 'The Penis Song'. Next up on stage were a captain and a first sergeant. They gave a flawless performance of 'Sweet Home Alabama' on acoustic guitars. An encore was demanded, and so the unlikely duo launched into Green Day's 'Good Riddance (Time of Your Life)', with altered lyrics. The audience chanted the chorus in unison: '*But for now this shithole is our home.*' I found myself singing along.

As Trux took back the microphone, I contemplated the night ahead: the floor mat and the freezing sleeping bag; the inevitable 2 a.m. gas alert; the fuzzy 5 a.m. wake up. And then the stale breakfast, the fear, the boredom, and the day made up of segments and routines. Then Trux said, 'And now I'd like to introduce you to the real stars of our talent show: THE MEDIA REPRESENTATIVES!'

The crowd cheered and booed simultaneously.

Rifles *ka-clacked*.

Someone shouted, 'Semper Fi!'

I turned to look at Nelson. He winced, and shrugged his shoulders.

'Come on, boys,' said Trux. *'Join me on stage . . .'*

# 13

## Shoe-*koo*, McKoo!

Before we go any further – and before things start to get *really* ugly – I should probably tell you what happened at the talent show. Trux, being a gentleman, didn't go through with his threat to haul the embeds on stage. Instead, we were asked to stand as he introduced us to the Marines. Through the gloom, scores of dirty orange faces peered at us with a mixture of curiosity and hostility. The only reporters they'd ever seen, after all, were in the movies; and most of them were scumbags. Likewise, the only Marines we'd ever seen were also in the movies; and they were mostly scumbags, too. 'Please give a big Camp Grizzly welcome to Chris Ayres, from *The Times* of London,' said Trux. There were low cheers and, I couldn't help noticing, a couple of boos. A solitary rifle *ka-clacked*. I hoped I wouldn't end up in a Humvee with its owner. 'Chris is from northern England, and his favourite band is Portishead,' Trux continued, making it up as he went along. I wished he'd chosen something more macho, like Limp Bizkit, or Rage Against the Machine. I also wished I worked for an American newspaper. To most of the Marines, being interviewed by *The Times* of London meant nothing. 'Why are the folks in London interested in *us*?' they kept asking.

That night the Marines were in a better mood. In the hooch, everyone was humming the captain's version of 'Good Riddance', writing letters to their families or girlfriends, and complaining about Gunny's 'Penis Song'. The good humour wouldn't last long. In fact this would be my last night at Camp Grizzly. After the next morning I'd never see Living Service Area 5, or First Lieutenant Joe Trux, again.

It was 3.04 a.m. when a captain from the 2nd Battalion burst into the hooch, flipped on the overhead lights, and yelled, 'GO! GO! DEVIL DOGS, LET'S GO!' I reached for my glasses and squinted up out of my sleeping bag. I checked my Xtreme 19 digital camping watch: the date was Tuesday 18 March 2003. The captain – a tall black man made entirely from skin and muscle – was already in MOPP level two. He was also wearing a camouflaged armoured vest with a hunting knife and a 9-mm pistol strapped to it. I wondered what he expected to kill with the knife. From my position on the floor, it looked big enough to disembowel a camel.

'*Oh no,*' I muttered, trying to shake myself awake. It was seven days since I'd arrived at Camp Grizzly, and I was getting used to the routine of Scud drills, MREs, infrequent bowl movements, and cold showers. I'd almost forgotten that war correspondents, at some point, had to go to war.

'That's it then,' said Trux, already half dressed and slamming rounds into the chamber of his M-16. 'This is for real.'

For the first time, I realized that Trux, like me, hadn't fully believed the war would happen. He'd probably convinced himself, like I had, that it was all part of a diabolical White House plan to mess with journalists' heads and scare the French. But we'd been wrong: *the President wasn't bluffing.*

I looked over at Nelson from the *Boston Globe*. Somehow he'd already got dressed and packed his rucksack. He was fizzing with nervous excitement. I might have shared his enthusiasm if I were covering the war from the nearest five-star hotel to the action, as journalists are supposed to do.

'Let's giddyup, folks!' said Nelson.

*Giddyup?* What the hell was wrong with him?

'This is a training exercise,' deadpanned the captain, who was still standing in the doorway of the hooch by the light switch. His right leg, I noticed, wouldn't stop jiggling, as though it had a battery in it.

'My *ass* this is a training exercise,' said Trux, matter-of-factly.

'Two other things,' said the captain, ignoring him. 'The President will address the nation at 1 a.m. Zulu Time – that's 4 a.m. local – and we have orders that all hands should grow a moustache.'

The men nodded blearily; no one asked why.

Then Trux exploded: 'Grow a *moustache?*'

'Yeah, that's right,' said the captain, slowly. 'A *moustache*. The general says we've all gotta grow one.'

'What – *now?*' asked Trux.

'Just do it, first lieutenant,' came the reply.

Covered in sand and reeking of stale body odour, I pulled on my hiking trousers, stained T-shirt and black tracksuit top. My body felt ruined. I knelt down and began the tedious routine of rolling up my sleeping bag and ground mat, then fastening them to the back of my rucksack with plastic clasps. When I was done, I heaved my blue flak jacket on to my back, put on my helmet, and stumbled outside to smoke a cigarette. It was 3.30 a.m. Within minutes my shoulders were aching from the weight of the Kevlar, which felt tough enough to withstand a small thermonuclear blast, never mind a sniper's bullet. I began to wonder if it was worth the pain.

Nothing prepared me for the noise outside. It was though hell had gone on tour and was making a one-night-only appearance in Camp Grizzly. The regiment's 2,000 vehicles clattered and groaned in a terrible symphony, like the cogs of a gigantic, murderous machine. For miles around, the desert glowed from the fake dawn of a thousand floodlights. I coughed, shivered and smoked, as a 10-ton truck rolled past the hooch. It was carrying two bulldozers, each the size of an office block. I assumed they'd be used to tear holes in the demilitarized zone that separated Kuwait from Iraq, creating a 'breach' through which the American tanks could pass. The 'DMZ' stretched 125 miles from the Saudi Arabian border to Umm Qasr – Iraq's only port city – and then onwards another 25 miles to the Abd Allah estuary, which eventually opens out into the Persian Gulf. The DMZ, I had been told by the Marines, was currently being 'guarded' for the United Nations by a 775-strong Bangladeshi infantry battalion. I imagined the Bangladeshis, like inept nightclub bouncers, trying to stop 150,000 Americans from crossing the border. If they had any sense they would have booked themselves into the Kuwait Marriott by now and ordered up the prawns and Wagyu-Kobe beef.

I trod on my cigarette and lit another one.

My heart, I noticed, was beating in a frantic 2/4 march.

I decided I should call the office. It was 12.30 a.m. in London, and there would still be a couple of night editors on the foreign desk. I pulled out my satellite phone, extended the chunky antenna, and started to dial.

The captain emerged from the tent as someone in London picked up.

'Y'ello?' said a distant voice.

'KILL THE GODDAM PHONE!' yelled the captain, making a furious throat-slitting action with his right hand. For a second I thought he was going to rugby-tackle me. The phone jumped out of my hands.

'We're in EmCon *Bravo*, for Christsake,' he bellowed.

We stared at each other.

'What's that?' I asked eventually, my hands still shaking.

'Radio . . . Emissions . . . *Control*,' he said, as if trying to stop himself doing something he would regret later. 'You switch that phone on and it gives out a radio signal. Ten seconds later a Scud lands on your head. It lands on my head too. And I don't want no Scuds anywhere near my head. Keep it SWITCHED OFF. We're gonna be in Bravo for the next forty-eight-hours. At least.'

I tried some of Dr Ruth's breathing exercises. Then a thought struck me.

'So how will I file any stories?' I asked.

'You won't,' said the captain. 'You're gonna be out of contact. You can send your stories when we go back to EmCon Delta.'

The embedding system suddenly seemed very flawed. I would be joining the front lines with no gun, no training and no means to send stories. It was as though I were tagging along just for the opportunity to get shot – or worse. Until now, the phone had been my only contact with reality. And now it was useless. The only upside was that Fletcher and Barrow might think I was dead.

I noticed the captain looking at my flak jacket.

'Why the hell are you wearing a *blue* vest?' he asked. His eyes moved upward with growing disbelief. 'And a *blue* helmet?'

'It's, er, Kevlar,' I replied. 'Bullet-proof, y'know?' I rapped my knuckles twice on my helmet and gave a weak laugh.

'Do you have any idea how many blue things there are in the Iraqi desert?' the captain replied, his eyes damp with anger.

I shook my head. I didn't want to hear the answer.

'Well, I'll tell you,' he said. 'There's one blue thing. And it's *you*.'

Trux appeared from behind me, his M-16 slung over his shoulder. He glanced at my jacket, which had the word 'PRESS' inscribed on the chest-plate in large, fluorescent white letters. Then he gave me a playful shove.

'What th—' I began to say.

'I'm *pressing*!' said Trux. He shoved me again, harder. 'Look, I'm pressing! It says here I have to press! What happens now?'

Trux slapped his palm on my back, then nearly collapsed with laughter. I thought I detected an upward curl of the captain's lips.

'That's very funny,' I said.

'Whoever gave you that vest, man, I wouldn't send 'em a Christmas card,' said Trux. 'I think they might want you dead. Why didn't they write "PRESS" in Arabic? As far as the Iraqis are concerned, that snazzy blue jacket might mean you're a goddam general. I hope the Kevlar comes with a warranty.'

I began to explain that, for ethical reasons, I shouldn't look too much like a Marine – even though I was wearing a camouflaged Marine chemical suit and travelling in a Marine convoy with a Marine artillery battery. But Trux was right. My jacket should have said, 'SAHAFFI', or, as Salman Hussein had said to me in the taxi outside the Marriott, 'LA TAPAR, ANA SAHAFFI.'

'Which unit are you assigned to, anyhow?' asked Trux. I could tell from the folds in his brow he hoped it wasn't his.

I tried to shrug, but couldn't because of the weight on my shoulders.

Then the captain said, 'He's with me.'

I almost choked on my Marlboro. The captain was still looking at me as though he'd caught me in a motel room with his wife.

'I don't think we've been introduced yet,' he said, offering me a bony hand. 'Captain Rick Rogers. The men call me Buck.'

'I'm Chris,' I said, presenting him with a fleshy, sunburnt palm in return. 'Chris Ayres. From the London *Times*.'

'OK, London *Times*,' said Buck. 'Follow me.'


By 3.52 a.m. I was standing next to an armoured Humvee on the dirt track that headed north out of Camp Grizzly, towards the Iraqi border. Behind the Humvee was a 7-ton off-road truck, stacked high with wooden crates of ammunition. It was towing a massive 155-mm howitzer cannon, which the Marines told me weighed more than the truck itself. I was surprised by how old-fashioned the big gun looked – as though it were only a couple of generations evolved from the wagon-wheeled, horse-drawn artillery that the British used to fire at the Americans. 'It has about as much in common with one of those pieces of crap as a Model-T Ford does with a pimped-up Cadillac Escalade,' the captain told me later. 'That gun can fire a rocket-propelled shell thirty klicks down-range at a rate of two per minute. That's why they call us the Long Distance Death Dealers. We kill more people on the battlefield than anyone else.'

Behind the howitzer was another 7-ton truck, also towing a gun, and then another, for as far as I could see. To the left of us were four identical artillery convoys, lined up side by side. I guessed there must have been at least a billion dollars' worth of military hardware parked outside the camp.

After leading me to the Humvee, Buck had disappeared for a briefing with the 2nd Battalion's commanding officer. While I waited for him to come back, I tuned into the BBC World Service. It was now 3.59 a.m. In less than a minute, President Bush would address the nation. A dozen Marines huddled around the V-shaped antenna of my short-wave radio: some of them smoked cigarettes; others ate MREs. In the field, I would soon learn, Marines eat whenever they can.

'*My fellow citizens*,' the President began, through a babble of interference, '*events in Iraq have reached the final days of decision . . . The United States and other nations have pursued patient and honourable efforts to disarm the Iraqi regime without war. That regime pledged to reveal and destroy all its weapons of mass destruction as a condition for ending the Persian Gulf War in 1991. Today, no nation can possibly claim that Iraq has disarmed. And it will not disarm so long as Saddam Hussein holds power.*' For a moment the President's voice faded out, to be replaced by a solemn Arabic voice and the echo of an Islamic call to prayer. I wondered if this was really the end of the world. I scrolled through the alternative frequencies for the World Service just in time to hear the President's fuzzy ultimatum: '*Saddam Hussein and his sons must leave Iraq within forty-eight hours. Their refusal to do so will result in military conflict, commenced at a time of our choosing. For their safety, all foreign nationals – including journalists and inspectors – should leave Iraq immediately.*'

The Marines shook their heads, cursed Saddam, and made their way back to their vehicles. It seemed inevitable: some of us would end up dying an unimaginable chemical death. Saddam, after all, had absolutely nothing to lose. Behind us, in a metal cage swinging from the cabin of a 7-ton truck, Speckled Ali, the NBC pigeon, cooed contentedly. Then I saw the captain, backlit by the glare of the floodlights, approaching the Humvee. He still looked pissed off, but I thought I could sense a slight mood improvement. 'So I've been told to look after you,' he said, without trying to hide his disappointment. 'This is the deal. As you probably know, the 2nd Battalion, 11th Marines, is made up of four firing batteries – Echo, Fox, Golf and Kilo – and a headquarters battery. I'm in charge of Kilo Battery. Our mission is to cover the infantry from the 5th Marines, who'll go through the DMZ ahead of us, when – or *if* – we get the order to cross the LOD.' I got the feeling Buck was the kind of military man who never used words when an acronym would do. With any luck, this meant I would never understand the true depth of the trouble we were in.

'Where would you rather travel?' asked Buck. 'In the Humvee with me, or in one of the 7-tons with the Devil Dogs?'

I turned to look at the Marines perched between the ammunition crates on the back of the truck behind us. I concluded that even Buck's company was preferable to sitting on top of several tons of high explosives.

'I'll go in the Humvee, if that's OK,' I said.

Buck nodded, and tightened his jaw.

'Where are your bags?' he asked.

'Outside the hooch,' I said. 'I'll get them.' Buck nodded, stalked around the Humvee, and climbed into the passenger seat.

A few minutes later I returned, dragging my metal dolly over the sand and gravel. By now, one of the castors had fallen off.

'You're bringing *all* of this?' asked Buck, through his wound-down window, as he surveyed my rucksack, laptop carrier, tent bag, travel wallet, toiletries case and flak-jacket holder. He saved his most contemptuous look, however, for my dolly. Before I had a chance to answer, Buck turned to the Marine in the Humvee's driving seat. 'Murphy, will you help the media guy with his shit?' he asked. The driver's door opened, a mouthful of chewing tobacco was spat, and within a few seconds a short, filthy Marine was standing next to me. He introduced himself as Lance Corporal 'Fightin' Dan' Murphy. His nickname, I was informed, came from his tendency to start nightclub brawls. I suspected he might have made this up. Murphy was twenty-four years old and came from an Irish family who'd settled somewhere in upstate New York. He wore his chemical suit extra baggy, like camouflaged skatewear.

It soon became clear my bags wouldn't fit. The Humvee was already overloaded with bullets for the rooftop 50-calibre machine gun, crates of hand grenades, an AT4 anti-tank rocket launcher, bottles of Saudi Arabian drinking water, and boxes of MREs. The rest of our water supply, meanwhile, was in a plastic tank on an open luggage rack bolted to the rear bumper. As a conciliatory gesture, I agreed to leave my dolly behind. After all, if my luggage was in the Humvee, I wouldn't need to carry it – or so I thought. Nevertheless, Murphy still had to unload two boxes of MREs and a few 'humanitarian' ration packs to make room for my rucksack. I contemplated dumping my fluorescent Two-Man Xtreme 19 Mountain Adventure Pod, but it seemed too painful after everything we'd been through together. Not, of course, that I had any intention of putting it up anywhere near Buck Rogers. If he was upset about my blue jacket, I didn't want to think about his reaction to a fluorescent yellow tent.

When the rear hatch of the Humvee was finally closed, I wedged myself on to the tiny, foam-cushioned back seat behind Murphy. The only way I could fit was to jam my knees up against the Kevlar chestplate of my jacket. That pretty much rendered all my body, apart from my head, immobile. I stared straight ahead, at the rack for the rifle that I wasn't allowed to carry, and began to groan.

'Are we ready?' asked Buck. The door opposite me clanked open and a much older Marine – I guessed he was nearly forty – jumped in. 'Yeah, we're ready,' he said, slamming the door behind him. 'Frank Hustler,' he added, turning to me and shaking my hand. Before I could ask his rank, age or where he was from, he said, 'If you're takin' notes, I'm a first sergeant, thirty-seven years old, from San Diego, California. Back home I have a beautiful Brazilian wife. And when I start shootin' that 50-cal on the roof you're gonna think your balls are on fire.' Hustler laughed, then dipped his finger into a tub of Vaseline and smeared it on to his tyre-tracked lips. With a grunt, he stood up on his seat, pulled a pair of black headphone over his ears, and poked his head through the hole of the machine-gun turret. Then he stepped up on to the metal plate to my right, where my armrest should have been. I couldn't stop staring at his boot tags, which had his blood type and social-security number written on them.

'OK, Murphy, let's CSMO,' said Buck.

The Humvee's V8 engine rattled and bellowed. I could feel the vibration of the blackened, vertical exhaust pipe behind my door.

We started to lurch forward – towards Iraq; towards fear; towards death.

'What does CSMO mean?' I shouted to the captain.

I could see his shoulders tighten. He *really* didn't like questions. I didn't blame him, to be honest. He had a war to fight.

'Clear Shit and Move Out,' he said, at last.

I hadn't expected to die so quickly. Even with my horror-flick imagination, I thought it would take at least a few days for one of Saddam's chemical Scuds, or diseased mortars, to find its way into my foxhole. Part of me even expected to survive the invasion, but get killed on the way home – in a helicopter crash over Baghdad, perhaps, or a friendly-fire incident in Kuwait. I certainly didn't expect it to end like this, a whole five minutes and twenty seconds after leaving Camp Grizzly.

We had been driving for only a couple of minutes when Buck realized we were lagging behind the rest of the 1st Marine Division. He began thumping his hand against a GPS device – which could allegedly calculate our position on the battlefield by triangulating our distance from three satellites – and swearing at it using words I'd never even heard before. Spread out over his knees was a map of the DMZ that had been drawn up from spy satellites. It looked about as reliable as the directions on the back of a Chinese take-out menu. 'LEFT, LEFT, GO LEFT!' he shouted at Murphy, who promptly swung the Humvee into a ditch, over a 3-foot sand berm, down a 45-degree rock face and on to the flat gravel of the wadi. '*Jesus Christ*, Murphy,' said Buck, 'you were supposed to take the *track*.' I twisted my neck to look at the speedometer over Murphy's shoulder. It was showing 50 m.p.h. It felt faster.

In a flash of rage, Buck tossed the GPS device over his shoulder, picked up the map, and shook the creases out of it. It was then he remembered something: 'LANDMINES! LANDMINES! MURPHY,

WATCH OUT FOR GODDAM LANDMINES!' The muscles in my buttocks clenched so tight I feared I might need surgery to unlock them. '*Oh shit*,' said Murphy, who started swerving violently to avoid anything that looked vaguely mine-like. Unfortunately, every other rock in the chalk-coloured desert looked mine-like. I winced as I remembered what the Lonely Planet guide had said about the dangers of 'wadi-bashing': '*People who keep track of these things emphasize that stuff still blows up every month.*' 'Just get back on the track, Murphy,' said Buck, wiping a dirty palm over his face. I noticed he'd hung a crucifix from dashboard in front of him. He'd also taped a brown prayer booklet, en-titled *Life & Death*, to the inside of the windscreen. 'Calm down, Murphy, and find the track,' Buck continued. 'Ain't no point in busting the tyres for the sake of some rocks.'

Then three things happened simultaneously: Murphy shouted, 'FUCK, FUCK, FUCK!'; the Humvee swung so emphatically to the left that it almost flipped over; and the door I was leaning on buckled and popped open. Suddenly my head was a foot from the desert floor and I was looking at the front wheels of the vehicle from an unusual and unwanted vantage point. After the initial shock, I soon worked out I was being held inside only by my legs, which were trapped under Murphy's seat. My door, meanwhile, kept slamming into my stomach, like a barnyard gate in a storm. I watched helplessly as the contents of my pockets – two notebooks, a packet of cigarettes and several ballpoint pens – fluttered out into the dawn breeze. It took perhaps thirty seconds for me to realize that no one inside the vehicle had noticed what had happened. *Or that they didn't care.* As I hung there, waiting for my legs to give way, forcing me to perform a fatal back flip under the Humvee's monster-truck tyres, I contemplated the sheer rotten luck of dying in a freak off-roading accident before cross-ing the Iraq border. The thought made me so angry I wrestled the flapping door and started to heave my Kevlar-plated torso upright. Eventually, with a bellow of pure animal rage, I threw myself back inside the vehicle and slammed the door shut behind me.

No one said a word.

Buck was still lost in his map – literally.

Murphy was still trying to find the gravel track. (I assumed he'd swerved to avoid a real or imagined landmine.)

Hustler's boots were still shifting nervously on the footplate.

'Bastards,' I muttered.

Then Murphy swerved again, my door popped back open, and once again I found myself staring into death's familiar face.

By the time we reached the so-called 'dispersal area' – the position from which the 1st Marine Division would invade – I felt as though I'd been at war for a year. My skin, which was white to begin with, had become even paler from the shock of dangling from the Humvee. Any remaining colour had been removed by the chalk-like dust that had blown into my face as I tried to avoid being crushed to death. 'Jeez,' remarked Hustler, when he ducked down from the gun turret. 'You look like you took a sand bath. Did you have the window open or something?'

'No,' I said, testily. 'The lock on the door's broken. It swung open every time Murphy swerved for a landmine.'

'Oh *yeah*,' said Hustler, absent-mindedly. 'We've been meaning to fix that. You just have to keep pulling it closed.'

'Right,' I said, nodding. The Marines, it seemed, had already changed me: I wanted to rip someone's head off.

At the dispersal area – another patch of hot, featureless gravel – Murphy and Hustler busied themselves putting camouflaged netting over the Humvee, creating an awning around the vehicle. The netting, I discovered, didn't actually provide any shade: it just gave me camouflage-patterned sunburn.

By mid-morning the sun was hard at work napalming the desert, forcing me to strip down to my soaked T-shirt and chemical-suit trousers. If the sun was bad, however, the bugs were worse. The air was an exotic soup of insects, some of them the size of meatballs. No matter what evasive action I took, they hovered around my face, taking exploratory bites out of my nose, neck and forehead. I began to feel as though my head had its own buzzing, snapping weather system. For the first time, the Kuwaitis' headwear began to make sense. I was relieved to remember I had a can of Xtreme 19 insect repellent in my pocket. Then I remembered it had fallen out during my near-death experience with the Humvee's broken door.

'These are big-assed bugs,' said Murphy, who was trying to punch away the insects without giving himself a black eye.

He eventually gave up, and decided to talk to me instead.

'Do they do much fightin' in London?' he asked.

I looked at the lance corporal. I could tell that, somewhere beneath all the dirt, his skin was pale and freckled like mine. The brownish colour of his hair, meanwhile, could easily have been a result of personal hygiene. If he'd taken a shower and come back a blond, I wouldn't have been surprised.

Murphy squinted back at me.

'There is on a Saturday night,' I said, picturing Leicester Square. That was a mistake. I suddenly felt overwhelmingly homesick.

'Do they fight Americans?' probed Murphy.

I wondered, for a second, if Murphy was trying to start a fight. He was small, but looked as though he could bench-press a bungalow. I imagined he could also get quite creative in his Marine-on-embed violence.

'No,' I said, emphatically. 'We *like* Americans. They're our allies. And friends. No one ever fights Americans.'

Murphy looked unconvinced, and slightly disappointed.

'Wanna learn how to fire an M-16?' he asked, unslinging his rifle.

It took me a while to process the question.

'I don't think that's, er, ethical,' I said.

Murphy gave me a disgusted look. He was now holding his gun so that it was pointing at me. I swallowed hard.

'So if there's a shitstorm,' he said, 'and you can shoot an Iraqi and save my life, or NOT shoot an Iraqi and let me die, *what you gonna do?*'

I thought about it for a second.

Then I said, '*I'd shoot the bastard.*'

After my gun tutorial – which basically involved learning how to switch off the M-16's safety catch – I quizzed Murphy about the war.

'Do you think this is it?' I asked.

'You mean . . . the invasion?' he said slowly.

'Yeah,' I said.

'Well, *last* time, they bombed the crap out the Iraqis for thirty-nine days before they sent in the ground troops,' he said. 'And that was with double the manpower. So I doubt it. Then again, they keep talkin about shock and awe, so maybe they'll just nuke the terrorist mother-fuckers and get it over with.'

Murphy, pleased with this analysis, lit one of my cigarettes. I'd grown so tired of him asking for them, I'd given him a pack. That was less than an hour ago. I noticed he was already down to the last three.

Hustler appeared from behind the Humvee carrying a shovel. He was all suntan and ribcage – like a Venice Beach bum. But he had the flat-iron head of a military man. This was a Marine whose youth had never involved voting Democrat. Hustler's hair was staging a retreat from his forehead, revealing the trenches of a life spent in foxholes and gun turrets, learning how to kill people.

'You can't dig a foxhole in this shit,' he said, throwing the shovel on to the gravel. 'You'd need a fuckin' bulldozer.'

Hustler was panting, with inlets of sweat trickling down his neck into the salt-water estuary of his lower back. I felt relieved: the first sergeant's failure to dig a foxhole meant I didn't have to try.

'What do *you* think, first sergeant?' I asked. 'Is this it? Are they gonna send the ground troops in this early?'

Hustler scratched the back of his walnut neck.

'Depends,' he said, lighting a filterless Marlboro. 'They're talkin' about shock and awe, but I don't see how they can do that if they're trying to win the hearts and minds of the Iraqi people at the same time.' His nose, I noticed, had been broken in two places. 'We need to go in, kill Saddam, and get the fuck out. Shock 'n' awe was Hiroshima; it was blitzkrieg. We're here to *liberate*.'

'I've heard they have this "e-bomb",' I said. 'It gives out an electro-magnetic pulse that melts the enemy's electrical circuits. Maybe they'll use that on Baghdad. Maybe that's what shock and awe is about.'

Murphy and Hustler considered my theory, which was based entirely on skim-reading one of Glen's old copies of *Newsweek*.

Hustler said, 'It's not much use if it lands next to a fuckin' hospital. And *everything* in Baghdad is next to a hospital.'

It was late afternoon when we got the order to move. This time I held on to the Humvee's door handle to keep it closed. I also wore my seat belt, just in case. It didn't take long for me to realize where we were going – in the distance I could make out several gigantic fireballs, with black wreaths of smoke drifting upward until they formed their own, thunderous weather front. I assumed the fires were in the Rumeila oilfields on the Iraq side of the border. 'Now *that* is a battlefield,' bellowed Hustler, from the Humvee's roof. He seemed almost boyishly excited. He had, after all, been waiting his entire adult life for this moment of violence.

We stopped just short of the razor-wire fence of the DMZ. Buck handed out painter's face masks, to protect us from the fumes. The sun hadn't set, but the sky was already black. Since leaving Camp Grizzly, I'd learned that the best way to keep track of what was happening was to listen to the radio in the Humvee's dashboard, instead of asking Buck questions, most of which he just ignored, feigning deafness. The radio was now saying something about 'twelve wellheads' having been destroyed. 'Saddam either set fire to them or blew them up,' it reported.

That night, I forced down an MRE and listened to the World Service. Saddam, it seemed, had rejected the option of going into exile. Another headline said that Iraq's 51st Mechanized Division had been armed with chemical shells. I also learned the most likely reason for the order to grow moustaches: Saddam had apparently equipped the Republican Guard with look-alike American uniforms, and was plotting to have Iraqi soldiers commit war crimes while wearing them. Saddam's Marine impersonators, however, would be clean-shaven. If all the Marines grew moustaches, therefore, his plan would be thwarted. It made perfect sense.

There was only an hour of light left – shortened by the oil fires – when I realized something awful: I had to use the lavatory – *urgently*. After a week of gut-clogging MREs, my aching bowels had finally surrendered.

The problem was, I didn't know where, or *how*, to go.

In the end, I just came out and said it.

'First sergeant,' I ventured. 'How do you use the bathroom out here?'

'Say again?' Hustler was busy trying to get his flameless heater to work.

'How do you, er, *take a shit*?'

'Did you bring an e-tool?' he asked, trying to contain a smirk.

'What's that?'

'An entrenching tool,' he explained, unhelpfully. Then he ducked inside the Humvee and pulled out his shovel.

'One of these,' he said.

'Oh, right,' I said, still not understanding what I had to do.

Hustler sighed.

'You dig a hole, take a shit in it, and cover it up again. Just think of it as getting back to nature. The great outdoors.'

It seemed simple enough. I looked around for a bush to hide behind. There wasn't one. There was only sand and gravel.

'Watch out for the scorpions,' said Murphy, who was aiming his M-16 at a vulture sitting on an abandoned propane tank next to a tumbleweed of razor wire. 'There's nine different species of 'em in Kuwait. All killers. They like coming out at night. So do the tarantulas and black widows.'

I was tired of being wound up, so I just grunted, took the shovel, and trudged off into the infinity of sand. I'd got about 20 feet away when I heard Murphy shout, '*And watch for fuckin' landmines, man.*'

How much worse could the war get? I remembered my grandfather's diary entry in 1940 after driving to Boulogne: 'Not very impressed by France at present. Although it may get better.' France, of course, got a lot worse for my grandfather. I wondered how much worse the Middle East would get for me. Or perhaps, I thought, I would get used to all this discomfort, and it would get better.

Now hyper-aware of landmines, I froze on the spot and, after hesitating for a second, plunged the shovel into a soft-looking piece of ground. Eventually I'd made a small, shallow hole. I wondered if the weight of my evacuation would be enough to trigger any 1991-vintage anti-personnel devices. I imagined the humiliation of dying from a landmine exploding in my buttocks.

In the end, nothing happened. But as I was covering up my mess I noticed several finger-sized holes, like animal burrows, all around me. Then I saw something glint in the reflected light from the fires. It looked like silk. I bent down. All of a sudden I was winded with adrenalin: *it was a spider's web*. I swore I could see a black, hairy leg behind it, climbing out of one of the holes.

Before I knew it, I was running back towards the Humvee, no longer caring about the buried explosives. '*Jesus*, stay on your tracks,

Chris!' I heard Hustler shout. But I wasn't listening. Murphy hadn't been kidding. There were killer spiders out here. And I'd just squatted over a tarantula's nest.

What with the cold, the wind, the fear and the cramped rear quarters of the Humvee, sleep was almost impossible. Work was also out of the question: Buck had lectured me on the importance of 'light discipline', which meant I couldn't use anything that glowed – including my laptop, satellite phone or digital watch – after sundown. 'At night, when the enemy sees a light, he shoots at it,' the captain explained. 'If you switch on that laptop screen at night, you might as well put up a goddam billboard and light it up with pink neon.' It was a long night. Still, I managed to pass out once or twice – a result of years of practice in economy-class seating. The dreams were the worst: wrenching hallucinations of home and family. I wanted to talk to the people in my dreams – my parents, my sister, Alana – but they couldn't hear me. They just stood around in a silent circle, looking down at me. 'I'm sorry,' I kept saying. 'I'm sorry.'

The next day – Wednesday 19 March – was a marathon of tense boredom. We just smoked cigarettes and fiddled with our MOPP gear, waiting for President Bush's forty-eight-hour deadline to pass. I worried about chemical weapons. I worried about the northern front, or the lack of it. I worried about being captured. I wondered what it would feel like to be blown up, or beheaded like Daniel Pearl. Before sundown, Buck handed me a printed sheet of A4 with the 1st Marine Division's blue, star-spangled logo on it. It was vaguely dated March 2003. At the top it said, 'Commanding General's Message To All Hands'. I knew it wouldn't be good news.

It continued:

> When I give you the word, together we will cross the line of departure, close with those forces that choose to fight, and destroy them. Chemical attack, treachery, and use of the innocent as human shields can be expected, as can other unethical tactics. Take it all in stride. Be the hunter, not the hunted . . . fight with a happy heart and strong spirit. For the mission's sake, our country's sake, and the sake of the men who carried the Division's colours in past battles . . . carry out your mission and keep your honour clean. Demonstrate to the world there is 'No Better Friend, No Worse Enemy' than a US Marine.

It was signed 'J. N. Mattis, Major General, US Marines'. I wondered if it was possible to wage war with 'a happy heart'.

The next morning, at 4 a.m., the deadline passed.

At 5.43 a.m., local time, a Baghdad correspondent for the BBC World Service reported hearing explosions near his hotel. The story was confirmed at 6.15 a.m., when President Bush announced that he had ordered an 'attack of opportunity', using thirty-six satellite-guided Tomahawk missiles and two F-117-launched GBU-27 bombs, in an attempt to 'decapitate' the Iraqi leadership. '*On my orders, coalition forces have begun striking selected targets of military importance to undermine Saddam Hussein's ability to wage war,*' the President declared over the radio. '*These are the opening stages of what will be a broad and concerted campaign.*'

At 10.38 a.m., as I was trying to eat some MRE peanut butter, Saddam fired back. Flying low under the radar, a Seersucker missile streaked towards us. The President's decapitation strike, it seemed, had failed.

'GAS! GAS! GAS!' shouted Buck.

I heard the 'crump' of a nearby explosion.

I always feared I would scream like a girl. In fact it turned out more like a baritone shout, starting out on key and then veering off into an atonal vibrato. I performed the scream in a crouched foetal position, with my arms wrapped over my helmet, behind the rear wheel of a 7-ton ammunition truck. In hindsight, of course, a gunpowder truck wasn't the cleverest place to cower. But it was the only protection I had, out there in the nothingness, amid the smoke and the flames.

It wasn't the Seersucker that made me scream. For a start, it was too far away (it whooshed over our heads and landed 600 yards outside Camp Commando, the headquarters of Lieutenant General James Conway, commander of the 1st Marine Expeditionary Force). And I was too busy putting my gas mask on to realize what was happening. Instead, the scream came later, at about 8 p.m. At the time, I was walking in almost total darkness from Buck's Humvee to the firing line, where six howitzers were pointing upward at the horizon. It was Hustler's idea: he'd suggested it would be a good idea to interview Kilo Battery's gunners.

Everything seemed fine – safe, almost.

Then came a flash of light so brilliantly white it bleached my eye-balls, followed by an overwhelming stench of cordite, and a pressure wave that right-hooked me in the face, almost knocking me over. All this was accompanied by an explosion so loud I thought I was the last thing I would ever hear. When I closed my eyes, I could see only a flood of white light. When I opened them again, the light was begin-ning to fade, like a lamp burn in celluloid. For a second, I wondered if I were dead, or blinded. Then the light bubbled and dimmed and I began to make out the dark outlines of the vehicles. No one was screaming, or running. Then, to the east, Echo Battery's guns went off, and I realized what had happened. *We had opened fire.*

The gun went off again. Stupidly, I'd continued to look at it, and I found myself blinded for a second time. I began to wonder if I'd done some permanent damage to my eyes. My ears, meanwhile, weren't just ringing, they were shrieking. I felt like Keith Richards after a two-nighter at Earls Court.

My panic attack lasted perhaps five minutes. When I finally brought myself under control, and got back to the Humvee, I began to feel relief that we hadn't been hit. That was when Iraq's 51st Mechanized Division started returning fire. 'SNOWSTORM! SNOWSTORM! SNOWSTORM!' said the radio. Buck threw himself out of the Humvee and shouted, 'GAS! GAS! GAS!' I got my mask on in record time, cracking the right lens of my glasses underfoot in the process. '*I thought the Iraqis were going to bloody surrender!*' I shouted to no one, through the valve near my mouth. '*And where's the Air Force?*' I hadn't spotted a single aircraft overhead. This didn't feel like a high-tech war. We were firing *cannon*, for God's sake. I thought this was supposed to be like a video game. Fortunately the Iraqis were fighting an even lower-tech war and shooting hopelessly long, their shells landing hundreds of yards to the south, in the giant car park of the desert. The better news was that no chemical weapons had been detected. Speckled Ali was apparently still in excellent health.

By the time the all-clear was called, the howitzers were still busy dealing out death, from a distance. I was told by a Marine that a bullet from an M-16 weighs barely more than 0.12 of an ounce. A shell from a howitzer weigh 13.5 lb. The round, known as DPICM, or 'dual purpose, improved conventional munitions', contains eighty-eight grenades, which soar over the heads of the enemy, separate, and then explode – piercing armour, dismantling body parts, and slicing through the pulp and gristle left behind. The howitzers turn the battlefield into a butcher's shop floor. And now, for miles up and down the DMZ, I could see the white flashes of the big guns going off. All four batteries were pumping out rounds at the same time: eighteen guns firing eighteen rounds, each one with eighty-eight bomblets, every thirty seconds.

Somewhere over the border, death was hard at work.

'Hey, Chris,' said Hustler at about 10 p.m., as the guns kept spitting out their fury. 'How would you like to fire one of the howitzers?'

'What?'

'Maybe we can arrange for you to shoot one of the big guns. That would make a pretty cool story, wouldn't it?'

'Er, yeah, maybe,' I stammered. I imagined being personally responsible for the deaths of hundreds of Iraqi soldiers.

'But, y'know, there might be an *ethical* problem with that,' I said.

'Damn right there'd be an ethical problem,' interrupted Buck, who was studying a map under a red night light. 'Both your asses would end up in Guantanamo Bay. Ain't no embeds firing no goddam howitzers.'

Hustler gave me an 'I tried' shrug.

Then Buck said, 'Oh, Chris, I forgot to tell you, we're in EmCon Delta now. You can use your phone and file a story. I think the enemy knows we're here. If they don't, they're either dead or about to be dead.'

The thought of writing a story seemed very strange. After all, I hadn't spoken to the office since leaving Camp Grizzly.

I switched on my satellite phone, waved the antenna around to lock on to the satellite, and dialled the foreign desk.

'Foreign new-*ews*?' said Barrow's familiar voice.

'Martin,' I said.

'Chris!' he said, almost choking with surprise. He sounded genuinely pleased that I was still alive. The familiarity of Barrow's voice suddenly made me well up. I got a horrible feeling I was going to burst into tears.

I tried to pull myself together.

'This is awful,' I said. 'This is really, really, awful.'

By now, I'd forgotten that the howitzers were going off in the background.

'Bloody hell, Chris,' he said. 'What are those, er, *loud noises?*'

'Guns,' I replied. 'Our guns, mainly. And some incoming. But mainly us.'

'Blimey,' said Barrow. 'Are you in a position to file us something? Just give me something off the top of your head.'

For the first time in my career, I blanked out. I couldn't think of anything. I was the world's worst war correspondent.

'Come on, Chris,' said Barrow. 'You've dictated stories a million times before. Just concentrate. You're going to be fine.'

But I wasn't fine. I was very much not fine.

And I had nothing to say.

The guns fired for six hours straight. I sat in the Humvee for most of that time, wishing I'd been able to dictate a more coherent news story to Barrow. Still, given that I was the only *Times* journalist with the front-line forces, I reassured myself that a news story with my name on it would appear on the front page. Not, of course, that it seemed worth it. What kind of nutjob would do *this* for a living?

Inside the Humvee, the disembodied voice of the radio informed us that the infantry had already blasted its way through the bulldozer-torn hole in the DMZ and into southern Iraq. '*We have contact, we have contact,*' the voice kept repeating. I looked out of the Humvee's window, but it was still suffocatingly dark outside. The only suggestion of the violence over the border was the distant echo of gunpowder, and metal hitting metal. For the first time since leaving Los Angeles, I thought about Oliver Poole, my rival on the *Daily Telegraph*. I thanked the God I didn't believe in that I hadn't been given Poole's place with the infantry. I imagined him crossing the DMZ on foot, with only a flak jacket and a notebook to protect him. *The poor bastard.* I wondered if he was as terrified as me. (He wasn't. 'I did feel remarkably unapprehensive,' he wrote of the first night of the war. 'I was confident in the ability of the soldiers I was with to protect me, and I had no doubt that somehow I would emerge unscathed, with a string of distinguished newspaper reports to my credit.')

Then one of the infantry commanders came on the radio. 'Hey, you artillery guys are doing a good job,' he said. 'All we're finding over here are arms and legs and pink mist.' Buck, Hustler and Murphy laughed. I wanted to vomit. But, to be honest, I was glad the Iraqis were dead. It meant they couldn't kill me.

We started moving just before dawn. By now we had a purple fluorescent sheet tied to the bonnet of the Humvee, so the Air Force wouldn't accidentally drop bombs on us. Our progress, however, was slow. A couple of tanks had broken down in the DMZ, creating a billion-dollar traffic jam of military hardware. Eventually, with a convoy of 7-ton trucks and howitzers behind us, we crashed through the breech and into the 6.2-miles of no man's land between Kuwait and Iraq. As the sun re-emerged from the cover of the horizon, I leaned out of my window to see that we were driving on a four-lane track marked by soft red and green lights, dug into the sand. It was as though we were on a runway, taking off into another dimension. 'Last week', announced Buck, 'this was a 10-foot berm and a 16-by-16-foot tank trench. *And now look at it.* Where have all those Bangladeshi United Nations dudes gone?'

A few yards into the DMZ we passed a sign saying, 'US TROOPS DO NOT ENTER!' and then another, which read, 'WELCOME TO THE DEMILITARIZED ZONE!' At the halfway point, two bearded Kuwaiti police officers stood beside their white squad cars, cheering and waving us on.

At the end of the 6.2 miles, there was no signpost welcoming us to Iraq, just an abandoned tent where the Iraqi border post used to be and the smouldering remains of a Republican Guard tank. Then another tank, and another. I tried not to look, fearing the charred and twisted human remains inside. The land was greener than Kuwait, and we started to pass dirty, withered farm animals and ranting Bedouin shepherds in black dishdashas. Some of them were flying white flags from their ramshackle, corrugated-iron huts, as they had been instructed to by Arabic leaflets air-dropped by the Americans. 'Shoe-*koo*, McKoo!' shouted Buck at one of them. The Bedouin saluted. It was hard to believe that only 90 miles to our south there was a city with Ferrari dealerships, KFC franchises and Armani boutiques. I looked at my wristwatch: it was now just after 9 a.m. on Friday 21 March: day two of the Iraq War.

'Here, take this,' said Buck, passing me a greenish, horse-sized tablet.

'What's this?' I asked.

'Doxycycline,' he said. 'It's for malaria.'

I examined the capsule, put it in my mouth, and gulped it down with a swig of lukewarm Saudi Arabian bottled water.

In front of me, Murphy did the same.

'I hate those fuckin' things,' he announced to the Humvee.

'Why?' asked Buck.

'The last time I took them', said Murphy, 'I was in Germany. I started to vomit, then I passed out. I had to be medevaced.'

Buck and I looked at each other. Then we looked at Murphy.

'Yeah, I get real sick with these tablets, man,' he reiterated. 'It sucks.'

'Murphy?' said Buck.

'Yeah?'

'Shit like that would've been good to know *before* you took the tablet.'

Murphy shrugged, and drove on.

It was 300 miles to Baghdad.

Basra, Iraq
2003

# 14

## While Shepherds Watched
## Their Guns by Night

'Murphy, *cover me*,' shouted Hustler, as he pulled out his Beretta 9 mm. He yanked open the Humvee's rear door and jumped out on to the gravel and mud. In front of me, Murphy grabbed his M-16 and also dived out of the vehicle. Then he crouched down behind the front wheel and aimed his gun over the bonnet. Buck stayed put in the passenger seat, chewing his lower lip, with a map of Iraq spread out over his lap like a tablecloth at a family picnic. I was in the back, as always, gulping down quick, shallow breaths and fingering the release catch of my diazepam auto-injector. If this was the end, I wanted to die happy. I didn't want to feel a thing.

We had made a terrible mistake. It was nearly sundown on Friday 21 March – the day we crossed the DMZ into Iraq – and we had been searching for a new firing position. Instead, we had ended up alone, our convoy of howitzers miles behind. When Buck finally got the GPS device to work, he realized we were *ahead* of the front lines. And now we were stuck in a dilapidated Iraqi hamlet which I guessed was somewhere near Basra International Airport. The dwellings – it was hard to call them houses – were made from stone, mud and corrugated iron, and guarded by razor wire and a sickly mutt with a hungry bark. White flags fluttered over the rooftops. It had been a muggy day, but now the infernal wind was blowing and it was getting cold.

I felt helpless – as though I were in the front row of a war movie, with the exits locked and bullets coming through the screen. I couldn't even call anyone, or file any stories, because we were back in EmCon Bravo. Buck, meanwhile, had given up trying to answer my questions, most of which were unanswerable anyway. ('Are you sure we're *safe* here?' was one of my favourites.) So, with nothing better to do, I just sat there and watched Hustler walk slowly forward, his pistol raised in the classic television–cop position. About 50 yards in front of him was a tall, robed man, gesticulating and shouting in Arabic. The Iraqi was standing on a steep berm, making it impossible to tell if he was alone, or whether this was an ambush. I wondered if I would be expected to fire the Humvee's machine gun if we were attacked.

'Shall I take him out, sir?' asked Murphy, hopefully. The lance corporal had spent the day cursing more than usual – making practically every word an expletive – and sweating feverishly. The hospital-strength doxycycline tablet had yet to knock him out, but I feared it wouldn't take much longer.

'Negative,' said Buck. 'Do *not* take the dude with the robe out.'

*Shoot him*, said a voice in my head. *Just shoot him*. I felt disgusted with myself. The Iraqi was probably terrified; we'd probably just turned his family into 'arms and legs and pink mist', as the faceless infantry commander had boasted. What I *should* have been thinking was, *Interview him; get out and interview him*. But I was more interested in staying alive than staying objective. The trouble was, I felt like a Marine. I was about as neutral as Murphy's trigger finger.

Hustler continued walking. You could see the power of the Beretta in his face: the possibility of being able to kill without going to prison. You could see the apprehension, too. He was old enough to know the consequences.

Murphy, on the other hand, was not.

'But I can waste him from here,' the lance corporal protested, his muddy index finger twitching with anticipation.

'He's civilian, as far as we know,' snapped Buck. 'Hearts and minds, Murphy. We don't shoot innocent people.'

I wondered if Buck would have said that if I weren't there.

'Maybe he's got explosives strapped to his fuckin' underwear,' suggested Murphy. 'Maybe he's an SEPW, sir.'

An SEPW, I remembered from one of the training sessions at Camp Grizzly, was a 'suicide enemy prisoner of war'. The Marines had been warned to expect Palestinian-style suicide attacks from insurgents.

'Maybe this is an ambush, cap'n,' he continued.

Murphy had a point. We were isolated, miles from any kind of support, and a perfect target. We didn't even have someone on the roof manning the 50-cal. The Iraqis must have known that taking American prisoners, torturing them, and then parading them on television was the best way to destroy support for the invasion back home. Earlier that morning I'd heard Sa'id al-Sahhaf, the Iraqi information minister (later to become known as 'Baghdad Bob' or 'Comical Ali') threaten Daniel Pearl-style vengeance on the invaders. '*Give yourself up*,' he said on the World Service. '*It is better for you this way, because if you do not we will cut off your heads, all of you. Curse you, you have put the US people to shame. We will destroy you.*'

'Well, we'll soon find out,' said Buck.

Hustler stopped a few feet in front of the Iraqi, who was wearing a stained grey dishdasha and leaning on a wooden stick. He looked more like a Bedouin shepherd than an insurgent. Not that Bedouin were harmless: they had a history of acting as battlefield surveillance for Iraqi commanders.

'Sir,' shouted Hustler. 'Please leave the area. This is a military operation. It is not safe to be here. *Please leave the area.*'

The man didn't budge. He continued his rant, pausing only to wipe tears from his face. He looked tortured, beyond reason.

Then I heard the explosion.

Kilo Battery was in good spirits after crossing the border. We were all still alive, for a start, and the resistance from the 51st Mechanized Division had been weaker than expected. More importantly, the intelligence about the Iraqis being armed with chemical shells turned out to be bogus. 'We killed a lot of motherfuckers,' reiterated the radio, as we passed the burning, smoking hulk of yet another Republican Guard tank. 'We keep expecting to see some infantry, but all we're seeing are body parts.' I wanted to look at the tanks, and the human offcuts strewn around them. But that way insanity beckoned. So I kept my eyes fixed straight ahead.

'Hey, cap'n, can we take pictures of the dead people?' asked Murphy.

'No,' said Buck. 'That is *not* cool.'

Iraq wasn't much to look at. I wasn't even sure if it was an improvement on the bug-infested sand pit of Kuwait. There were no landmarks or signposts, just endless tank trenches, sand berms and dirt roads – how the Wild West might have looked in the 1840s. Perhaps, I thought, it would get better.

After crossing more open countryside – which, in Iraq, means baked scrubland covered with a thin green weed – we hung a left on to fresh tracks, which I guessed had been made by the infantry in front of us.

Every single muscle and sinew in my body felt stiff, as though fear had given me rigor mortis. I could hardly believe I'd made it over the border. I was excited, in a warped way. I felt like a hero. I also felt like a fool. How would I get out of this? Back in England, I'd promised my grandfather I would leave Iraq if it became too dangerous. 'What on earth makes you think you'll be able to do that?' he replied, with a dark chuckle. My grandfather, after all, had spent *five years* trying to leave Czechoslovakia. The thought of me going to the Middle East made my grandmother cry. She still remembered the single-page telegram sent by the British War Office to my grandfather's father on 1 November 1940. It informed him that 'Dvr. Ross Selkirk Taylor' was missing in action, presumed dead or captured.

We continued heading north-east, towards Basra.

By late morning I became aware of a voice trapped inside my head. It was a female voice, squeaky and bubbly, with an 1980s backing track. '*Borderline,*' it sang. '*Feels like I'm going to lose my mind/ You just keep on pushing my love over the borderline.*' So much for war having a rock 'n' roll soundtrack. My war, it seemed, would be fought to the teenie-bop of early Madonna. *Great.* I started to zone out, the song still looping interminably in my head. I hadn't slept for twenty-four hours. Perhaps I was becoming delirious. My trance was interrupted, however, by the rhythmic thump of a helicopter overhead – the first aircraft I'd seen since the invasion began. About bloody time, I thought. Where had the Air Force been? 'Look up,' instructed Hustler, lowering himself into the Humvee from the gun turret. 'That's a Marine Huey up there. I'll bet you Colonel Mattis is in it. Man, he *loves* the fight.'

This was an understatement.

'Actually, it's a lot of fun to fight,' the general would tell a war conference in California two years later, causing public outrage. 'You know, it's a hell of a hoot; it's fun to shoot some people. I *like* brawling.'

Apart from the handful of Bedouin who lived near the border, we didn't see any Iraqis for miles. The nearest we came was a stray dog, trotting contentedly, and with no urgency, in the direction of Kuwait City.

Murphy, meanwhile, sweated and grunted as he drove. Every so often he seemed to slump in his seat, and the Humvee would veer right, causing Buck to shout, 'MURPHY! LANDMINES!' I expected the lance corporal to pass out at any second. Even Buck kept giving him worried looks. I wondered who would drive if Murphy had to be medevaced. I hoped it wouldn't be me.

Eventually we joined a paved road.

The Humvee speeded up. Now we were doing 20 m.p.h.

It was a shock when we saw the first Iraqis: about thirty prisoners of war, sitting cross-legged in a roadside ditch, their hands fastened behind their backs with plastic flexicuffs. Their eyes were hard and shiny. Two Marines brandishing M-16s stood over them. The Iraqis looked gaunt and shell-shocked; some of them had traces of blood on their white dishdashas and no-brand jeans. An empty white pick-up truck – the Iraqi equivalent of a Humvee – was parked opposite them. I felt as though I'd become trapped inside a television newsreel. It's easy to ignore the destitute and bleeding when you're at home on the sofa, dunking biscuits into your tea. It's easy to avoid asking all those difficult, unanswerable questions about how they got there and whether or not your country had anything to do with it. It's not so easy when they're sitting a few yards away, next to their confiscated mortars and AK-47s.

I felt sorry for the Iraqis: they'd been screwed by Saddam Hussein, screwed by the war with Iran, screwed by the first Gulf War, screwed by the sanctions, and now screwed by the 1st Marine Division. They'd also been screwed, of course, by the British, who invaded Mesopotamia back in November 1914 and considered introducing the country to mustard gas. 'I do not understand this squeamishness about the use of gas,' declared Winston Churchill, then Colonial Secretary, in a memo. 'I am strongly in favour of using poison gas against uncivilized tribes.'

So there the Iraqis were, in their own country, only a few miles from one of the world's largest oilfields – and barely two hours' drive from the Rolex retailers of Kuwait City – and they had *nothing*. I didn't blame them for hating us. I didn't blame them for returning fire. I might not have blamed them for using chemicals. Perhaps the invasion would one day be worth it; perhaps one day Iraq would be a rich, democratic republic. But what reason did *they* have to believe that?

'What you do with them at night?' I asked Buck.

'We shoot 'em,' interrupted Murphy.

Buck gave him an accusatory look.

Murphy spat tobacco out of the window. 'Just kidding,' he said.

'Actually,' said Buck, 'we release them. That means they can go back to their weapons and try again tomorrow night.'

The downside of being in Buck's Humvee soon became clear. Our job was to drive ahead of the howitzers and find new firing positions, where the Long Distance Death Dealers could set up shop and cover the infantry during another push forward. We were essentially the forward reconnaissance unit. And so, after passing the prisoners of war, we left the howitzers on the relative safety of the road and went off in search of a new location. We drove for an hour, eventually reaching Highway 8, a four-lane motorway that runs from Safwan on the Kuwait border to Basra, then on to Baghdad. Instead of taking the road, we roared over a bulldozed crash barrier, across the central reservation, and down the embankment on the other side.

Highway 8, I noticed, had been blocked by a company of tanks, in front of which was a solitary Iraqi. He was lying bleeding on the tarmac next to a green motorcycle. 'Is he dead?' asked Murphy as we passed. 'No,' came Hustler's shout from the roof. 'He's alive, but he sure as hell looks shell-shocked.'

The tanks reassured me. I felt as though we were surrounded by friendly forces. And so, as Murphy steered the Humvee through ditches and barren fields, I began to relax. As the fear subsided, I started to feel strangely bored. So I pulled out my Walkman, loaded up a CD, and dozed off. I felt like a child again, in the back seat of my dad's Renault 9, on a French summer holiday. In my dream, the familiar figures returned, standing in a sunbleached room from my childhood, all swirly carpets and patterned wallpaper. There was Mum, Dad, Catherine, and Alana. I was looking up. My dad was telling me something I couldn't make out. He said it again. Now I could hear. *'Proud line of cowards,'* he was saying, over and over again.

When I awoke, the Humvee had stopped and Buck and Hustler were arguing.

'Are you sure?' said Buck.

'I'm fuckin' sure!' replied Hustler.

'Hey, wakey-wakey,' said Buck, turning to me. *'Sweet dreams?* Do you have any batteries for that tape recorder of yours?'

Glad to be finally of some use, I dug deep into my North Face laptop bag and produced a twelve-pack of Duracell. The batteries were, in fact, for my electric toothbrush. But I wasn't going to tell the captain that.

Buck opened up his GPS device, tore out the dud batteries, and replaced them with my Duracells. Then he waited.

*'Goddamit,'* he said, finally. 'You're right. We're here.' He pointed to the middle of an empty white grid on his map.

'Where's the front line?' asked Hustler.

'There,' said Buck, moving his finger down and to the left.

Then, on the berm in front of us, a robed figure appeared.

For a fraction of a second, Buck, Hustler, Murphy – and, of course, the cowering blue-helmeted embed in the back of the Humvee – thought we'd been ambushed. Then we realized the explosion was too big, and too distant, to be aimed in our direction. It was an industrial noise, like machinery pounding metal into metal, and on a totally different scale of violence to the artillery fire I'd grown used to. I guessed it was an Air Force bomb, taking out an Iraqi weapons bunker.

'Boy, someone's gettin' all messed up over there,' declared Buck. 'I sure as hell would not like to be gettin' some of that . . .'

'That shit would *suck,*' agreed Murphy, who was still kneeling down and peering through the sights of his M-16.

The Bedouin, I noticed, had ducked. Now he was back on his feet, and Hustler was trying to communicate with him using hand signals. The exchange began with Hustler saluting, then giving the Iraqi a questioning look. The nomad began frantically shaking his head. This, I assumed, meant he wasn't an Iraqi soldier. Then the Bedouin cupped his hands towards his mouth. This was followed by a patting motion, as though he were tousling the hair of a young child.

'He's saying he needs water for his family,' said Buck, getting restless.

Hustler turned and started jogging back to the Humvee, his gun now back in its holster. He stopped outside Buck's window.

'Hey, captain,' he said. 'Do we have any spare water?'

'What did you tell him?' asked Buck, passing the first sergeant his own bottle of al-Qassim through the window.

'I basically told him I'd give him the water if he would take his fuckin' sheep somewhere else and keep them there.'

'Good work,' said Buck, through a snorted chuckle.

'Man, that dude was old and crusty,' said Hustler, grinning. 'He kind of looked like the guy from *Lord of the Rings*.' With that, the first sergeant turned, jogged back to the Bedouin, and handed him the water. The tribesman waved thank you with his wooden crook and hobbled off over the berm.

'How do you know he's not going to give away our position?' I asked Buck.

'I don't,' said Buck.

Hustler, now coughing up sand and sweating, jumped back into the Humvee.

'Let's get the fuck out of here, Murphy,' said Buck – 'before we meet someone who isn't from *Lord of the Rings*.'

'Foreign new-*ews*?'

It was 7.10 p.m. and we were back in EmCon Delta, which meant I could use my satellite phone. Buck had found a position for the Long Distance Death Dealers near Highway 8, and the howitzers were hard at work again, raining down death and dismemberment on some poor bastards 18 miles to the east. According to the World Service, that was where the 1st Marine Division and the British 7th Armoured Brigade were trying to take Basra. In a few hours time the 51st Mechanized Division would surrender. Not, of course, that I knew that.

'Martin,' I said.

'Chris! How's it going?'

Barrow sounded chipper. He probably knew more about the progress of the war than I did. Buck wouldn't tell me anything.

'Great,' I said, in a voice thick with phlegm. '*This is so much fun.*'

One of the howitzers went off, drop-kicking me in the stomach with the back blast. By now, however, I was used to it.

'Still at war, then,' said Barrow.

'Yeah. Did my story go in on Thursday night?' I asked.

Barrow suddenly sounded distracted. His keyboard clacked in the background.

'Oh, er, yeah. It went through.'

*It went through?* This, in Barrow-talk, meant the story went through the computer system, but didn't get in the newspaper.

'Martin, did it make it into the *paper*?'

'I'm not sure,' said Barrow, now bullshitting for Britain. 'I think something went in the first edition. Don't know about the second . . .'

'*What?*'

The first edition, as Barrow knew, was shipped overseas to news-stands in Europe. No one else in Britain, apart from the night editors of rival papers and the drunks who bought *The Times* from Leicester Square tube station at midnight, would ever see it. It probably wouldn't even make it into the electronic archive. *The Times spiked my story from the first day of the war!* I felt winded with betrayal. This, I knew, was punishment for dictating 'mucky' copy.

The silence, transmitted via space at $10 per minute, was uncomfortable.

'Not to worry,' I said, eventually. 'I've got another story – this one about the Bedouin. I'll file it over the weekend.'

'Good stuff,' said Barrow.

The line went dead.

I felt so utterly dejected I almost didn't hear the Iraqi mortar when it exploded less than 200 yards outside the camp.

'Incoming! Incoming! Incoming!' bellowed Hustler. We looked at each other, both thinking the same thing: *the Bedouin.*

As he masked up, Hustler shook his head in frustration.

Still upset with Barrow, I flung my cracked, mud-smeared glasses into the sand and pulled out my own mask.

I wondered if this story would get spiked too.

War makes you feel special. It makes you feel better than your office-bound colleagues, gossiping over the water cooler, or wiping Prêt-à-Manger mayonnaise from their mouths as they hunch in their veal-fattening pens. War gives your life narrative structure. The banal becomes the dramatic. When you're at war, you don't worry about American Express bills. War spares you the washing–up. Life at the brink of death makes all other life seem trivial. You're a *hero* when you're on the front lines. Here's another thing about war: as much as you hate the fear and the MREs and the mutilated corpses and the incoming mortars and the freezing nights in the Humvee, you know you'll be a more popular and interesting person when, or if, you return. Because war is all about death, and everyone wants to know what death is like.

These, as far as I can tell, are the upsides of war. But I suspect war doesn't make you any better. All life, ultimately, exists on the brink of death; war just makes it obvious. Besides, no matter how close to death you come, you never get any closer to understanding it. 'Death is easy,' as one veteran combat correspondent once said to me. '*Life* is hard.' War, I fear, makes it impossible to go back home. And then you have to go to war again, to make sure you're still special.

So this was what I did on the weekend of 21 March. On Friday night I lay in a shallow foxhole wearing a chemical suit, with my fingers plugged in my ears, as the Iraqis threw mortars at us and we killed them in return. We killed a lot faster than they could throw, and soon the mortars stopped.

On Saturday morning I squatted in Kilo Battery's FDC, or 'fire direction centre', writing a story about Bedouin nomads on my laptop, which I had wrapped with plastic sheeting to stop the sand getting between the keys. The FDC was constructed from two Humvees parked back to back, with a heavy tarpaulin canopy in between. Under the canvas were a whiteboard, a table with a map flattened out on it, and a steel-cased computer. The computer, I was told, could analyse weather, wind, map coordinates and other variables – including the colour of the Iraqis' underwear, probably – and then decide how much gunpowder should be put inside the shells, and at what angle the howitzers should be pointed. Using mathematical rules that the Mesopotamians themselves probably discovered, all this ensured that Kilo Battery produced the maximum possible number of body parts per round.

The big guns may have looked primitive, but they were deceptively ambitious in their destruction – and more accurate, I suspected, that any billion-dollar Air Force gadget. From my dusty corner of the FDC I heard new targets being called in over the radio by 'forward observers', who were somewhere out in the kill zone ahead of us. I was grateful I wasn't embedded with *them*. Seconds after each new coordinate was processed, the pompous bolero of the howitzers resumed.

I wondered how many we'd killed. Hundreds? Thousands?

On Saturday afternoon we filled up with fuel. This was more complicated than it sounds. It involved skidding down into a dried river bed, where four jumbo-sized oil tankers had been parked behind a cover of yellowing palms – the only vegetation I'd seen so far. The tankers were guarded by a semicircle of unsmiling Marines, pointing 50-cals out into the murk. One by one, Kilo Battery's vehicles filled up with diesel then wobbled and grunted out of the mud forecourt. Behind us, other units were lined up in a perfectly choreographed ballet of military logistics.

With full tanks, we rejoined Highway 8, this time using the four-lane tarmac surface. The road seemed to be littered with rubber, which I assumed must have come from the tanks. Then I realized the rubber was in fact black leather. As we began to pass makeshift paddocks with barefoot prisoners inside, I understood what had happened. The 8,000 or so soldiers of the 51st Mechanized Division had surrendered – by taking off their boots. And now there was a cobbler's nightmare of scuffed leather and snapped laces flung all over the asphalt. Iraqis civilians stood on the roadside and cheered at the military convoy as it thundered past. I wondered if they were genuinely happy to see us, or if they just wanted our rations. It was hard, however, not to feel stirred by the welcome. Perhaps the Iraqis – mainly Shi'ites in this part of the country – wanted to be liberated after all. The cheering and waving continued for miles, until I felt a stinging pressure behind my eyes. I looked at Hustler. He was smiling like he'd just won the lottery, and smoking a victory cigarette. 'Boy, this sure makes you feel good,' he said. 'Now I *know* we're doing the right thing.'

I was growing to like Hustler. I respected the way he'd handled the Bedouin, and the fact that he'd turned down my offer to call his wife on my satellite phone. 'If I call the missus it'll just make it worse,' he said. 'She'll hear one of the howitzers go off and think I'm about to fuckin' die.' Murphy, in contrast, had jumped at the chance to use the phone. 'No shit, I'm in Iraq,' I heard him say to his girlfriend, a college student in Nevada. 'There are dead guys *every*where.'

We spent Saturday night in a camp outside Basra. Surrounding us was enough military hardware to invade China, never mind Iraq. For the first time since crossing the border, I felt safe. I felt so safe, in fact, that I contemplated putting up my Two-Man Xtreme 19 Mountain Adventure Pod. I thought better of it, however, and decided instead to sleep on the floor beside the Humvee. I hoped there were no tarantulas in Iraq. Before I passed out, I called Alana, then my mum. It was the first time I could talk without a backing track of artillery fire and incoming alerts.

'Are you *safe*?' asked my mother. 'A man from the Iraqi information department says he's going to cut everyone's heads off . . .'

'Yes, I'm fine,' I said. 'Don't listen to the Iraqis. They don't have a chance. This will all be over pretty quickly, I'm sure.'

After seeing the welcome party on Highway 8, I almost believed it.

'Can't you come back?' asked my mother.

'Leaving would be more dangerous than staying,' I said.

I wished I'd been making this up. But it was true. There was simply no way of going south. Even if there were, it would be career suicide. As far as I knew, I'd managed to get only one story published, in one edition of the paper. And, besides, I didn't have my passport, so I wouldn't be able to leave Kuwait anyway. I was stuck with Captain Buck Rogers and his men until the end of the war.

Or at least until I could come up with a better plan.

The next morning the 1st Marine Division went on a Sunday drive. Iraq was supposed to be the worst camping trip of my life, but it felt more like the worst road trip – a crawl to the seaside on a sweltering August bank holiday, on an empty stomach, with the locals taking pot-shots at you from the hard shoulder. We set off at dawn, in a steel fist of a convoy that stretched further than I could see in either direction. This, I was told, was known as a 'thunder run'. We headed north, up Highway 8, in the direction of Baghdad. We were well covered: on either side of the motorway were formations of US Army missile launchers, raised into the firing position. Then we saw the Army's bridge-building division, composed of hundreds of amphibious lorries, each one carrying gigantic folding metal structures. In spite of the firepower, I flinched every time an overpass loomed. Each one had a sinister brick sentry box on top, with narrow slits for windows – perfect for lobbing out grenades.

By early afternoon we had followed the Shatt al-Arab waterway towards the town of al-Qurnah. With bleached desert on one side and sparkling blue water on the other, it almost felt as though we were in California. The asphalt of Highway 8, however, was virtually unmarked. Road signs, in Arabic and English, were few and far between. And I hadn't seen a single petrol station.

I kept my short-wave radio switched on, and listened to furious Arabs being interviewed by the BBC. They predicted apocalpyse, and defeat for the Western infidels. There seemed to be no reports about the Marines' steady progress northward. I did learn, however, that Basra International Airport had been secured, and that the Marines were encountering 'pockets of resistance' near al-Nasiriyah, the capital of Iraq's date-growing region. I remembered reading in my Lonely Planet guidebook that al-Nasiriyah is only a few miles from Ur – Prophet Abraham's alleged birthplace – which was excavated by Sir Leonard Woolley in the 1920s. The royal tombs of Ur had survived 4,500 years. I wondered if they would make it through 2003.

As we chugged forward, rarely getting over 10 m.p.h., I tried to eat an MRE, but I'd left my appetite behind somewhere in the Kuwaiti desert. Every few miles we'd see Iraqi civilians standing on the side of the road with young children on their shoulders. They would wave, make peace signs, and point at their mouths. Sometimes a Marine would throw them a yellow bag of humanitarian rations. At one point we passed a Marine who had constructed a roadside lavatory out of an upturned ammunition crate. He sat on it, ignoring the passing traffic, reading a book. The cover looked like Hemingway. Surrounding him was a junk yard of Western consumer culture: crushed Marlboro packets, dented Coca-Cola cans, torn M&Ms wrappers, and hundreds of empty bottles of al-Qassim water. I later read that the coalition troops in the Middle East got through 45 million 50-ounce water bottles *every month*.

'The second we take Baghdad,' muttered Murphy, 'someone's gonna get a fat-assed contract to clean this shit up.'

'I wouldn't bet on it,' said Buck. 'That's probably *our* job.'

At about 4 p.m. we left Highway 8 and crossed the Euphrates on a temporary iron bridge. Murphy, who had taken another doxycycline tablet at the camp in Basra, was starting to look a bit perkier, although his face was still streaked with sweat and mud. On the north side of the river, Iraq changed for the worse. We found ourselves in a ghoulish landscape of desiccated mudbanks. The place looked as though it had been hit by a nuclear bomb. Dying reeds slumped in pools of brown water. Then, through a gritty fog, came men who looked like apparitions: skeletons with torn robes, bare feet, and festering blisters on their legs and faces. They held up bony infants, as diseased mutts snapped at their feet. We drove on, throwing out rations as we passed. As the sun ducked under the bloody horizon, I wondered if we'd descended into Purgatory. Was this really what had become of the Babylonians: the people who'd invented the number zero; who'd split the day into twenty-four hours, and the hours into sixty minutes?

'Welcome to the marshlands,' said Buck – 'the most fucked-up place on earth.'

I kept thinking we would stop, but we never did. We just lumbered onward, at 3 m.p.h., down a recently bulldozed surface of dried mud. To the right of us, over a berm, Saddam appeared to have been building a new motorway. Either that or it was one of the Iraqi president's drainage plants, installed after 1991 to destroy one of the world's largest freshwater ecosystems, and make half a million marsh Arabs homeless. Saddam apparently saw the Shi'ite marsh-dwellers as a political threat. I wondered what the mudflats would have looked like back in the 1950s, when the Ma'dan still crossed the marshes in wooden canoes, raised water buffalo, and made cathedral-like *mudhifs*, or huts, out of dried reeds. It was almost too depressing to think about.

As we pushed on, we were overtaken by white Nissan pick-up trucks. One of the drivers, I noticed, wore a black dishdasha and a New York Yankees baseball cap. The vehicles streaked past like grounded comets, leaving behind tails of stinging orange dust. One of them almost clipped the Humvee.

'Who the fuck are those dudes?' asked Murphy, coughing.

'Special forces,' said Buck, with a sneer. I wondered if any of them were SAS – the next generation of David Silvers.

'They need special fuckin' driving lessons,' concluded Murphy.

For the first time since Kuwait, we all laughed.

The convoy continued. By now it was almost completely dark outside, so Buck handed Murphy a pair of night-vision goggles. When he put them on, Murphy looked as though he had a telescope strapped to his forehead. I recalled what the colonel had told the Marines in Kuwait: 'Your average Iraqi, when he sees a Marine with night-vision goggles and an M-16 rolling past his house in an armoured Humvee, is gonna think he's having a close encounter of the third kind.'

We drove with our lights off, as did everyone else. From the back of the Humvee, without the benefit of night vision, it felt suicidal. Our progress came in short, jerky bursts, with Murphy stamping on the brakes, making us crunch violently to a halt inches from the luggage rack of the Humvee in front.

I'd been at war for almost seventy-two hours now, and the nights were turning out to be a lot worse than the days. I kept wondering what was lurking behind the berm to our right. I'd once read that some of the Ma'dan were descended from the Zenj – a race of cannibal slaves who revolted under the leadership of Ali the Abominable in the year 869, until they were driven back into the marshes by the Babylonians. The image of the slave warriors made me shiver. I wished I had no imagination. I pulled my North Face jacket over my shoulders and tried to fall asleep. My limbs, however, were aching too much. And, as always, the reports over the Humvee's radio were getting more horrifying as the night progressed. At 10 p.m. the first medevac requests were called in: a 7-ton had overturned; a Humvee had crashed; a tank had fallen into the Euphrates. These hellish dispatches were all delivered by the same disembodied bass mono-tone – like a voice from the underworld, coming out of the darkness.

Five hours later, at 3 a.m., we finally stopped. We had been driving for twenty hours. I fell out of the Humvee and dry-heaved. I looked up to see a corporal from the vehicle behind us. 'Christ, I'm saddle-sore,' he said.

Murphy, exhausted, pulled off his goggles, threw down his sleeping bag in a ditch, and collapsed on top of it. He passed out with his arms over his head. He had, I realized, pulled off an astonishing feat of phys-ical endurance. Buck, as usual, made his bed on the Humvee's bonnet; Hustler curled up on the roof. By now it was savagely cold. Each gust of wind whistled through the Humvee's panel cracks. I wished my chemical suit was lined with wool, not charcoal. I lay in an inverted U-shape across the rear seats, my back arched over the gunner's foot-plate in between. The armour of my flak jacket, useful for once, helped support my shoulders. My head, meanwhile, drooped backwards, as though I were in the recovery position. I started to shiver uncontrol-lably – probably because I hadn't eaten since Kuwait. *I couldn't sleep.* Wouldn't this be the perfect time for Republican Guard to attack?

We were in EmCon Bravo, so calling Alana was out of the ques-tion. If I powered up my satellite phone now, a klaxon would prob-ably go off in Baghdad. Instead, I flicked on my short-wave radio and plugged in the earbud headphones. This was a mistake. The World Service informed me that the Republican Guard had captured five American soldiers, including a woman, and killed eight more. The report said the Americans had been ambushed near al-Nasiriyah. *Wasn't that where we were?* Two of the American prisoners had already been interviewed on Iraqi television, in contravention of the Geneva Convention. They said they were from the 507th Maintenance Company. I tried not to imagine the horror of being caught alive.

My heart changed tempo.

There was more to come: the ITN correspondent Terry Lloyd had been killed in Basra; a cameraman for Australia's ABC network had died after a car bomb had exploded in northern Iraq; an American soldier had been arrested for throwing a grenade into a hooch in Kuwait; two British pilots were presumed dead after being downed by a 'friendly' Patriot missile; ten Marines had been slaughtered in a fake surrender in the marshlands; and the Iraqi information minister was claiming that the Americans' advance up Highway 8 was all part of an elaborate trap. '*We have made them enter the quagmire and they will not be able to get out,*' he declared. What the short-wave radio didn't tell me was that the Army's 3rd Infantry Division – in which Oliver Poole was embedded – was already less than a day's march from Baghdad.

After the onslaught of bad news, the BBC announcer changed tone. '*And now*', she crooned, '*we go live to Hollywood.*' It was then I remembered: tonight – still Sunday 23 March in California – was the seventy-fifth Annual Academy Awards. Somewhere, in an alternative universe, I would be 8,500 miles away, in a bow tie and a black tuxedo, sipping champagne in the press room of the Kodak Theatre. After the show, perhaps, I would take Alana to the *Vanity Fair* post-Oscars party at Morton's steakhouse. Perhaps I would meet Kate Winslet, Brad Pitt or Julia Roberts.

But there was no alternative universe.

I was stuck in some god-awful swamp, in a faraway country, on the front lines of an invasion; shivering, lonely, and waiting to die.

I was woken at 6.30 a.m. by a voice in my head.

'*We live in fictitious times,*' it said. '*We live in the time where we have fictitious election results that elect a fictitious president. We live in a time where we have a man who's sending us to war for fictitious reasons.*' For a while I thought I was still dreaming. I wanted to sit upright, but there was no blood in my limbs. I released a low groan of pain. 'My back,' I said. 'Oh no. My back . . .' Somehow I managed to shift the dead weight of my legs. Then I realized my short-wave radio was still switched on and the headphones were still jammed into my ears.

'*We are against this war, Mr Bush,*' said the voice, which I now recognized as belonging to the film-maker Michael Moore. '*Shame on you, Mr Bush. Shame on you.*' I could hear booing and whistling in the background as an orchestra started to play cheesy show-business music. I released another groan.

For a moment, I wanted Moore to be out there with Kilo Battery. I wanted him to make his anti-war speech in the marshlands, to the Marines. I wanted him to see what Saddam had done to the Ma'dan. I wanted him to know what it feels like to wake up in a Humvee, surrounded by people who want to kill you, and listen to a tuxedoed film-maker in California tell you that it's all based on a lie.

It was then I realized the true genius of the embedding scheme: *it had turned me into a Marine.* I was thinking like a fighter, not a reporter. And yet I wasn't a fighter. I was an idiot in a blue flak jacket. The Marines didn't even want me there. Being an embed, it seemed, was the loneliest job on earth.

Buck, Murphy and Hustler were already awake.

'Did you hear the World Service?' I asked, stretching my legs.

'If you listen to the BBC World Service,' declared Buck, 'we lost this goddam war four days ago. It's depressing.'

'Want some coffee?' asked Hustler.

I didn't respond. I thought I must have misheard him.

'Coffee?' he said again.

Then I smelled it: hot, chocolatey coffee, like an olfactory orgasm.

'God yes,' I said, walking around the Humvee.

Behind the rear wheel, Hustler had lit a camping stove and was boiling water. In it he'd poured MRE cappuccino powder. I winced at the thought of what it would taste like: I was used to $10 tins of gourmet espresso.

'Welcome to Starbucks,' said Hustler, grinning.

He handed me a steaming metal mug. I slurped the hot liquid warily. It was the best cup of coffee I'd tasted in my life.

'First sergeant,' I announced, 'if you were a girl, I'd marry you.'

'Fuck off,' he replied.

I didn't blame Hustler for not wanting to marry me. I hadn't washed or changed my underwear for four days. I lived like an animal. My morning routine involved digging a hole for my morning evacuation, washing my face with a dollop of foam hand sanitizer, then shaving in the Humvee's rearview mirror using cold bottled water. (By now the Marines had been told to get rid of their moustaches, because they interfered with the gas masks.) Then I'd try to eat breakfast – usually a sachet of peanut butter or raspberry jam. More often than not it would make me retch.

Today, however, Hustler's coffee, along with the relief of surviving the night, had cheered me up. By the time I climbed back into the Humvee I was humming 'Borderline' again. Then I realized it: I was actually *proud* of myself for having lasted this long. I was proud of myself for not backing out of the embedding scheme at the Kuwait Hilton. I was even proud of my stinking four-day-old underwear. What's more, the stress of the invasion seemed to be using up all my excess adrenalin, so that during my fleeting moments of safety I felt in better physical form than I had in years. Perhaps Dr Ruth had been right all along. I remembered what she'd told me about 'fight-or-flight' anxiety at her clinic in New York, before September 11. 'It's called "acute stress response",' she said. 'Young men used to need that on the battlefield.' I almost wanted to call Dr Ruth and tell her that my adrenalin had finally come in useful. At last *it was doing its job*. That was when I realized it: part of me was actually enjoying this.

It didn't take long for the part of me enjoying the war to come to its senses. It took until sundown, in fact, when the fighting resumed. The attacks weren't the organized, tank-led assaults we'd expected from the Republican Guard. Instead, they were opportunistic pot-shots from Iraqi 'irregulars', who appeared out of the mud and vanished just as quickly. Even tracking their mortars by radar was pointless: by the time we fired back, the insurgents had moved. They were clearly smarter than their recently slaughtered comrades in the 51st Mechanized Division.

The 1st Marine Division was much further north now, towards the city of al-Diwaniyah, and the convoy had split up into tactical units. Kilo Battery had spent the day, as usual, looking for a safe place to park the howitzers, eventually finding a suitably grim stretch of marshland in the late afternoon.

The Marines went through their usual routine of surveying the site twice, using a plumb line and an arc, to make sure the guns would fire in the right direction. No sooner were they done, however, than a herd of camels began strolling haughtily through the camp. Buck groaned. 'I'm sure the goddam Iraqis are dressing up as camels now,' he muttered. Then came the inevitable Bedouin shepherd, ushering his animals with a bent wooden stick. He wore a look on his face that said, 'Who? Me?' Buck thumped his palm against his forehead. 'Lance corporal,' he said to Murphy, 'will you get the Arabic phrasebook, find the word for 'danger', and write it on some big pieces of cardboard from the MRE boxes. I wanna put up signs.'

Murphy did as he was told. Before long our camp was surrounded by notices telling the Bedouin to bugger off. It was too late now, however. We all knew what the incident with the camels meant: our position had been compromised. At just after 9 p.m. this was confirmed by the Humvee's radio. 'You have about a dozen technicals heading your way,' the deadpan voice informed us.

'What's a technical?' I asked, hoping for the best.

'It's like what they had in Somalia,' explained Buck. 'The insurgents take a civilian vehicle and put a machine gun on the roof. We call 'em technicals.' The name, Buck told me, came from the days when the Red Cross used to buy vehicles for militias in return for not being attacked. The bribes were written off as 'technical expenses'. I wondered who'd paid for the Iraqis' vehicles.

'So we're . . . being attacked?'

Buck looked at me for a while.

Then he said, 'Don't you *ever* look on the bright side?'

I gave a weak, humourless laugh.

'Pass me the night visions,' said Hustler from the back seat. He put them on and heaved himself up into the gun turret.

'They're still approaching,' announced the radio. 'You've got three mikes before contact.' That meant three minutes.

Hustler's boots tap-danced on the footplate beside me as he swung the 50-cal from side to side, trying to see the technicals.

Buck and Murphy started klacking rounds into their M-16s.

I wished there was something I could do other than just sit and wait. I almost wanted to take Hustler's place in the machine-gun turret. Instead, I concentrated on trying to silence a hysterical internal monologue. It reminded me of what Wilfred Owen had once written in a letter from the front lines: 'There is a point where prayer is indistinguishable from blasphemy. There is also a point where blasphemy is indistinguishable from prayer.' I felt slightly ashamed of my prayers, even in their current blasphemous form. I'd stopped going to church as soon as my parents would let me, and it seemed corny and predictable (not to mention convenient) that I would convert while under gunfire. But praying is rational. I'd prayed on September 11, while watching the office workers fall from the floors of the World Trade Center. Unless you knew for a fact that it wouldn't do any good, *why wouldn't you*?

I looked over at Buck, who was now playing with the crucifix on the dashboard. I knew that Buck hated having me around (on several occasions he'd tried to get me to ride in the back of one of the ammunition trucks), but I respected him nevertheless. After all, the captain had a war to fight, and I wasn't just a distraction: I could get him killed. Although there was a permanent knot of worry in his brow, he had remained supernaturally calm since Kuwait.

Before I could finish this thought, Buck exploded.

'GODDAMMIT! GODDAMMIT!' he screamed. 'FUCK! FUCK!'

'What the hell's wrong?' hollered Hustler from the roof.

Murphy launched himself out of the Humvee, and crouched down in the firing position. I put my head between my knees.

*Perhaps this was the end.*

'It's OK,' said Buck, sounding embarrassed.

'What?' came the hoarse shout from the roof.

'I thought I'd lost my M&Ms,' admitted Buck.

Hustler and Murphy cursed simultaneously. I wanted to throw up.

'One mike,' said the radio.

Then we heard it: a hateful chorus of gunfire, blasting through the mudflats. It was followed by a clap of man-made thunder and a white flash from our own camp, as one of the howitzers spat out more heavy metal.

The noise continued for a while.

When I opened my eyes and took my fingers out of my ears, Buck, Murphy and Hustler were laughing in disbelief.

'What is it?' I asked, wondering if I was the punchline of the joke.

'The guys upfront asked for support,' said Buck. 'So they sent up a whole company of tanks. *A whole goddam company.*'

Hustler gave a low whistle.

Murphy slapped the dashboard.

I wondered how many tanks were in a company.

The next morning we drove past what was left of the technicals: molten heaps of charred and smoking metal that looked as though they might once have been Toyota pick-ups. After their late-night rendezvous with *fourteen* Marine Corps M1 Abrams tanks, however, it was hard to tell. I tried not to look at the human outlines in the crushed, upside-down cabins. 'They thought they were being real sneaky,' tutted Buck as he surveyed the wreckage. 'They probably didn't realize we have night-vision goggles and can see them coming. We had all freakin' day to engage.'

'What I don't understand', said Murphy, 'is why they wanna fight anyway. Why do they still love that cocksucker Saddam?'

'It's probably more of a hatred of Americans than a liking for Saddam Hussein,' said Buck. 'They think we're imperialists, and that we're gonna change their way of life and make them all Christians. Hopefully they'll think otherwise when we take Baghdad and get the hell out of their stinking country.'

Later, after we'd found a new position – this time raiding the surrounding houses and confiscating AK-47s and Iraqi uniforms – I saw a familiar face approach across the mud. He was an older Marine, bespectacled, slightly overweight, and with a silver cross on his lapel. I noticed a scar on his neck. For a while I couldn't work out why I knew him. Then it came to me: he was the chaplain I'd met on my first day at Camp Grizzly. He brought bad news: a nearby Marine unit had opened fire on a civilian truck, killing its driver, after it refused to stop at a roadblock. 'I don't think the Iraqis realize that you've gotta stop for the Marine Corps,' he said. The chaplain also told us that a lance corporal from a tank unit had been killed by one of his own company's 50-cal machine guns. The screws on the gun's safety catch had worked themselves loose during our twenty-hour convoy. Someone had grabbed the 50-cal while pulling himself out of the tank, and it went off. The round from the gun virtually sliced in half the lance corporal, who was smoking a cigarette nearby. The sheer pointlessness of the Marine's death depressed me. Another Marine, the chaplain said, had shot himself in the leg with his own 9-mm pistol, probably in an attempt to get sent home. The Marine had survived and got his wish: he was medevaced to Germany.

The chaplain, I soon realized, got to hear all the hard-luck stories. Then he said, 'Have you seen the white buses yet?'

'What white buses?' asked Buck.

'The Iraqis are driving around the towns, picking up all the fighting-age men and taking them to the front lines,' said the chaplain. 'We found a few of the buses, and at first we couldn't work out what the heck they were for. We found one guy, no more than nineteen years old, lying outside one of them with a gunshot wound to the back of his head. It didn't make any sense. Then it dawned on us.' The teenager had been shot by the Republican Guard, explained the chaplain, for refusing to fight. In other words, he'd been killed for refusing to get on the bus which would have driven him to the front lines, where the Marines would have killed him instead.

Yes, the chaplain heard all the hard-luck stories.

'I've never seen nothin' like this before,' said Murphy, the next day. 'This is just crazy.' It was now Wednesday 26 March – day seven of the war – and we were still stuck in the marshlands. It wasn't yet noon, but the sky was the colour of tangerine and we could see only a few yards ahead. Something very bad was happening. The conditions, the Marine Corps meteorologists told us, were the result of an anticyclone sitting above Europe, forcing the jet stream into two paths, one through Scandinavia and the other straight through our camp. The gale was whipping up dried mud from the marshbanks, creating a thick, acrid fog. Even Murphy looked scared.

It had been another miserable day. After a week spent in a Humvee with three Marines, I was desperate to talk to a civilian, or at least another embed. I tried calling David Willis, the BBC reporter I'd met at Camp Grizzly, but I couldn't get through. From what I'd heard on the World Service, he was still stuck in al-Nasiriyah, which, like Basra, was proving to be harder to secure than expected. I also tried Glen, who I assumed was still embedded at the Al Jaber airbase, but his line was dead too. Instead, I stumbled over to the FDC and charged up my laptop by plugging it into Kilo Battery's diesel generator. Even fully charged, my beleaguered Sony had only a hour of battery power. My satellite phone wasn't much better. Convinced we weren't going anywhere in the storm, I took advantage of the power connection and wrote 600 words on the technicals, then filed it to Barrow via Copymaster. I internally congratulated myself on becoming a slightly less incompetent war correspondent.

I would tell you about the rest of morning, but you already know: the foxhole; the sunblock; the explosions; and finally the leaflet telling Buck 'how to deal with a dead media representative'. It ended, of course, with the order to move positions. It must have come straight from General Mattis – he was determined to prove we were an 'all-weather fighting force'. I hoped he was right. I jumped into the Humvee's back seat while dialling London on my satellite phone. This would probably be my last chance to call Barrow before we went back into another radio blackout. As I listened to the phone ring, I restarted my laptop. The battery indicator, for some reason, was flashing red. I wondered if my Sony was about to raise the white flag.

'Foreign new-*ews*?'

'Hi, Martin,' I said. 'Do you want something on the weather? We can't see a bloody thing. Are you watching Sky?'

There was a pause.

'Crickey, yeah,' said Barrow. I pictured him looking up at the television in the newsroom. 'Can you file us a few words?'

'We're going back into EmCon Bravo,' I said, sounding like a professional. 'Shall I dictate you something now?'

'That would be great,' said Barrow, taken aback.

I leaned out of the window and spat out a gobful of orange slime.

'It was like fighting a war in the depths of hell,' I began. 'Howling winds blew up mud from the marshbanks of central Iraq . . .'

# 15

## Thirty Mikes Later

By the time I'd finished dictating the story, my face was a mask of orange mud. The stuff was running out of my nose and down the back of my throat, forcing me to cough and spit every few seconds. It was in my eyes. I could even feel it dripping out of my ears. I tried wearing the painter's mask I'd been given for the oil fires, but it didn't do any good. I'd never imagined I could be so *involved* in the weather. The visibility in our tangerine world had shrunk to just a few feet. Buck's GPS device had stopped working. Murphy's night-vision goggles were useless. And somewhere out there the Iraqis were waiting for us. They were probably as at home in the mud as I would be in the bar of the Beverly Hills Four Seasons. The Marines cursed in disbelief. 'When this shit clears, I keep thinkin' we're gonna be surrounded by the motherfuckers,' said an exasperated Buck, again playing with his crucifix.

Eventually he ordered Murphy to stop. 'We're all gonna die in a goddam crash if we don't pull over,' he said. 'Kill the engine.'

The Humvee shuddered to a halt, and its big V8 died with a mechanical belch. The southern jet stream seemed to be blowing right through the vehicle, making it shake violently on its suspension. We were on another bulldozed dirt track, having turned west off Highway 8. To our right was a berm. I wondered if there was an infantry unit on the other side, or whether we were alone. To our left was a billowing curtain of fog.

'Dammit,' said Buck, from the passenger seat. 'We've lost the convoy.'

I got out of the Humvee, still finalizing my story with Barrow on the phone, and looked behind us. I could see only a couple of other Humvees through the murk. *We were stranded.* I cursed General Mattis.

Some of the Marines were doing the same. Moving positions in this weather was surely insanity.

'Is everything all right?' I heard Barrow say, from 2,600 miles away.

'Not really, Martin,' I replied. 'We've just stopped on an unprotected stretch of marshland. I think we've lost our unit.'

I was amazed that the satellite phone was still working.

Buck, I noticed, was now sweating and thumping the GPS device.

'Hang in there, Chris,' said Barrow. 'And look on the upside.'

'What's the upside?'

'It's nice and sunny here in Wapping.'

'*Cheers*,' I said.

Barrow gave a strangled chuckle. He was trying to cheer me up.

'I hope we get through this,' I said, shakily. I felt a convulsion somewhere deep inside my stomach. It was the second time in seven days that I'd nearly choked up on the phone to Barrow. This had to stop.

'You will,' said Barrow. '*You'll be all right.*'

I heard thunder, or an explosion of some kind. The weather, it seemed, was determined to kill someone today.

I wondered if Fletcher or Barrow really knew what it was like out here.

'OK, let's talk tomorrow,' I said. 'Is my stuff getting in the paper?'

'Yeah,' said Barrow. 'It's all running. Speak later, OK?'

*It's running*? That didn't sound very reassuring.

'OK,' I said, and hung up.

In fact my stories *were* running. Fletcher and Barrow were only just beginning to realize the importance of the embedding scheme. At this point in the invasion I was the only *Times* reporter anywhere near the front lines. It was laughable – and terrifying. Even our Baghdad correspondent, Janine di Giovanni, had been ordered out of the city by Robert Thomson, *The Times*'s editor. 'Reporters are pulling out their hair with boredom in Kurdistan,' di Giovanni wrote at the time. 'There's a real war in the western desert on the Jordanian–Iraq border, but no one can get to it; and on the border of Kuwait most of the press corps are miserably camping out in their cars, unable to get into the desert.' These so-called 'unilaterals' had been shaken by the death of ITN's Terry Lloyd, who had charged into Basra without the support of American troops. According to one account, he'd suffered a shoulder wound from friendly fire and had then been hit again by a US helicopter as he was being taken to hospital in an Iraqi minibus. Now his body was lying in one of the city's teeming hospitals.

In fact most British reporting from Iraq was being done by relatively unknown war correspondents. Take the BBC: John Simpson was stuck in the north, while Fergal Keane was reporting from a hotel roof in Jordan. The BBC was instead relying on David Willis and his embedded colleague Gavin Hewitt. As for the front-line coverage of *The Times* and the *Daily Telegraph*, it was all coming from their two respective Hollywood correspondents – one of whom was handling the challenge with more grace than the other. I later saw a photograph of Oliver Poole as an embed. Shirtless beneath an unzipped Army flak vest, he was casually smoking a cigarette in front of a blackened mural of Saddam Hussein. To his right, an Iraqi truck was on fire. His Goa necklace, I noticed, was still intact. He looked good – dashing almost. The *Telegraph*, meanwhile, had come up with a name for the phenomenon of war veterans being stuck at checkpoints miles from the action: 'Nick Wapshott Syndrome'.

The phone call over, I got back inside the Humvee and wished for sleep. There was nothing else I could do. Sleep, I had discovered, was the only way I could relax. It was almost worth the sadness of the dreams. Since Kuwait, I had developed an almost Zen-like ability to fall into a meditative doze.

You'll probably recall what happened next: the darkest night in Iraq's history; the trucks overturning in the wind; the lightning that was confused with a chemical alert, forcing us to clamp gas masks to our mud-drenched faces; and, worst of all, the bass monotone on the radio informing us that we had 'contact'. This time the attack was serious. The dark shapes moving towards us weren't customized pickup trucks: they were Republican Guard tanks. A dozen of them had been spotted by an artillery unit to the south, which had fired a few rounds of white phosphorus above our heads, so the forward observers could see what was ahead.

The shapes were grunting south with only one purpose: to kill. Behind us, the artillery started firing, hopelessly off target. There was no way they could have surveyed their position, I thought, never mind used their GPS targeting. I pictured the Marines aiming the howitzers manually, like rifles. I hoped they knew what they were doing, otherwise we would end up suffering the fate of Iraq's dismembered 51st Mechanized Division. Then, finally, came the impossible news: the Air Force, making a belated entrance, was sending some F-15s to the marshlands. There was, however, a horrible catch. It would take them thirty 'mikes' to get there.

There was no doubt about it: we were dead.

So what do you do when you think you have less than thirty minutes to live? In ideal circumstances, I'd pour myself a martini, put on a record, and write down some final thoughts. Perhaps I'd make a few phone calls: thank-yous, goodbyes, good-riddances – that kind of thing. If drunk-dialling is bad, imagine death-dialling. That could really get you into some trouble in the morning – if you were unlucky enough to survive whatever it was you thought was going to kill you. But here was my problem: I was with three Marines in the back of a Humvee, in a mudstorm so thick I could barely see my hand in front of my face. There was no booze. And I couldn't use my phone. Death, it seemed, was not going to happen on my terms.

I'd expected death to feel profound, or at least cinematic. But this felt strangely underwhelming. For a start, I was more angry than scared. What's the point of dying at the age of twenty-seven? It's like walking out of a play after the first act. It's meaningless. It's a waste. *So that's it then*, I thought. I wished I'd done more. I wished I'd tried harder at everything. I wished I hadn't spent so much of the past decade worrying. I thought about all my visits to Dr Ruth's clinic. I wished I'd known then what I knew now: *you're stronger than you think*. Then again, I'd been right to be anxious. I'd always thought the 1990s were a scam, and that the war virgins' dot-com lifestyles would end in violence and tears. Now I'd proved myself right.

I thought about the consequences of my death. My grandparents' final years would be ruined, as would most of the rest of my parents' lives. My father would blame himself for giving me permission to go to war. Perhaps my parents would divorce, as married couples who lose a son or daughter often do. As for Alana, who knows how my death would affect her? She'd at least become richer. I'd felt so rotten about leaving her alone in Los Angeles that I'd made her the biggest beneficiary of my News International life-insurance policy. Perhaps I should have married Alana. Perhaps I should never have dragged her to California in the first place.

I looked at the timer on my glowing digital watch, which I'd set to count down from thirty minutes. There were seventeen more to go.

So did I still consider myself a coward as I sat there waiting to die? Hemingway neatly defined cowardice as 'a lack of ability to suspend the functioning of the imagination'. But how are you supposed to turn off the imagination when you're trapped in the dark, waiting to find out what it feels like to be dissected and burned by a round from a Soviet-built tank? I'll be honest: I didn't feel like a coward for being *scared* of war. I felt like a coward for agreeing to go to war. I felt like a coward for letting my journalist's ego get the better of me. I felt like a coward for being so selfish. Because there was more at stake here than *my* life.

With less than ten minutes remaining on the stopwatch, the howitzers were thumping out rounds of DPICM almost indiscriminately. I wondered if it was a good idea to hose down such a large area: after all, the rounds from the big guns had a 'dud rate' of up to 14 per cent, and we'd have to drive through our own unexploded munitions if we advanced any further north towards Baghdad.

On the other hand, that wouldn't be a problem if we all died tonight.

I couldn't bear to listen to the World Service. If I had, I would have learned that American aircraft carriers in the Persian Gulf were having to ground flights because of the weather conditions. I would also have learned that some 2,000 Iraqi troops, plus 1,000 irregulars, were managing to keep the coalition forces out of Basra. Other reports, meanwhile, were claiming that Iraq's Special Republican Guard was advancing south from the Iraqi capital, towards the marshlands.

'Contact in five mikes,' said the radio.

'What are you gonna do when this shit is over?' asked Murphy, who had been sitting in silence, staring at the steering wheel.

'Sit in my backyard and have a fuckin' beer, probably,' said Hustler, who was standing rigid in the Humvee's gun turret.

'Maybe I'll go back to Trinidad and see my folks,' suggested Buck. 'My old man can't fly. We ain't seen each other in a while.'

'What are you gonna do, Murphy?' I asked.

'I'm gonna get the fuck out of this shithole swamp and go snow-boardin',' he said. 'I'm gonna get my truck from my parents' house, put some Bob Marley on the radio, and drive up to Vermont. It's gonna be *sweet.*'

I'd never thought of Murphy as the Bob Marley type.

I looked at my watch: three minutes now.

The fear was making me cold. I pulled my sleeping bag around me. I closed my eyes.

Then it started. There was a low boom, followed by what sounded like a machine stripping the threads off a bolt. The boom came from ahead of us; the ripped screech from somewhere above. The noise that followed was so loud I thought it would shake the flesh off my bones. I imagined a steel trapdoor being slammed shut, amplified by Wembley Stadium's PA system and played back through the echo chamber of the Grand Canyon. The mudbanks shook to the rhythm of unconditional annihilation. *Someone was gettin' some,* as the Marines would say. I found myself shouting involuntary expletives. Then another trapdoor was shut. The noises kept coming, until I felt as though someone had torn the membrane out of my eardrums.

The F-15s, I later learned, had arrived just in time. They'd turned off their GPS guidance systems, swung low into the orange fog, and used manual overrides to target the tanks, which had started to flee up Highway 8. The tank drivers mustn't have been expecting the Air Force on a night like this.

I almost felt sorry for them.

When the destruction was finally over, everyone in the Humvee was shouting. This, I thought, is what the will to live sounds like. 'YEAH! YEAH! OH, YEAH!' we all howled in unison, like the animals we were.

'Targets destroyed,' said the monotone on the radio.

By dawn the mudstorm had cleared. I'd never felt better in my life. We were lucky, of course: we hadn't lost anyone. But the nightly purging of terror, followed by the relief of the sunrise, was making me feel superhuman. When you're not scared, it's impossible to remember what fear is like. Ironically, the war had probably improved my health: my bowel movements had slowed to one every other day, and the face mask of mud I'd worn since crossing the Iraq border had cleared up my stress acne. Hustler's morning coffee, meanwhile, was more refreshing than any Starbucks cappuccino. My happiness was pure – childlike almost. It was the joy of being able to wiggle my toes, or jump up and down. It was the elation of simply being alive.

As we prepared to move north, and reunite with the rest of our convoy, I heard one of the lance corporals from the FDC singing the 'Oompa Loompa' song from *Willy Wonka and the Chocolate Factory.* '*Oompa loompa, doompadee doo,*' he chanted '*I've got a perfect puzzle for you . . .*' The movies, I thought, have got the soundtrack to war all wrong. War isn't rock 'n' roll. It's got nothing to do with Jimi Hendrix or Richard Wagner. War is nursery rhymes and early Madonna tracks. War is the music from your childhood. Because war, when it's not making you kill or be killed, turns you into an infant. For the past eight days I'd been living like a five-year-old – a non-existence of daytime naps, mushy food and lavatory breaks. My adult life was back in Los Angeles with my dirty dishes and credit-card bills.

By 8 a.m. we were on the move. As we roared back on to Highway 8, we realized that the previous night's attack had been more ambitious than imagined. Bloodied Iraqi bodies were strewn over the road, some of them heaped on top of each other next to more obliterated white pick-up trucks. Iraqi mortars, never to be fired, were lined up in the ditches. The dead wore olive-drab jackets, headscarves and civilian shoes. I found it sad, in a way, that they couldn't even afford proper uniforms. Ahead of us, meanwhile, were the flattened remains of the Republican Guard tanks. I wondered if the tank crews had been as reluctant to fight as the nineteen-year-old that the chaplain had found on the white bus. 'We took quite a number of prisoners last night,' said the voice over the Humvee's radio, 'including a brigadier general.' In fact the coalition forces had so far taken nearly 9,000 Iraqi prisoners of war. General Mattis, it seemed, had been right all long: the Marines *were* an all-weather fighting force.

By noon, after several unexplained delays, we were rumbling up Highway 8 at 50 m.p.h. The post-nuclear landscape of the marshlands had finally ended, replaced by green farmland and adobe-style home-steads in palm-tree-lined tracts. I assumed the properties belonged to the local Shi'ite landowners. At about 11 a.m. we passed the first blue overhead motorway sign since al-Nasiriyah. On it were three white arrows pointing north towards Baghdad and Hilla, with the place names written in English and Arabic. This meant we were now only about 80 miles south of the Iraqi capital – barely a two-hour drive on smooth tarmac. I remembered reading about Hilla after the first Gulf War. It was one of the towns where Saddam had quashed the Shi'ite uprising by murdering 170 men and boys at the al-Mahawil garrison. Other Shi'ite insurgents were allegedly thrown from the top floor of the city's hospital, or pushed into the Euphrates with weights tied to their feet. Some victims were hung from electricity pylons. Members of the Republican Guard from Hilla who refused to fight their own people were also executed. I wondered how much these people could hate the Americans, given what Saddam had already done to them.

At 11.30 a.m. Barrow called my satellite phone. I felt as though we hadn't spoken in years, even though it had been only twenty-four hours.

'Just so you know,' said Barrow, 'the editor's very keen for you to file anything you can. You're the only one at the front.'

'OK,' I said, my muscles tightening. 'I've been a bit, er, busy. But I'll try and get something over to you by the end of today.'

'That would be great,' said Barrow. 'As much as you can.'

The familiar pressure of newspaper deadlines almost made my life in Iraq feel more normal. But fear returned, like an unmissed com-panion, the further north we went. On the Humvee's radio we heard reports of sniper fire from the roadside ranches. 'Two Marines down,' said the calm, bass voice.

Buck, as usual, was giving away nothing about our mission. Eventually, after covering perhaps 30 miles since setting off that morning, we skidded left off the motorway and started looking for a new position. My knowledge of the routine made it no less terri-fying, especially when we resumed our job as the forward recon-naissance unit. Predictably, the faces of two Iraqi shepherds bobbed out of the long grass as soon as a suitable location had been found. 'These guys are sheep herders by day and warriors by night,' announced Buck. 'I've had enough of this shit. Let's go search their house.'

Murphy swung the Humvee into a U-turn and headed in the direction of a small mud-and-brick dwelling in the adjacent field. I wondered how the Iraqis would react to the Marines storming into their home. Hustler was in the gun turret, chewing loudly. I could tell he was itching to let loose with the 50-cal. I didn't blame him. I felt as though a gunfight might break the tension. Another Humvee from Kilo Battery followed us. The vehicles stopped about 15 feet from the house and four Marines, including Buck, jumped out. They crept up on either side of the doorway, their rifles locked and loaded, then burst in, shouting. They emerged a few minutes later carrying two AK-47s and four rounds of ammunition, plus a couple of Republican Guard uniforms. The property had been empty, even though the Iraqi shepherds had sworn that their wives and children were at home. 'This is getting like Vietnam,' said the sergeant who led the raid. 'We can't fight 'em during the day, because we don't know who the fuck they are.' It was the first time I'd heard the V-word since leaving Camp Grizzly.

We drove back to our position, and I started digging another coffin-sized foxhole – probably my tenth since the war began. I'd just finished when we got the order to move again. 'We're gonna CSMO in about ten mikes,' declared the radio. 'We're drawing some sniper fire, so keep your grapes down.'

I was sweating and filthy, with a ring of sunburn around my neck. I had changed my underwear only once since leaving Kuwait.

Soon enough, we were on the move again. It took me a while, however, to work out what was happening: we were going *backwards*, towards the marshes. Was this a retreat? By the time we joined Highway 8, every other vehicle in the 1st Marine Division seemed to be going in the same direction. The rest of the afternoon was spent in a DMZ-style traffic jam, going nowhere. Tanks, burning up gallons of diesel, wheezed and choked around us. I caught sight of Speckled Ali, the NBC pigeon, swinging in his cage from one of the 7-ton trucks. He looked well. At one point, we heard the *phfut-phfut* of sniper fire from a building 1,000 yards from the roadside. Minutes later a Navy F-14 Tomcat howled overhead, making a steel-trapdoor sound with its payload of 500 lb bombs. The Marines cheered. The scale of the destruction, however, seemed disproportionate to the threat of the rifleman.

By dusk we were back where we'd started, in the ocean of mud. There were rumours that we'd tried and failed to take an airport, or that the advance was a feint – a giant bluff – to divert the insurgents' attention from al-Najaf, where they were fighting the 3rd Infantry Division, in which Oliver Poole was embedded. Whatever the reason, it was a right hook to morale: especially mine. I began seriously to question what I was doing in Iraq. How much more fighting could I take? And what was the point of being an embedded journalist anyway? Proper war correspondents write about *both* sides of a conflict. I might as well have been paid by the Marines. Also, I had no idea what was going on. Buck made sure that the only information I got was what I heard on the Humvee's radio or saw with my own eyes. Perhaps he was worried that I would be captured and interrogated by the Iraqis – Saddam had already imprisoned four journalists, including a *Newsday* reporter and photographer, calling them 'spies'. My battlefield perspective, therefore, was about as useful as Baghdad Bob's. My mum knew more about the war than I did. Sometimes I felt as though all I did was stand next to the guns and describe how loud they were. *Was that worth dying for?* The alternative, of course, was to go unilateral. But that seemed like suicide.

It was about 6 p.m. when I trudged over to the FDC, plugged my laptop into the diesel generator, and started to write an account of the previous night's tank ambush. It had taken me a while to realize that it even merited a story, probably because I was so involved in the action – I remembered suffering exactly same problem on September 11. I'd worked out that by pre-writing most of my stories in longhand I could made the best use of my time in the FDC, using it mainly to just type and edit. So by 8 p.m. my first-person tank narrative was done, along with a shorter piece about the house raid near Hilla. Pleased, I walked outside to send it all.

'Hurry up,' said Buck. 'We going back into EmCon Bravo any second. It might be a couple of days before we go back to Delta.'

I panicked: this was probably my last chance to get something in the paper by the weekend. After that, the tank story would be out of date. Besides, Barrow had told me the editor wanted as much Iraq material as possible.

'Hey, captain,' I said, as Buck jogged back towards one of the guns. 'Yeah?'

'Where are we? Can I put a dateline on this story?'

'Just say we're near al-Diwaniyah,' he said, turning away.

By now I was an expert at getting around the problem of 'light discipline' on the battlefield. I simply put the computer inside my sleeping bag and crawled in after it. Using the zipper, I created a hole at one end big enough for my hand and the satellite phone to poke through. Then I waved the phone around, my fingers over the glowing LED display, until it locked on to a satellite. After that, I loaded up Copymaster and started the erratic process of sending a story to London. Although my laptop was fully charged, the battery icon was flashing red. I was amazed, however, that the trendy purple-and-blue computer had survived this far. Even though it was wrapped in plastic sheeting, it now looked like a 5,000-year-old relic from the royal tombs at Ur. *Please work*, I thought. *Just one more time.* 'Welcome to Wapping,' said Copymaster. 'Waiting to connect . . .' My laptop gave a strangled beep and a message popped up the screen: 'Change power source immediately!' it said. 'Come on, hurry up for God's sake,' I muttered under my breath. The laptop squawked again and the screen flickered. *Oh no.* I held my breath. Then, with a wheeze and a sigh, the little machine died.

I exhaled, thumping my fist on the ground.

Just before the laptop had crashed, I could have sworn I saw a message pop up in Copymaster's low-tech blue dialogue box.

'2,134 words sent,' it had said.

I called Barrow immediately to check that my words had made it to London. The moment he picked up, the howitzers started to fire. I knew it was only a matter of time before another chemical alert and an EmCon Bravo radio blackout, so I tried to get the conversation over with as quickly as possible.

'Bloody hell, Chris,' said Barrow, as the back blast from one of the guns almost knocked the phone out of my hands.

'Yeah, *I know*,' I said. 'Did you get my stories?'

I head the plastic rattle of Barrow's keyboard.

'Yeah . . .' he said. 'Good stuff. Thanks.'

'OK, Martin,' I began. 'I have to go n—'

'Hang on, Chris. Ben Preston would like a word.'

*Oh no.* I'd never worked directly with Ben, but, given that he was *The Times*'s deputy editor, I knew he'd been involved in getting me the job in Los Angeles. He'd probably also had a say in sending me to Iraq.

I stood in the mud, listening to Vivaldi, as Barrow patched me through. Even in my chemical suit, NBC boots and flak jacket, I felt like a schoolboy. I wondered how much more surreal my life could get.

'Chr-*is*?' said Ben. I pictured him in Wapping: he was sporty and boyish, with short, dark hair and modern, rectangular glasses. His father, Peter Preston, was a legendary former editor of *The Guardian*. It was always worth thinking carefully about what you said to Ben. I shuffled on the spot.

'Hi, Ben,' I said.

'How are you holding up?' he began

'Not that great, to be honest,' I blurted. 'But, y'know, it's OK.'

I was trying hard to sound nonchalant and professional, like most of the other war correspondents I'd met in the Middle East.

'I hear you're having second thoughts about being a war correspondent,' said Ben. I wondered if Barrow had told him about my incompetent performance on the opening night of the invasion.

'You're getting some great stuff from Iraq,' he continued, 'and you're the only person we've got on the front lines. But, as much as we need you there, if you want to leave, no one's going to think less of you. It's a decision only you can make. You can say I ordered you out, if you want.'

I couldn't believe what I was hearing. At last I knew *The Times* understood how dangerous the embedded scheme had become. I felt like a madman who'd realized that it was the world, not him, that was insane.

'OK . . .' I said, warily.

'Could you get out even if you wanted to?' asked Ben.

'I don't know,' I said, honestly. 'It could be more dangerous than staying.'

'Well it's your call,' said Ben. 'No one's going to second-guess you.'

'Thanks,' I said. 'Can I, er, sleep on it?'

'Of course,' said Ben, sounding surprised. 'And keep the stories coming.'

Across the mudbank I saw Buck making the throat-slitting action. 'KILL THE GODDAM PHONE,' he was shouting.

# 16

# AWOL

*Sleep on it.* I could hardly believe I'd used the phrase. This was how the evening progressed: at 10 p.m. a Marine from a nearby infantry unit had one of his legs blown off after tripping over one of our unexploded shells; at 11 p.m. the artillery behind us shot white phosphorus into the air, illuminating thirty Iraqi pick-up trucks advancing south; by midnight the irregulars had retreated, or been killed, but only after the howitzers had scattered yet more unexploded ordnance around our position; and at 1 a.m. came a chemical alert, accompanied by a rumour that Saddam had authorized the Republican Guard to use 'dirty' mortars anywhere north of Karbala, the most northern of Iraq's Shi'ite cities. The rest of the night was enlivened by 500-lb satellite-guided bombs, small-arms fire, the occasional incoming shell and, at 4.30 a.m., another Scud warning. The violence ended at 5.50 a.m., when the sun rose wearily over Friday 28 March: day nine of Operation Iraqi Freedom. I hadn't slept at all.

I like to think that by morning my mind hadn't been made up. I like to think that I was still deciding whether to stumble on ineptly towards Baghdad, or give up and return to the JW Marriott Hotel, with its luxury spa and room-service menu. But perhaps there was no decision to make. Perhaps I knew exactly what I was going to do, the moment Ben Preston offered to 'order me out' of Iraq.

Buck, of course, was of no help. He wouldn't tell me if Kilo Battery was even heading towards Baghdad, or whether we would bypass the capital and go north to Tikrit, Saddam's birthplace. He had other things on his mind. Kilo Battery was running short of MREs, water and fuel, and the supply lines were under attack. After the first week's dash, we seemed to have skidded to a muddy halt.

Murphy, meanwhile, was baffled by my dilemma.

'So you don't *have* to be here?' he asked.

'No,' I replied.

'But you get a big-assed bonus for this shit, right?'

'No. Nothing.'

'So you're not getting paid . . . *and you don't have to be in Iraq?*'

'No, not really.'

'Then what the fuck are you doing here?' he asked.

I couldn't think of a good answer.

Then three extraordinary things happened.

First came an unfriendly tap on my blue, Kevlar-plated shoulder.
I was squatting in my foxhole, wiping smears of mud from my broken
glasses and smoking one of my last Marlboro Lights. Beside me was
the short-wave radio. It was saying that the Iraqis were being helped
by 'volunteers' crossing the border from Syria and Iran. As I turned
and looked up, I almost yelped with surprise. Looming above me was
Captain Jim Hotspur, the public-affairs officer from the Kuwait
Hilton. Hotspur looked sunburnt and irritated. I wondered what I'd
done wrong.

'Ayres?' he said.

'Yes,' I replied, trying to stand up. I fell backwards instead.

'I've got something for you.'

This couldn't be good. Had I broken the 'ground rules'? Was I
going to be disciplined? *Would I get court-martialled?*

Hotspur reached into his pocket and produced a maroon booklet.

'Congratulations,' he said, handing it to me. 'You're a Kuwaiti
resident.'

I stared at the worn, royal-crested passport in my hands. It seemed
as though it had come from another world, another era. I opened it
up and saw three pages of Arabic script, which would no doubt cause
a lifetime of problems with US immigration officials. The visa, I
noticed, had cost me nearly $100.

'Thank you,' I said, as Hotspur about-turned and marched away in
an orange haze. He was carrying a plastic bag full of passports belonging to other embeds. I could hardly believe the captain had found me.

*I was free.* With my passport, I could theoretically get on the next
flight out of Kuwait International Airport (not, of course, that there
were any flights to London – they'd all been cancelled because of

the war). The problem, of course, was that I was more than 200 miles
north of the airport – 200 miles of death and anarchy. I remembered
what my grandfather had said about leaving Iraq if it became too dangerous: '*What on earth makes you think you'll be able to do that?*'

By now it was 10 a.m. The sun was crouching low on the muddy
horizon, preparing for another hard day's work.

I tried to forget about my passport and any question of going home.
Instead, I decided to find out what had happened to my tank-ambush
story. The only way to do this was to call Alana, who could look it up
on *The Times*'s website. We were back in EmCon Delta, but I still
flinched when I switched my satellite phone on, half expecting it to
trigger another Scud alert. It was 7 a.m. in London, and Friday
morning's edition of the paper had already been online for a few hours.

In Los Angeles, the other side of the world, it was 11 p.m.

I'd managed to call Alana once a day from Iraq, sometimes more,
and by now she was used to the ambient noise of 155-mm gunfire in
the background. I asked her to look for my article in the 'World News'
section. I wondered if the story had been shortened, or if it had even
made it into Friday's paper.

'Can't see anything,' she said.

Behind me, the big guns shouted. Somewhere, more Iraqis died.

'Isn't there a section on Iraq, or something?' I asked.

I heard the hollow clatter of my office keyboard.

'Yes, I'm looking at the Iraq section now. Can't . . . see . . . anything . . .'

I sighed, which unsettled the mud, sand and phlegm that coated my
lungs. The sigh ended as a dry heave. I couldn't believe it: my front-
line dispatches had been spiked, *again*. All that fear and death for
nothing.

'That's it,' I said, bitterly. 'I've had enough. This is pointless.'

'Hold on,' said Alana. 'I can see your photograph here.'

'What?'

'Your picture. It's . . . it's on the, *wow*, it's on the FRONT PAGE.
There's a long story underneath – something about tanks?'

'You're kidding?'

'Actually, your story isn't *on* the front page . . .'

'Uh?'

'It *is* the front page.'

For a brief, exhilarating moment I realized why people become war reporters: the thrill of writing an I-nearly-died-a-gruesome-death story is unbeatable. It feels like a middle finger to anyone who's ever doubted you, including yourself. I remembered hearing about two journalists who'd gone to Iraq because their girlfriends had dumped them. I couldn't understand it at the time. Now it made sense. *War makes you feel special; it makes you feel better than all the war virgins back home.* But here's the downside: writing an I-nearly-died-a-gruesome-death story requires you to nearly die a gruesome death. I wondered what my next big story would be: a chemical attack on Kilo Battery? An outbreak of smallpox? Next time, perhaps, I wouldn't be so lucky. And was it all worth it, for a fuck-you and a front page?

'What's the headline?' I asked Alana.

'*We were stuck when the Iraqi tanks came,*' she read. '*Stranded, 90 miles from Baghdad . . . from Chris Ayres near al-Diwaniyah.*'

I thought about my first week at *The Times* and the 'nib' I'd written for Barrow. How did I end up on the front lines of a war?

Then I looked up and saw Buck. He seemed even less happy than usual. His eyes were pinpricks of violence and determination.

'Finish your phone call,' he said. 'We need to talk.'

What happened next would change everything.

I got off the phone and walked over to Buck, who was now standing beside the FDC and sucking on a pen. His hunting knife, I noticed, was still strapped to the front of his flak vest, next to his 9-mm Beretta. Sleeping rough for nearly two weeks had taken almost no visible toll on the captain – he still looked like a pro athlete – but I could tell the nightly attacks were getting to him. The Marines hadn't expected so much resistance. The previous day's retreat, even if it was a bluff, must also have been disheartening. Before the war, there'd been talk of a 'ten-day sprint' to Baghdad. The mudstorms, and the heavy fighting in Basra and al-Nasiriyah, had made that plan look hopelessly optimistic. To me, it now seemed impossible that the Americans could win a quick and relatively bloodless victory in Mesopotamia. The same thought must have occurred to Buck. Forget hearts and minds. This was going to be about blood and entrails.

'OK, Chris,' he said. 'You ain't gonna like this one bit, but I have orders. I have no choice. You understand that?'

I stared at the captain's lean, muscular face, and wondered what could possibly call for such a melodramatic opening.

'Yeees,' I said slowly. 'I understand.'

'What kind of satellite phone do you have?' asked Buck.

The phone was still in my hand. I looked at it.

'It's a Thuraya,' I said.

'I'm going to have to take it,' said Buck. 'I have orders to confiscate all Thuraya phones being used by media representatives.'

My jaw slackened in a visual cliché of surprise.

'*What?*' I said, in a slightly alarming falsetto. 'What do you mean?' I continued, making an effort to lower my pitch.

My main concern, of course, should have been my ability to send stories. But it wasn't. I was more worried about not being able to tell anyone I was alive. My family, who were being kept up to date by Alana, would think I was dead. (Apart from once, near Basra, I hadn't called my mother directly, for the same reason Hustler hadn't called his wife: the soundtrack of death in the background was too much.) Even *The Times* would probably think I was dead. There were no other journalists in my unit, so I could hardly borrow anyone else's phone. I couldn't believe this was happening.

'I need your phone,' reiterated Buck.

'Are you serious?' I asked. '*Why?*'

I could tell the question irritated him. Warriors don't ask for orders to be explained. He turned to the Marine behind him.

'Staff sergeant,' he said, 'did the order for the phone ban give a *reason?*'

'It says the French sold the codes of the phones to the Iraqis, sir,' came the reply. 'It means the enemy can trace the signals, sir.'

'There you have it,' said Buck. 'The goddam French. I'm not being an asshole, Chris. It's an order. I don't have a choice.'

*The French sold the codes to the Iraqis?*

'Thuraya isn't even a French company,' I blurted. 'It's based in Abu Dhabi, for God's sake. There's got to be a better reason.'

'Nothing I can do,' said Buck, now walking away.

I knew it was pointless arguing. He was right: it was out of his hands.

'What about the other embeds' phones?' I shouted to Buck, who was now 30 feet away. 'Are they being confiscated too?'

He pretended not to hear.

'It's only Thurayas,' the staff sergeant explained. 'Iridium phones are fine.'

He held out an apologetic palm.

I bit my upper lip with frustration and handed him the Thuraya. He ripped out the battery and gave me the empty handset back.

Perhaps the Marines were right. Perhaps the phones had been compromised. I certainly wasn't going to risk getting myself, or anyone else, killed. *But to blame it on the French?* I knew that the Thuraya handsets had a built-in GPS feature, allowing phone calls be pinpointed accurately, but wasn't that why we had daily EmCon Bravo radio blackouts? Besides, Thuraya's investors were all from supposedly friendly Middle Eastern countries, including the United Arab Emirates and Qatar, where the Pentagon's central command was based. But there was nothing I could do. I felt helpless. Without a satellite phone I was of no use to anyone.

I was dead weight.

So this is it. This is the moment, 90 miles from Baghdad, that will stay with me for ever. This is what I think about when I find myself awake at 5 a.m., shouting at the red glow of the bedside clock ('Kill the *fucking* light!'), and wondering if I did the right thing out there in the mud and the sand. As I tug at the damp and twisted sheets, I feel ashamed for letting myself down – and Fletcher; and Barrow; and the Marines. And I want to go back to the marshlands, to prove that I'm not a coward. By sunrise, however, the moment has always passed. And I don't go anywhere.

After handing over the phone battery, I went to my foxhole to brood. What should I do? I had my passport; I had my front-page story; I even had permission to leave from *The Times*'s deputy editor. Was this the end of my war? Surely, I told myself, I could get around the Thuraya ban. Maybe I could go to Kuwait City, buy a new handset, and hitch a lift back into the war zone. Or perhaps I could try to leave Kilo Battery, find a fellow embed with an Iridium phone, and ask to borrow it. What about David Willis from the BBC? I shook my head. I remembered that he also had a Thuraya, and an unreliable one at that – he'd spent most of his time at Camp Grizzly borrowing an ancient device belonging to Scott Nelson of the *Boston Globe*. I remembered Scott's phone being the size of a small photocopier, with two floor-mounted antennas for locking on to the Iridium satellite. Besides, I'd be lucky if anyone would let me make a $10-per-minute call, while draining their battery, more than once. And how would I physically *get* to David Willis, or any of the other Marine Corps embeds? I'd probably have to embed myself with the bloody infantry, or go unilateral.

'Sod that,' I said out loud, to no one.

I realized, of course, that the Thuraya ban was an extraordinary excuse: a get-out-of-Iraq-free card. *Sir, the dog ate my satellite phone.* But no one in London would believe it. They'd all know I'd lost my nerve. This was worse than Nick Wapshott being stuck on the *QE2* on September 11. This was voluntary.

I climbed out of my foxhole, took off my helmet and flak jacket, and trudged over to Buck, who was now standing by the gun line. By now I'd abandoned my hiking boots and was wearing a pair of Nike running shoes. After Thursday night's conversation with Ben Preston, I'd stopped feeling like a Marine.

I couldn't believe what I was about to do.

'Captain,' I said, taking a quick, shallow breath.

He gave me an expectant look, as though he knew what was coming.

The moment felt freeze-framed. *This was it.* I tried not to think about the consequences of what would follow.

Then I said, 'Can you get me out of here?'

Buck looked at me for a while. Perhaps he was relieved. Perhaps he was disappointed. Perhaps he didn't care.

'OK,' he said, carefully. 'I can probably get you back to Kuwait down the supply line. But I don't want anyone thinkin' I had anything to do with this. I don't want anyone thinkin' I wanted rid of you.'

'They won't,' I said. 'I'll make that clear.'

Buck stared over my shoulder and said nothing. Then he nodded. 'Let me talk to HQ,' he said.

*What had I done?* Leaving the front lines of Iraq after nine days seemed like failure by any measure. I thought of all the reporters who'd lasted months, or years, in arguably worse places: Bosnia, Rwanda, Chechnya, even Baghdad under the 1991 bombing campaign. Janine di Giovanni, a veteran of all these terrible datelines, once told me that her career was a result of 'an abnormal lack of fear'. Perhaps I suffered from an abnormal *excess* of fear. Even Oliver Poole, my fellow member of the Hollywood foreign press, was able to butch it out in Iraq with the 3rd Infantry Division. Historically, my nine-day career as a war correspondent became even more meaningless. Ernie Pyle reported from the battlefronts of World War II, on and off, for nearly five years, until his death. And Winston Churchill, at the age of twenty-two, lasted six weeks in Afghanistan's Swat Valley with Sir Bindon Blood and his troops.

It could, of course, take me a week to get back to London. When added to the time I'd spent in the Marriott and Camp Grizzly, my war would have lasted more than a month. But who was I kidding? *Nine days.*

After talking to headquarters, Buck told me that a Humvee from one of the supply camps in the rear would come out and get me in an hour. I couldn't believe it was that easy. The captain warned me, however, that it could be a long and dangerous route back. The supply lines, after all, were easy targets for insurgents. But it seemed to me that I'd be taking a risk no matter which direction I went. And at least there was less chance of chemical or biological warfare in the south.

Back at the Humvee, Hustler and Buck were more sympathetic than expected, although I felt as though I was letting them down. By leaving, I was no longer suspending disbelief: I was admitting that the war was dangerous, and that we could all get killed. And no one wanted to be reminded of *that*.

'If I were you, I'd get my ass out of here too,' offered Murphy. 'You didn't sign up for this shit. You're a reporter.'

But I had signed up for this, no matter how naively. And I was a *war* reporter. This was supposed to be my job.

The Marines, I realized, were different from what I'd first imagined. Their motivation, of couse, was as alien to me as mine was to them. They wanted to prove themselves as warriors; I wanted to watch from a safe distance. But during the invasion they'd been more quiet and determined than gung-ho and macho. And they'd kept a nihilistic sense of humour throughout. Perhaps they'd toned themselves down because of the 'media rep'. But I somehow doubted it.

I walked to the back of the Humvee, and started to pull out my bags. Everything was slathered in mud and reeked of desert filth. My dolly was long gone, so I was going to have to work out a way to carry everything. I tried to lift my rucksack on to my Kevlar-plated back, but I soon gave up. I'd have to drag it. As for the yellow tent, I was almost tempted to leave it in the back of the vehicle. It was taking up vital MRE space, however, so I decided it had to come with me.

When I looked up, Hustler was standing awkwardly in front of me. He looked tense and exhausted. I remembered that he was nearly two decades older than the high-school-age Marines. Hustler hadn't been called up for the first Gulf War, however, and this was his last chance to use his training.

'Hey, Chris,' he said, in a stage whisper. 'Can you do somethin' for me?'

'After all that coffee you've given me,' I said, 'I'll do anything.'

Hustler held out a square piece of cardboard from one of the MRE boxes. He'd cut it out with a knife. On it was a message: 'Carolina & Kids: I'm doing fine. Hope everything is okay at home. Hope this ends soon so I can come home to you. I promise to stay low. Love You.' Underneath, in a childlike blue print, Hustler had given me his wife's home and mobile-phone numbers.

I looked at the first sergeant. He seemed slightly embarrassed. He was probably wondering if this was a good idea.

'If you get time, call my wife and read this out to her,' he said.

'I will,' I said. I wanted to shake his hand, but we just looked at each other. I felt a sudden weight of sadness. I wondered how many men from Kilo Battery wouldn't make it out of Iraq. I remembered what Robert Capa, the *Time–Life* combat photographer, had written in his autobiography: 'The war correspondent has his stake – his life – in his own hands, and he can put it on this horse or that horse, or he can put it back in his pocket at the very last minute . . . Being allowed to be a coward, and not be executed for it, is his torture.' This was my torture: Buck, Hustler and Murphy didn't have the option to leave. Even if they did, *they wouldn't*. Marines get court-martialled for cowardice; journalists get a suite at the JW Marriott.

It wasn't long before the Humvee from the supply camp arrived. When I looked at it, I realized what I was about to do. The vehicle was nothing like Buck's. It had a canvas roof, no armoured plating, and no rooftop machine gun. The left wing had been punctured and torn by rounds from AK-47s.

Maybe I should have listened to my grandfather: leaving Iraq was probably more dangerous than staying. *Was I making an awful mistake?* I threw my bags into the back of the vehicle, then went to say farewell to Buck.

'Thanks for looking after me,' I said.

'Any time,' he replied, with a quick handshake. 'Now you can go back to England and tell everyone about that jerk of a captain who confiscated your satellite phone in Iraq.' He gave a sardonic grin.

And that was it. I would never see Captain Rick 'Buck' Rogers ever again.

Before I got into the Humvee, Hustler tapped me on the shoulder.

'You don't have to call my wife, y'know,' he said. 'Don't worry about it. You're gonna be busy when you get back. No big deal.'

I couldn't believe Hustler was trying to spare me the guilt of not calling.

'I *will* call her,' I promised.

'Thanks,' he said. 'But you don't have to.'

The Humvee spluttered and wobbled, then pulled slowly out of the camp. Soon we were back on the sniper's gauntlet of Highway 8. I looked out nervously at the wasteland around us. We seemed to be alone.

For three minutes we rattled south.

Then the Humvee's engine cut out.

'Shit!' said the driver.

The vehicle, now in neutral, began to lose momentum.

'Shit!' said the driver, as the Humvee's starter motor laughed like a wounded hyena. '*Start*, you fucking piece of crap.'

There was nothing in front of us and nothing behind.

We creaked to a halt.

We sat there for about a minute on the open highway, in our canvas Humvee, before the engine coughed back to life. I almost passed out with fear. This was even worse than the broken rear door in Buck's vehicle. I wasn't surprised that the Marines ambushed in al-Nasiriyah had been travelling in a supply convoy. The good Humvees, it seemed, were reserved for the front lines. This one looked as though it had barely survived 1991. In my head, I started to write the headline of my own death: *Tragic Reporter Killed While Fleeing Battlefield*. That's the trouble with being a journalist: you see a morbid headline in every situation. You've written them all before. There was, of course, a worse scenario than death: becoming an unwilling celebrity on Iraqi television. Or, even more terrible than that, the star of an al-Qaeda webcast.

Our journey south continued for another three minutes with the engine cutting out intermittently, in defiance of the driver's howled expletives. Then, after perhaps a mile, we swerved right into a new camp. The sickly V8 died, and everyone climbed out. I could still feel the vibration of Kilo Battery's guns.

'You can stay here for the night,' said the driver. 'We'll see if we can get you a ride back sometime over the next few days.'

I tried not to groan. One mile down, 199 to go. I didn't even have any cigarettes. At this rate I'd be in Kuwait by Christmas. I dumped my bags by the front wheel and lay on the floor, using my laptop case as a pillow. If we weren't going anywhere, I might as well get some rest. I fell into a meditative doze.

Hours vanished. The heat soaked up my energy. Insects started to crawl inside the charcoal lining of my chemical suit, which probably made a nice change from all the mud. I was too drowsy to shake them out.

It was late afternoon when I heard a voice. 'Hey,' it said, 'we got you a ride outta here.' I opened my eyes and saw the tall, rickety-Humvee driver. Like me, he looked as though he was having a bad war. The vehicle's malfunctioning engine had probably already taken a decade off his life. Not that a decade would make much difference if he ended up being ambushed on the open road.

'Great,' I said, stretching my sore joints. 'When are we leaving?'

'Now,' he said. 'We've got a delivery to make. MREs and whatnot.' He climbed into the Humvee and started the engine. It sounded like it needed an emergency oil transfusion. I started hauling my luggage back into the vehicle, then yanked open a rear door and folded myself into the narrow seat. Two Marines grunted in after me. I hoped this journey would be less traumatic than the last one. It wasn't. Minutes later we were gliding in neutral again as the Humvee's engine took more time out. I closed my eyes, stopped breathing, and waited for the inevitable.

The engine restarted. We hadn't been ambushed.

This time we kept moving for a while, passing formations of tanks, Humvees, troop carriers and grounded Marine helicopters. The equipment was lifeless – as though someone had unplugged the American war machine. I wondered if they'd simply run out of fuel. 'Looks like we're takin' a pause,' said the driver. 'Before we get to Baghdad.' Was this part of the Pentagon's war plan?

Our destination turned out to be a roadside trench in which the Marines had built a camouflaged village of wooden Portakabins and net awnings. As the Humvee grumbled through the entrance, I saw dozens of men stripped to the waist and taking sponge baths, washing their underwear, or just sunbathing on the bonnets of their vehicles. Others sat at fold-down tables, playing card games and listening to the BBC World Service. It was as though Butlins had opened a holiday camp in hell. One entrepreneurial Marine had set up his own outdoor barber's shop. He sang jazz standards as he worked the electric clippers. He offered two styles – bald or nearly bald – and stood knee deep in clumps of hair that hadn't seen shampoo since Kuwait. He could have been an extra from *M*A*S*H*.

I got out of the Humvee and headed towards what looked like the camp headquarters. The temporary cabin seemed almost luxurious, making me realize how close to the front I'd been. There were embeds everywhere, wandering around with notebooks, wounded laptops and satellite phones. For once, I felt almost safe. I stared hard at one journalist, who was obviously talking to his news editor in America. There was something familiar about him. Then it dawned on me: it wasn't the reporter, but his phone, that I recognized. He was talking on a bloody Thuraya! I dropped my bags in a makeshift courtyard and jogged over to him.

'Wasn't your phone confiscated?' I asked him, after he'd hung up.

The embed was older – possibly in his sixties. He was the first person I'd seen since Kuwait City without a chemical suit. Instead, he wore khaki hiking trousers and a white shirt, decorated with a pin from Vietnam.

'No,' he said, taken aback. 'Why?'

'They told me the Thurayas have been banned. Something about the French selling the codes to the Iraqis . . .'

'That sounds unlikely,' he laughed. 'I had one of these in Afghanistan. They're incredible, aren't they? Just like a cellphone.'

I couldn't believe what I was hearing. The implication was just too awful. *Had Buck lied to me? Was this all a horrible joke?*

'Did they *take* your phone?' asked the embed.

'What?' I said, still thinking about Buck. I wanted to throw up.

'Your phone. Did they take it?'

'They took the battery,' I said.

The embed gave me an experienced look.

'If I were you,' he advised, 'I'd get a new battery and forget about it. We're all using them here. No one mentioned a ban.'

He raised a conspiratorial eyebrow.

It was then I remembered: somewhere in my laptop case I had a bagful of Thuraya accessories. Perhaps there was a battery in there somewhere. I ran over to my luggage, got down on my knees, and began pulling out zip-locked freezer bags full of cables, power adaptors and torn instruction booklets. Seconds later I triumphantly held up a spare, dead battery. Now all I needed to do was find somewhere to charge it up. So I rapped on the door of the headquarters cabin and squeezed inside. It was full of embeds, typing on computers plugged into wall sockets. A few officers stood around, eating MREs and swapping competitive banter.

'You know what General Patton said about going to war without the French, dontcha?' one of them was saying. His face was the colour of a burst blood vessel. The other Marines shrugged innocently.

'HE SAID, "IT'S LIKE GOING DEER HUNTING WITHOUT AN ACCORDION!"' came the punchline.

There was riotous laughter. Palms slapped walls. Boots stomped.

'Am I OK to use my phone?' I interjected, holding up the Thuraya.

'Knock yourself out,' said the joker.

Minutes later I was talking to Fletcher. Again, the twenty-four hours since I'd spoken to the foreign desk felt like a year.

I tried not to think about Buck.

'Nice front page yesterday,' said Fletcher. 'We need more from you today.'

I felt myself click back into professional mode. Then I remembered: I hadn't told him about my decision to leave the front lines. I suddenly realized the almighty mess I was in. This was going to be awkward.

'Martin,' I began. 'The Marines have, er, confiscated my phone.'

This seemed like the best way to approach the subject.

There was a short silence, as my voice was relayed to London via space.

Fletcher: 'So what are you using now?'

Yes, this was *definitely* going to be awkward.

'My, er, phone,' I explained. 'Because . . . I'm using it without permission. I found a spare battery. But I'm not going to have it for long.'

'A spare battery?'

I felt as though I'd just swallowed a chilli.

'They took my battery. The phones have been banned, so they took my battery, which means I can't use my phone. But now I have a spare battery. And the ban seems to have been, er, lifted. So I'm . . . er, *yeah*.'

'Can you file something today?' said Fletcher, eager to move on.

'Yes, of course,' I said. 'That's fine. Absolutely fine. Yes.'

'Gd. We need something on the supply lines being attacked: Marines Get Bogged Down in Marshlands, that kind of thing.'

'OK. Will do.'

'Send over 700 words,' said Fletcher. 'It's for the front again.'

*The front page?*

'OK,' I said.

I still hadn't told him about my decision.

'Oh, er, Martin?' I said, casually.

'Yes?'

'I'm heading back towards Kuwait. There's no point in me staying on the front lines if I can't use my phone.'

There was a baffled $10-per-minute silence.

'File your 700 words,' said Fletcher. 'Let's talk about it later.'

The phone call was over.

I welcomed the distraction of having to write a story: the situation with Buck, Fletcher and the satellite phone was starting to get overwhelming. I asked the officers in the Portakabin if they knew who was in charge of the supply line. They told me to go outside and find Lieutenant Colonel Keil Gentry. It didn't take long. Gentry was a boyish, fair-haired Marine, probably in his late thirties, who could have been a British Spitfire pilot in another war. I introduced myself and asked if food and water rations were getting through from Kuwait, or whether the invasion was becoming 'bogged down', as Fletcher had suggested on the phone. 'Well, we need everything: beans, bullets and Band-Aids,' he said, with a martini-bar grin. I asked him if the supply convoys were being attacked. 'Everyone's been taking a few pot-shots,' he said. 'The big threat is these "irregular" forces.' He grinned again. After a day of bullshit, Gentry's honesty was reassuring. He told me that part of the supply problem was the speed of the Marines' advance into Iraq, which was faster General Patton's 600-mile sprint through Europe after the Normandy landings. And, of course, there was the issue of storms, particularly the one on the night of the Iraqi tank ambush. But the insurgents were the biggest worry. 'We planned for it, we trained for it, but we really hoped it wouldn't happen,' Gentry said. 'We thought this would be a liberation. We thought the Iraqis would be throwing flowers at us. But it's been a lot more hostile than that.'

The interview was over: I had my story.

After I'd filed the 700 words, Fletcher didn't call me back. So on Saturday morning I hitched another lift south. Regardless of whether Buck had been lying about the phone ban, it was too late to turn around now. I'd made my decision. Besides, the 1st Marine Division didn't seem to be going anywhere. This was clearly affecting the morale of some Marines, who'd expected Operation Iraqi Freedom to be as quick and decisive as Stormin' Norman's walkover in 1991. 'As far as I'm concerned, *we're* the only people in shock and awe,' one of the men confided.

I used my recently liberated Thuraya to call Alana and my mother. They both sounded pleased, but nervous, that I was on my way out of Iraq. I didn't blame them: I was pretty nervous too. My mother was worried that even Kuwait wouldn't be safe: an Iraqi Seersucker missile had apparently hit Souq Sharq, the luxury shopping mall on the Persian Gulf that I'd visited before the war.

The journey down the supply lines was made in short, terrifying bursts, usually via the back of canvas-covered Humvees. Each Marine camp seemed bigger than the last. Eventually I reached a base of perhaps 100 hooches, surrounded by tanks and UH-1 'Huey' helicopters. One of the pilots offered me a lift back to Kuwait. It sounded too good to be true. It was. In an agonizing 100-yard sprint, I managed to haul my rucksack, tent bag and laptop to the take-off site, while still wearing my flak jacket and helmet. Then I found out that a colonel had taken my seat.

'Sorry,' said the pilot, giving me the thumbs down.

I stood in the dirt, sweating and exhausted, as the downdraft from the Huey's blades sandblasted my face. I was devastated.

By late afternoon I'd resigned myself to spending the night at the camp and resuming my journey south on Sunday. I was surprised, therefore, when Captain Jim Hotspur turned up in a Humvee and offered to take me futher down the supply line. I'd never felt pleased to see him before. We sat together in the back of the vehicle, with Hotspur pointing his M-16 out of the window. '*We've got the package!*' he yelled into his radio. I felt as though I'd been kidnapped.

'Why are you leaving?' asked Hotspur, as we drove.

'My editor wants me back in Kuwait,' I lied.

'Interesting,' he said.

Hotspur knew the real reason. He knew I'd bottled it.

'By the way,' said Hotspur, 'do you have a Thuraya phone?'

I couldn't help smiling. I knew what was coming. It was almost a relief: Buck Rogers hadn't been lying to me after all.

'Yeah,' I said.

'We're gonna have to take it,' he said. 'It's an order, I'm afraid. The phones have been compromised: the Iraqis are using 'em to track our positions. You're gonna have to give me the phone *and* the battery. Some sneaky bastards have been giving us their goddam spare batteries. Write your name, media organization and address on the handset and we'll get it back to you whenever we can.'

*Yeah, right*, I thought. But I wasn't going to object: it was pointless. And at least my excuse for leaving Iraq was genuine.

I reached into my bag for the phone.

'It's OK,' said Hotspur. 'Give it to me at the camp.'

★

It was nearly dusk when we reached the 1st Marine Division's headquarters, a familiar desert metropolis of hooches, Portakabins and military vehicles. It seemed as though there were enough Marines at the camp to fill Baghdad. I ended up in a semi-covered press area, where an older American reporter, raw from the sun, was talking loudly into an Iridium phone. A few other embeds hung around, smoking cigarettes and taking notes in bored longhand. After I'd surrendered my Thuraya to one of Hotspur's men, a Marine offered me his camping chair. I gratefully took it. I couldn't help wishing, however, that I'd managed to get on the damn helicopter. After all, I guessed that I was still 170 miles north of Kuwait City. And, although I was scared of flying over the southern war zone, I wanted to get home so badly I didn't care.

'Who d'you write for?' asked the older American when he'd finished dictating a story update to his Washington bureau chief.

'London *Times*,' I said.

'Did you hear about the Swede?' he asked, with gleeful eyes.

'No, I didn't.'

'He was a unilateral,' said the embed, who sounded like a New Yorker. 'Thought he could get into Iraq by driving over the border in a Hertz rental. He ended up being stopped by a couple of Republican Guard at a checkpoint somewhere near Basra. They took his car, stripped him of all his clothes, pointed him in the direction of Kuwait City, and told him to walk back.'

The embed gave a staccato laugh.

'Christ!' I said.

'Apparently the only thing that saved him was his Swedish passport. The Iraqis told him that if he'd been an American, or a Brit, they would have shot him in the head. Gotta love the Swedes, right?'

I imagined the horror of having to walk, naked, back to Kuwait.

'Perhaps the passport was fake,' I said.

'Whatever,' said the embed, laughing. 'Now he's got to put a Ford Taurus on his expenses sheet. Somewhere in Sweden there's gonna one unhappy sonofabitch of an editor. But at least he's still alive.'

'Did he survive the walk?' I asked.

'I assume from the fact I heard the story that he survived. The Army probably picked him up near the DMZ. They must have laughed their asses off when they saw a naked Swedish unilateral approaching them.'

I looked around me. If I'd been assigned to the 1st Marine Division's headquarters, I thought, I would probably have lasted the whole war. Then again, the embeds looked like caged animals. That's the military's big secret: it makes you so sick with boredom that fear comes as a relief.

The rest of the day passed slowly, one second at a time.

That night, after managing to eat my first MRE since leaving the front lines, I sat in one of the hooches and watched a DVD of *Dr Strangelove*, starring Peter Sellers, on a sergeant's laptop. I fell asleep before the end.

For the first time since Camp Grizzly, I didn't dream of anything.


'YOU! AYRES!'

This wasn't a good way to start Sunday morning. I was sitting on the borrowed camping chair, snoozing, with *The Quiet American* on my lap. Somewhere behind me, a chaplain with a camouflaged cassock was giving communion. I felt exhausted and depressed. The war was catching up on me.

I opened my eyes to see Hotspur. He was gripping a clipboard and fizzing with barely controlled rage.

'Hi,' I said, optimistically.

'I read your story on the Early Bird, Chris,' announced Hotspur. The Early Bird, I vaguely remembered, was the Pentagon's news-clippings service. A daily edition was faxed to senior officers in the field.

'Oh, right,' I said.

My stomach went into free fall: had I made a factual error?

'*Beans, bullets and Band-Aids in short supply*,' quoted Hotspur, spitting out the words as though each one was an insult against his mother. '*This is a force of Marines that has run out of energy.*'

'That's my story,' I confirmed.

'You broke the ground rules, Chris,' said Hotspur, unexpectedly. 'You think it's OK to give our position away? "*From Chris Ayres near al-Diwaniyah*"? You know what, Chris, I'm glad you're leaving, because otherwise I'd be kicking your sorry ass out of here. You're a pisspoor journalist, Chris.'

'What?' I exclaimed. 'Captain Rick Rogers gave me permi—'

'*Morale was at an all-time low*,' quoted Hotspur. 'I don't understand, Chris. I don't see what you see. Your story's bullshit.'

I started to mouth silent objections. How could I have broken the ground rules when Buck was the one who'd told me to say we were near al-Diwaniyah? Besides, my front-page tank-ambush story on Friday had also been datelined al-Diwaniyah, and no one had said anything about *that*. What's more, my account of the supply-line jams had all come from the lieutenant colonel. I felt more depressed than angry. I'd been shocked by the openness of the Marines during the invasion, in spite of Buck's tendency to ignore my annoying questions. Sometimes I'd even wondered if the openness was in the Marines' best interest. Perhaps Hotspur had come to the same conclusion. Perhaps the Marines were thinking twice about embedding.

Hotspur curled his lip with disgust and stomped away.

I felt something tug at my back. I looked around to see the Marine who'd lent me his chair. His neck was taut with anger.

'Gimmie my fuckin' chair back,' he said, pulling the chair harder. This time I fell on to the mud. I couldn't believe this was happening. 'You can sit in the fuckin' dirt,' he muttered. 'I ought to shoot you in the head.'

What could I say? I just sat there, feeling tired and miserable.

This made everything so much worse.

After dinner, as the dusk turned the sand an unmanly shade of pink, Hotspur returned. I was sitting in the same spot, staring into the disappearing sun, and willing Monday morning to arrive. The captain crouched down and looked me dead in the eyes. 'I was pretty hard on you earlier, Chris,' he said. 'You're a good guy, I've been reading your stuff. I shouldn't have gone at you like that.'

'It's OK,' I said, and I meant it. 'It's been pretty tense around here.'

Hotspur gave a quiet laugh and nodded.

'So are we cool?' he asked, offering a raw, blistered hand.

'Yeah, we're cool,' I said, shaking it.

'Good,' said Hotspur, slapping my blue shoulder. 'I'm gonna try and get you a ride outta here ASAP. Hold tight. I'll be back.'

At 3 a.m. on Monday 31 March – day twelve of the war – Hotspur, my unlikely saviour, delivered on his promise. 'We got you a helicopter,' he said, shaking me awake in my Beverly Hills sleeping bag.

'Get your shit together. You're leaving in five mikes.' I almost didn't
want to believe it was true, after what had happened the last time with
my promised flight back to Kuwait. Still, I knelt on the floor and
rolled up my ground mat and sleeping bag as fast as I could, hands
shaking with anticipation. By the time Hotspur returned, I was ready.
I prepared myself for another physical ordeal. 'Follow me,' said the
captain, picking up my laptop case. I jogged on numb legs after him,
leaning forward to spread the weight of my flak jacket and rucksack.
I kept thinking my knees would give out, throwing me down into the
mud. But they held fast, using some secret reserve of strength. When
we finally reached the take-off site, I realized my ride wasn't just a helicopter: it was a massive, twin-rotor CH-46 Sea Knight – the kind that
used to carry American teenagers to their death in the jungles of
Vietnam. The twin turbines shrieked as the blades created their own
extreme weather system. '*Holy shit!*' I shouted, looking up at the enormous blacked-out war machine, almost invisible against the night sky.

'This is the package,' shouted Hotspur to one of the Sea Knight's
co-pilots, who was wearing a green flight suit, helmet and night-
vision goggles. 'He's going to Kuwait. Take him as far south as you
can tonight.'

The co-pilot handed me a pair of black earmuffs, then used his
M-16 to usher me to the back of the helicopter, where there was an
open metal hatch. Still wearing my rucksack, I hiked up the ramp,
flinging the rest of my bags in front of me. I sat on one of the wooden
benches that ran down either side of the cargo area, and pulled the
earmuffs over my head. I felt as though I were watching a television
newsreel with the sound turned down and an industrial vacuum
cleaner next to my head. My eardrums were buzzing so violently I
almost expected them to bleed.

It was dark in the helicopter, with only a fuzzy green glow coming
from the cockpit. I could see the outlines of the pilots, backlit by the
instruments. My only fellow passenger was a major, who sat on the
bench opposite. He said something, but I couldn't hear. So I just
smiled and nodded dumbly.

Eventually the pitch of the turbines changed, and I felt the strange
vertical thrust of the rotors. The rear hatch, I noticed, was still open.
I thought about how much easier this was than the twenty-hour convoy

from Basra into the marshlands. I also thought about Fletcher, who was probably in bed somewhere in London. I hoped he wouldn't be too angry about me leaving Iraq. He would probably regret ever asking me if I wanted to go to war. And then I pictured Kilo Battery, still taking mortar fire somewhere near al-Diwaniyah. *Should I have stayed?* For now, I didn't care. I just wanted to get home. I wanted my parents and grandparents to see me alive. I wanted the fear to be over. We gathered speed. I remembered reading that Sea Knight helicopters were vulnerable to attack because they flew lower than 10,000 feet, with a relatively slow top speed of 166 m.p.h. – not to mention the noise. I looked out of the open hatch at the infinity of darkness below. There were no street lamps, no car headlights, no stars, and no moon. Just a terrible, empty blackness. If you see light after sundown in Iraq you're either about to kill or be killed. I thought about all the pain and death of the past twelve days. How could this wrecked and tortured country ever recover? Would the Americans ever leave? I wondered how many Marines would be flown out of Mesopotamia in plastic bags, and how many Iraqis would be killed by their liberators. *Was the war right?* I wished I had a stronger opinion. I just wanted to go home. I looked at the major in front of me. His head was slumped back and his eyes were shut.

I can't remember what came first: the orange flash on the ground, the popping sound, or the stink of cordite, carried over the cold night breeze. But I remember a delay before the fear and the sickness took hold.

'*What the hell was that?*' I shouted silently to the sleeping major. The turbines thrummed inside my head. I looked right, through the glass screen of the cockpit, and saw cyborg outlines against a green background. The aircraft shook and banked. I wondered if I was already dead. *An orange flash.* The Iraqis must have aimed at the noise coming out of the clouds. *A popping sound.* The bastards must have fired an RPG, or rocket-propelled grenade. I imagined the fate I'd avoided by a few lucky yards: the mangled blades, the fiery hulk, the blackened human shapes. War is so random, I thought. In war, no one is special. In war, you always die for someone else's cause.

And so we continued, thrashing south through the darkness.

Towards the border. Towards the lights.

# Epilogue

*So this what I found out yesterday: Saddam Hussein has a Thuraya satellite phone. That's right. The exact same model as mine, before Hotspur confiscated it. You can't always believe wartime rumours, of course, but it makes sense. The Pentagon wasn't worried about the embed in his blue flak jacket giving away the Marines' position: it wanted to clear the battlefield of background noise, so that when Saddam switched his phone on – BOOM! I'm just grateful I didn't think of a way to hang on to my Thuraya at the front. Being mistaken for Saddam Hussein would have been an unlucky end to an unlucky career in war journalism.*

*The day after I left Iraq, the Americans started winning the war. On Tuesday, a captured Army supply clerk was rescued from a hospital in al-Nasiriyah by an elite unit of Navy Seals and Army Rangers. She was Private Jessica Lynch, a nineteen-year-old from Palestine, West Virginia. Even Bush-haters found themselves punching the air with gung-ho satisfaction. Somewhere in Washington a Pentagon public-affairs officer must be laughing himself to sleep at night. The headline in* The Times, *as in every other newspaper, was 'Saving Private Jessica'. Yes, the luck of the Americans is changing in Mesopotamia. Even the Iraqi information minister is now regarded as an international joke. They're calling him Comical Ali.*

*Victory is expected any day now. But I worry about the insurgents, the shepherds by day and the warriors by night. I doubt they'll recognize any conventional defeat on the battlefield. For now, however, the Americans have taken Saddam International Airport and there are star-spangled tanks in the suburbs of the capital. On news-stands across London, Oliver Poole's photo byline stares out from the front page of the* Daily Telegraph. *'The first newspaper reporter to reach Baghdad,' it says, in a heavy, bold type. Glen was right: Poole is fearless.*

*The war, however, isn't getting any safer for the war reporters. Statistically, journalists are ten times more likely to die than coalition soldiers. The latest*

*victim is Michael Kelly, editor-at-large of* Atlantic Monthly. *The circumstances of Kelly's death seem horribly familiar: the Humvee under enemy fire,
swerving and crashing into a ditch. Both Kelly and the driver drowned.*

*For others the war is proving to be perilous in different, less lethal, ways.
Geraldo Rivera, the Fox News reporter, has been escorted out of Iraq after
sketching a map of his position in the sand. Then there's Peter Arnett, Pulitzer
Prize winner and CNN hero during the first Gulf War. He's been fired by
NBC News and* National Geographic Explorer *for giving an interview to
Iraqi state television: he told the Iraqis that the American war plan had failed.*

*But enough of all this. You probably want to know how I got back to
London, how my final, shameful deed of the war was completed. Here's the
funny thing: the Sea Knight didn't get me back to Kuwait. Soon after the
RPG attack, we landed to refuel. I had no idea where we were. In total darkness, I was led out of the helicopter by a Marine with a lens on a stalk where
his eyeballs should have been. I stood there, blind and choking on the vapour
of aviation fuel, while the tanks were filled. Around us were more Marines,
pointing their M-16s out into the unknown. If a shell hit us now, I thought,
our bodies would land on the moon. We climbed back on board, flew for another
twenty minutes, then landed again. We were still in Iraq. I might still be there
now if it wasn't for my fellow passenger, the major, who offered me a ride on a
cargo plane. We touched down in the northern Kuwaiti desert at 6 a.m. After
waiting all day at the tiny, dusty airfield, I talked my way on to a supply convoy
going to Al Jaber, the Air Force base where Glen was embedded. I imagined a
night of hot coffee and war stories. When I called Glen's mobile, however, I
found out he'd left Kuwait weeks ago. Now he was back in London, preparing for his next trip: central command in Qatar.*

*After Iraq, Al Jaber felt like Disneyland. There was hot food, Fox News, a
supermarket, tents with 'cot beds', and – best of all – a press room with leather
seats and English newspapers. Getting off the base, however, proved almost
impossible. After an exhausting, anguished night of cancelled convoys into
Kuwait City, I decided to call my old friend Salman Hussein, the taxi driver.
It took me a while to convince him to come: he doubted the Americans would
let him anywhere near a high-security base. Eventually, at 11 a.m. on Tuesday
morning – April Fool's Day – Hussein arrived in his white Taurus. It took me
another hour to persuade an Air Force public-affairs officer to give me a lift to
the pick-up spot. Meanwhile, Hussein's misgivings were confirmed when the
guards wouldn't let him past the front-gate checkpoint. I ended up staring at*

*his taxi down an empty 100-yard stretch of tarmac, with the public-affairs officer protesting that we didn't have permission to go any further. Finally, after more bureaucratic squabbling, a deal was done. By the time Hussein pulled up beside me, I wanted to give him a hug. Instead, I gave him $100. He smiled, nodded, and said, 'Thank you very much.' Then he told me the fare to Kuwait City was $200.*

*My reunion with the staff of the JW Marriott Hotel wasn't a happy one. In fact they didn't seem at all pleased to see me. Perhaps it was the smell: I hadn't washed for fifteen days. Arabs in white dishdashas gave me disapproving looks as I clomped over the marble foyer, each step creating an Aladdin's puff of dried mud. To be fair, I didn't look much like a guest at a five-star hotel. I was still wearing my chemical suit and gas mask, for a start. My glasses were broken and smeared with mud. My remaining hair had turned into a single matted dreadlock. Nevertheless, I booked myself into a corner suite and immediately ordered up the Wagyu-Kobe beef, the dozen Gulf prawns with lobster tail, and three cappuccinos. I had some catching up to do. The mirror in my room confirmed the worst: I hadn't lost an ounce of weight. Not that I cared. I ran myself a bath of almost intolerable heat and lay there for two hours. Then I tried to wash my bags and belongings, with limited success. By the time I was done, the bathroom looked like a slaughterhouse, with orange-brown slime splattered all over the walls.*

*I stayed at the hotel for a couple of nights, making $50 phone calls to Northumberland and California, and writing stories from the business centre. Fletcher, who took my decision to leave Iraq surprisingly well, tried to convince me to go back into Iraq with the British. 'The trouble is, Chris, after the tank-ambush story everyone thinks you're a war correspondent,' he complained. I was having none of it. I flew back to London, via Dubai, on Thursday. I visited the office for an hour to give back my flak jacket, helmet and change from $5,000.*

*That was yesterday. Now I'm sitting at Prêt-à-Manger near Leicester Square, wiping mayonnaise from my mouth after an English-breakfast sandwich. This was my fantasy back when I was in the marshlands.*

*I already feel changed by war. My anxiety, for example, is gone. Dr Ruth would be proud. Life seems shorter, more urgent. Here in London, where chemical drills don't ruin your morning coffee, I feel invincible. I've stopped looking both ways when I cross the road. I took a cab yesterday, and didn't fasten my seatbelt. Why not? I've lost my war virginity. And, now that I know what war is like, I've stopped worrying about death. I no longer dread the dirty bomb on the Underground, the nuke in Times Square, the anthrax in the post. Battlefield fear has put all other fear into perspective. Perhaps that's what my generation needs: urgent, mortal terror. I sang in the shower this morning because the water was hot and because no one was trying to kill me. It was a pure, uncomplicated happiness. I can only hope this lasts.*

*And now I'm sitting here, at an outdoor table, amid the lunchtime crowd. Freedom is a novelty: the thrill of spending money; of eating your own choice of food; of not doing what the captain says.*

*I spent the morning in Covent Garden, touring the shops and replacing my war clothes, which I was still wearing. First came the jeans, then the loafers, followed by the sweater and the waterproof jacket. In every dressing room my outfit changed, until the visual memory of Iraq was erased. At one point I went to a cash machine and sniggered at the number on the screen: my March salary was untouched. Now I'm in full civilian uniform, with bags of dirty combat-wear at my feet, my mobile phone on the table, and a folded copy of* The Times *in my hands.*

*Tomorrow, Alana arrives from another solar system: Los Angeles. Our relationship will not survive the Iraq War, but neither of us know that yet.*

*Look – here come some children. I feel all fuzzy and sentimental. The kids look Asian or Eastern European; the eldest is perhaps ten years old. They're holding a tourist map. Perhaps they've lost their parents. I smile as they approach, the map held out for me to read. Perhaps I can help them. The map's now under my nose, and they keep pushing it towards me. I ask them where they want to go, but all they say is 'Please, sir. Please, sir.' Something feels wrong. My right hand moves down to feel the familiar leather bulge in my pocket. I'm disappointed with myself, at my lack of trust. Then they're gone – lost in the crowd. I look at the table and see the empty space where my mobile phone used to be. The map, it seems, provided cover for a tiny, thieving hand. I curse and get up, ready to sprint after them.*

*Instead, I start laughing. I've travelled halfway across the world, escaped mortars, tanks and snipers, and returned to London, only to be robbed by a ten-year-old near Leicester Square. I'm laughing harder now – I'm laughing so hard there are tears in my eyes. Pedestrians stare; a toddler points.*

*But I can't stop.*

# Acknowledgements

The late Peter Cook had some excellent advice for reporters willing to write risky stories: publish and be absent. Hence Cook went to Tenerife after identifying the Kray twins as East End gangsters in *Private Eye* magazine; and hence I found myself holed-up in a Cotswolds hotel after writing an article for *The Times* entitled 'I Made My Excuses and Left', which explained why I'd run away from the Iraq War. There is nothing necessarily wrong, of course, about running away from a war. Unless, that is, you're a soldier. Or a war correspondent for *The Times*.

*The Times* should probably have fired me for giving up my embedded position with the US Marines. Instead, the paper made the best of a difficult situation and turned my incoherent 5,000-word confessional, rattled out on an IBM in the business centre of Kuwait City's JW Marriott Hotel, into a 2,500-word cover story for its *Times 2* section. If it wasn't for the executives and editors who agreed to publish it – Robert Thomson, Ben Preston, Sandra Parsons, Anne Barrowclough and Jonathan Gornall, who kindly compared my stint in Iraq to his transatlantic rowing career – *War Reporting for Cowards* might not have been written. They probably have mixed feeling about that now. But I'd like to thank them all nevertheless.

It's worth mentioning that *The Times* has treated me exceptionally well during my eight years as a staff reporter; and that I'm hugely indebted to all those editors, particularly Robert Thomson and Ben Preston, who have given me the freedom to write bad jokes in the first person. It also says a lot about the culture of *The Times* that my decision to leave the front lines was treated with sympathy, in spite of the short-term consequences for the paper's war coverage.

I must also thank Martin Fletcher, *The Times*'s foreign-news editor, for taking the risk of sending his Hollywood correspondent to cover an invasion, and Martin Barrow, for his soothing sarcasm throughout the war. The 'two Martins', who still wake me up at 6.30 a.m. every day with bizarre requests ('Chri-*is*?, We need you to buy an AK-47 in Las Vegas' was a recent Barrow classic), have been supportive, patient and, most importantly, forgiving editors. They were particularly understanding while I was writing this book. Or rather I'm sure they would have been if I'd answered any of their phone calls. Thanks must also go to my early mentors at *The Times*, Patience Wheatcroft and Robert 'Lunch Tutorial' Cole (formerly of the *Evening Standard*), who were probably as shocked as me when they saw my face next to a Middle Eastern dateline. All of the aforementioned *Times* personnel, particularly Martin Barrow, have been extremely good sports about their descriptions in the book, as was Oliver Poole of the *Daily Telegraph* (who wrote his own account of being embedded, entitled *Black Knights: On the Bloody Road to Baghdad*). Similar tolerance was shown by Joanna Coles, now executive editor of *More* magazine in New York; Toby Moore, the novelist; and Glen Owen, now at the *Mail on Sunday*.

Thanks must also go to my parents, Peter and Jenny Ayres; my sister, Catherine Newton, and her husband, Tom; and my grandparents, Ross and Florence Taylor, for their overwhelming love and support during all the difficult times mentioned in this book. It's also about time I apologized to Tom for nearly giving him anthrax. Special thanks must go to my grandfather for letting me interview him about his capture during World War II. Those conversations inspired me to write this book – because I wish *he*'d written a book.

*War Reporting for Cowards* could not have been written, of course, without the US Marines. I will always be grateful to them for looking after me in Mesopotamia. My own experiences in Iraq are trivial compared with those of the Marines; but warriors are rarely writers (when they are, they win Pulitzers), and I hope that their bleak humour in this book helps readers understand what these men's lives are like. My own wimpish performance under hostile fire should give some idea of the bravery required to stay on the front lines.

Nor could this book have been written without the help of Mark Lucas, my agent at Lucas Alexander Whitley, whose pitching and proposal-editing skills are almost as good as his Des Lynam impression. My New York-based agent, George Lucas, at Inkwell Management, has been similarly invaluable. I would also like to thank the others who gave me advice on the book and showed early, morale-boosting enthusiasm for it. These include Toby Young, Graham Broadbent at Blueprint Pictures, and Tobin Armbrust and Basil Iwanyk at Thunder Road Entertainment in Los Angeles.

The efforts of all these people would count for nothing, of course, unless someone had agreed to publish the book, and I couldn't have found a sharper or more encouraging editor than Roland Philipps at John Murray. His interest was enormously flattering, as was the enthusiasm of Morgan Entrekin at Grove/Atlantic, who is publishing the book in the United States.

I used many reference materials during my research. Some of the most helpful books were *Ernie Pyle's War*, by James Tobin; *Trying Not to Go Deaf on the Gun Line*, by Scott Bernard Nelson of the *Boston Globe* (his report can be found in *Embedded: The Media at War in Iraq*, edited by Bill Katovsky and Timothy Carlson); *Churchill*, by Roy Jenkins; *The Poems of Wilfred Owen*, edited by Jon Stallworthy; *A Reed Shaken by the Wind*, by Gavin Maxwell; *The Anthrax Letters: A Medical Detective Story*, by Leonard A. Cole; *Hostage*, by Chris Cramer and Sim Harris; *Give War a Chance* and *Holidays in Hell*, by P. J. O'Rourke; *In Harm's Way*, by Martin Bell; *Iraq: The Bradt Travel Guide*, by Karen Dabrowska; *Iraq: An Illustrated History and Guide*, by Giles Munier; and the Lonely Planet guide to the Middle East. I found Microsoft Encarta and Wikipedia.com to be invaluable resources. I also used many newspaper and wire-service reports – far too many to list

Finally, I would like to thank my fiancée, Lucie, who agreed to marry me weeks before I disappeared into my office to write this book. I emerged, months later, exhausted, ratty and even balder than when I began. She must have wondered what she had done.

Without Lucie's patience, support, advice and proof-reading, *War Reporting for Cowards* might never have been completed. She assured me she was laughing *with* me, not *at* me, when she giggled over early drafts. On several occasions, however, she couldn't resist asking: 'You didn't *really* do that, did you?'

Unfortunately, I did.